DESTINATION

DESTINATION
TRIBULATION
& BEYOND

THOMAS FARR

TATE PUBLISHING
AND ENTERPRISES, LLC

Published by Tate Publishing & Enterprises, LLC
127 E. Trade Center Terrace | Mustang, Oklahoma 73064 USA
1.888.361.9473 | www.tatepublishing.com

Tate Publishing is committed to excellence in the publishing industry. The company reflects the philosophy established by the founders, based on Psalm 68:11,
"The Lord gave the word and great was the company of those who published it."

Book design copyright © 2011 by Tate Publishing, LLC. All rights reserved.
Cover design by Kenna Davis
Interior design by Lindsay B. Behrens

Published in the United States of America

ISBN: 978-1-61346-749-7
Religion / Eschatology
11.11.14

There are a number of people who have been especially helpful to me in the writing of this book series. First, I need to thank Joe, who encouraged and helped me from the start; also, I need to thank Jim, who can do all the red-tape items that drive me crazy. I also need to thank Barb and Sharon, who kept me supplied with pertinent information. I need to thank my son, Joshua, who is literate in the ancient Greek and was a great resource and aid in explaining difficult linguistic questions. Thanks to those who provided material and financial support to enable these publications. I need especially to thank my wonderful wife, because without her faith in Christ and in me, I would not have had a chance to write anything. This work would have been impossible without all of them. But most of all, I need to thank God, because this is truly His book series; I'm merely a secretary.

This is the word of El Shaddai, Almighty God, the great I Am That I Am, through the prophet Isaiah.

Isaiah 46:11:
> "From the east I summon a bird of prey;
> from a far-off land, a man to fulfill my purpose.
> What I have said, that will I bring about;
> what I have planned, that will I do."

Isaiah 55:10–11:
> "As the rain and the snow
> come down from heaven,
> and do not return to it
> without watering the earth
> and making it bud and flourish,
> so that it yields seed for the sower and bread for the eater,
> so is my word that goes out from my mouth:
> It will not return to me empty,
> but will accomplish what I desire
> and achieve the purpose for which I sent it."

TABLE OF CONTENTS

TERMS AND DEFINITIONS

Term	Definition
NIV	New International Version Bible
NASB	New American Standard Version Bible
KJV	King James version Bible
ASV	American Standard Version Bible
AMP	Amplified Bible
YLT	Young's Literal Translation
Rosh Hashanah	"head of the year" or "first of the year" beginning of Jewish New Year – a time to make resolutions and a time of reflection (true Rosh Hashanah is yet to come)
Yom Kippur	Jewish "Day of Atonement" (true Day of Atonement is yet to come)
Shofar	Shofar is a ram's horn - used for calling an assembly of the people and/or call to war.
synagogue	From a Greek root meaning "assembly." The most widely accepted term for a Jewish house of worship. The Jewish equivalent of a church, mosque or temple.
Shabbat	The Jewish Sabbath, a day of rest and spiritual enrichment
Strong's	Strong's Exhaustive Concordance and/or Strong's Exhaustive Concordance and Lexicon
Sukkoth or Succoth	(Also transliterated as **Succoth** or **Sukkoth**) known as the **Feast of Booths**, the **Feast of Tabernacles**, **Tabernacles**, or the **Feast of Ingathering**
Jerusalem	Capital and largest city of the modern state of Israel (although its status as capital is disputed); it was captured from Jordan in 1967 in the Six Day-War; a holy city for Jews and Christians and Muslims; was the capital of an ancient kingdom
Zion	1) An imaginary place considered to be perfect or ideal. 2) Originally a stronghold captured by David (the 2nd king of the Israelites); above it was built a temple and later the name extended to the whole hill; finally it became a synonym for the city of Jerusalem; "the inhabitants of Jerusalem are personified as 'the daughter of Zion'" 3) Jewish republic in southwestern Asia at eastern end of Mediterranean; formerly part of Palestine
States of Jordan	1) Administrative subdivisions: Twelve governorates--Irbid, Jarash, Ajloun, al-'Aqaba, Madaba, al-Mafraq, al-Zarqa, Amman, al-Balqa, al-Karak, al-Tafilah, and Ma'an. 2) Approximately 1.7 million registered Palestinian refugees and other displaced persons reside in Jordan, many as citizens 3) http://www.state.gov/r/pa/ei/bgn/3464.htm
Gog	Ruler/leader of Magog
Magog	Land/country at the "utter most" north from Israel. Go to North Pole from Israel and look back at the last country passed through (Russia).
kanaph	the edge of extremity, a wing, a flap, a quarter
1 biblical month	30 days (1 cycle of the moon) – established by God at Creation
1 biblical year	360 days (12 cycles of the moon) – established by God at Creation
time	1 biblical year (given in Daniel and Revelation)
times	2 biblical years (given in Daniel and Revelation)
half time	½ biblical year (given in Daniel and Revelation)
Jewish month	1 biblical month
Shidduhim	the making of a match – a couple
kiddushin, or eirusin	the betrothal, the engagement
nisuin	The ceremony of the marriage. (Means elevation) the couple was elevated to full marriage status with all the aspects of marriage.
huppah	symbolizes the consummation of the relationship
ekklesia	Greek meaning a called out assembly - "church"
rapare	Latin - snatching away (Rapture – part of Paul's 'mystery' message)
mystery	Secret (to shut the mouth)
Eschatology (ˈeskuˈtālujee)	the study of end times

PREFACE

I feel that it is advisable to explain to the reader the process I used to arrive at the conclusions found in this book series. God gave me an interest in this subject some time before I actually began writing. He also impressed upon me that perhaps I would someday write a book on this, so this idea was with me before I felt the need to actually begin writing. For some years, several things delayed my beginning this book. Perhaps the biggest was the fact that I knew that it would be a daunting task. I honestly didn't know where to begin. When God finally impressed it on my heart to start this work, I also found myself in a position where I was able to devote much more time and resources to this study. God provides! Never underestimate the power of God!

As I began to study for this book, I had a very basic understanding of end-time prophecy, and as I read through God's Word, much of what I read was a mystery to me. I was convinced, though, that God wasn't just wasting words when He revealed these prophecies to the Bible authors. He gave them these prophecies to be understood by the reader if he or she were to spend the necessary time to search out the answers. Of course, there are some prophecies that we won't fully understand until the events are fulfilled. The reason for this is that God wishes for them to remain secret until that time.

But when God wishes for them to remain secret, He tells us so! The identity of the antichrist is one such example! God's Word makes it perfectly clear that we won't know who he is before he comes to power as the antichrist. Another example is dates. When will these things occur? Paul tells us that we don't need to know. That is God's word on it, so people need to quit second guessing God! When God says that we don't need to know the times or the seasons, He isn't lying! Very little bothers me more than an otherwise godly person giving dates for future prophecy, first, because God says we won't know, and second, because when these dates finally pass and inevitably nothing happens, it makes believers look either like fools or deceivers. I know the scriptures about being fools for Christ's sake, but second guessing God isn't "for Christ's sake." Fortunately, most of future prophecy can be understood by an in-depth study of God's Word with much prayer. The information is there!

One of the things that spurred me to write was the fact that as I spoke to believers, I was amazed at the number of different theories I encountered. Even in my own church, the number of different ideas was amazing, and for the most part, these theories were directly opposed to each other. They simply couldn't all be correct! If I were to go to a bookstore and browse the prophecy section or surf the web, the same is true. I was inundated with many "experts" who completely contradicted each other. All of them supposedly were grounded on God's Word! At that time, I couldn't understand why anyone would see prophecy any differently than a pre-millennial, pre-tribulation, "God raptures the believer away for the tribulation to follow immediately, and then the thousand years of Christ's reigning on earth, followed by eternity in heaven for believers" view. At that time, this was basically how I viewed prophecy in a nutshell. Boy, was I shallow! But as I talked to believers of their different viewpoints, I found that these people who disagreed with me were sincere, God-loving, intelligent people. Suddenly, it struck me; am I so arrogant as to assume that I'm right and they are wrong? I knew that my understanding of prophecy was shallow, a sort of ignorance-is-bliss attitude, but I was comfortable with it. Suddenly, I was no longer comfortable. I have found that when God has something for me to learn, He begins with making me uncomfortable. So I began praying about it. God laid on my heart something that went beyond discomfort. It filled me with dread! I was to empty myself of all preconceived ideas on prophecy. I also decided to not go to any "expert," simply because I could find an "expert" that would say anything that I wanted, so what's the point in that? This was perhaps the most difficult thing I've ever had to do as a believer. Emptying yourself of beliefs you've had from the time you were a child is frightening. It left me feeling unsure and exposed: vulnerable. I didn't like this at all. I frankly knew that I had work to do. I also knew that I had to study with the help of just one scholar, one expert. This expert was God's Holy Spirit, and I claimed the promise of Christ in John 14:26. Here, Christ tells us that the Holy Spirit will teach us all things. This is a promise from God.

When you study God's Word you need to study, not to prove your point. Most errors in studying God's Word are made due to this attitude. Most cults erupt from this kind of study. This is called subjective Bible study, and it will prove nothing! You've wasted your time and done God a great disservice! Also, beware of any deep study where you don't change your mind on something! This isn't to suggest that you couldn't be correct on the first try, but study with an open mind and be willing to change your mind when Scripture suggests the need. Never, ever, ever go into a study assuming that you have all the answers to begin with. That is what I had to do. At that point, God could use me; I was teachable.

I began with a study of rapture verses: 1 Thessalonians 4–5 and 1 Corinthians 15. With these, I also studied Christ's Olivet discourse of Matthew 24, Mark 13, and Luke 21, which are also commonly considered rapture verses. I studied not only their content, which is paramount, but the timing of each passage and the audience that it was written to. When Christ made His Olivet discourse, Paul wasn't preaching. In fact, Paul (as Saul) was an enemy of Christ. This is a very important consideration. The audience that this was addressing had never heard of Paul's teaching to the Thessalonian believers or, for that matter, the Corinthian believers. Christ's ministry was before Paul's and was frankly to a different group! God's Word tells us that Christ was a minister to the circumcision (Matthew 15:24, Romans 15:8). Paul's ministry was to the Gentiles (Romans 11:13). Don't misunderstand this; Christ's work on this earth *applies* to all humanity, His sacrifice on the cross, His burial and resurrection, His intercession, etc., but His earthly ministry was to Israel. Paul tells us this throughout his work. But Paul's ministry came years later and was directed to a gentile audience. This understanding is very important. Then I did a careful word study of each of the above-mentioned portions. You will find the result in this book series. After I finished this, I collected future prophetic portions and studied them. I looked for "markers" in each portion that may be referred to in other passages. I learned many things doing this but was still unable to put them in any particular order. I was reluctant to study one particular passage of prophecy, though, because it had always confused me. This was the Magog battle passage of Ezekiel 38–39. The reason it confused me in the past was that I had been busy placing other portions in the wrong place! Finally, I had to study this daunting and detailed portion. The first thing I noticed was that it was loaded with important "markers" that I considered likely to be found in other portions. I was absolutely blown away with the information God had provided in this passage. I had never previously studied this portion without trying to study it in light of some "expert's" viewpoint. That had been my mistake! Now I was free to study solely based on what God was going to show me, not on what an "expert" was going to show me. I traced these markers to other portions and found that they do, indeed, lead to a wealth of other scriptures. At that point, the sequence of end time's prophecy began to fall into place. I will list here some of the markers to show how the process works.

Ezekiel 38:2–3 and 5–6 tell of the attacking countries involved. To a certain extent, this can be followed elsewhere, but in a comparative study, it doesn't give much help, because these specific countries aren't named in other portions. What are named are general locations which cover the areas of these countries in dealing with this in other portions. The name Magog isn't even mentioned in other portions in conjunction with this battle. But the general directions are mentioned, and that's important. We find that the details of this battle are mentioned in many other portions, and that is very important. Several key markers are found in Ezekiel 38:8 (we will look at a few markers from Ezekiel 38 and go into Ezekiel 39). The phrase "invade a land that has recovered from war" shows us that this attack will be against a land that has been involved with a war. This may have been a notable war, because it is noted here, so I began looking in other prophetic portions that involved a war. (As you may have guessed, there are some!) I noted them. Also, we found that they "recovered" from this war. Also in this verse, we found that they were gathered from many nations to the land of Israel. From this, we can understand that it is Israel after they are gathered from being scattered around the world. We know that Israel had only become a nation in 1948 in modern times, so this prophecy can only be future. There hasn't been a war of this magnitude since (or for that matter, before) that time. Another key is the phrase, "now all of them live in safety." At this point, today, they don't live in safety! I decided to search Scripture and see if I could find any portions dealing with this battle. I found many references of battles that were still future. None mentioned specifically the countries mentioned here, but there were enough references dealing with certain details of this battle that it became obvious that it was referring to what I was calling the "Battle of Magog." There were other battles mentioned that clearly didn't involve this battle. The details were wrong, and the countries were wrong. Some battles were already fulfilled. I needed to be careful to not include already fulfilled battles as future prophecy. Again, there were differences in detail that made the battles obvious as to which ones were being referred to in the context.

There was one battle in particular that had several references that wasn't the Battle of Magog. I called this the "battle of Damascus." I called it this because the city of Damascus today prides itself as being the oldest perpetually inhabited city on the face of the earth. Its habitation probably goes back to prehistoric times. Now, before anyone gets upset with me because Damascus has been overthrown several times throughout history, it was never rendered uninhabitable. The point of these scriptures is that it will no longer be inhabited. Isaiah 17 tells us it will no longer be a city, just a heap of ruins. That has never happened in all of history! So this battle is future! Aha, another piece of future prophecy. But which one comes first? We will find the answer to this momentarily. I searched and found several references to this battle, and these references do name city names or the names of the people that inhabit these cities or countries!

I found in this battle that not only is Damascus destroyed, all of Syria apparently is destroyed as well, along with several other countries. One of the countries that are nearly totally destroyed is Israel! I wondered if this could be the war that Israel has recovered from as mentioned in Ezekiel 38:8. Certainly, the "battle of Damascus" would be a notable war—Israel is nearly wiped out! We find also in Isaiah 17 that Israel recovers from this war; they are farming the land. But in Isaiah 17:12–14, we find that Israel is involved in another devastating war. The evidence is mounting! Another thing that I've noted in the Isaiah portion is Isaiah 17:10. It is a sad commentary on Israel's spiritual condition. It says, "You have forgotten God, your savior…" This comment is placed after the Damascus battle and before the next devastating battle. This is why, while they are farming the land, it doesn't do well; God doesn't prosper their work. They have forgotten Him. This is during the great recovery. In Isaiah 17:14, we find in reference to this next battle: "This is the portion of those who loot us, the lot of those who plunder us." Now I had enough clues to do a comparative study of these two portions. I referred back to Ezekiel 38–39, looking to see if there were any cross markers. There were! When God intervenes on Israel's behalf in the Battle of Magog, the attacking army is utterly devastated, and we find that Israel takes the goods left behind from the attacking army and uses it for their own benefit. In Ezekiel 39:10, we find: "They will plunder those who plundered them and loot those who looted them." Now, while this wasn't conclusive, the agreement in the phraseology between Isaiah 17:14 and Ezekiel 39:10 did at least catch my attention. In Isaiah 17:13, we find that this battle (the one after the recovery from the battle of Damascus), Israel wins because of God's intervention. In Ezekiel 38:18–23 and Ezekiel 39:2–6, we find that Israel wins only by God's intervention. It's looking more and more like a match! Then in Ezekiel 39:22, we find perhaps the most important marker in all of end-times prophecy: "From that day forward the house of Israel will know that I am the Lord their God." This is a once-and-forever event and certainly should be mentioned in other scriptures. Being as it occurs at the height of a mighty battle, it should appear much in scripture, and it certainly does. Now, referring to the timing of this Battle of Magog with the battle of Damascus, we found that after the battle of Damascus, Israel had "forgotten God your savior," but after the Battle of Magog, "from that day forward the house of Israel will know that I am the Lord their God." The Damascus battle thus has to come before the Battle of Magog. Israel will never forget God after the Battle of Magog, but they will forget God after the battle of Damascus. So the order of these two battles is set: Damascus will come first, and Magog will come second!

Now also in Ezekiel 38:8, we find that Israel is living in safety until they are attacked by Gog and his cohorts. This is referred to in I Thessalonians 5:3: "While people are saying 'peace and safety,' destruction will come on them suddenly." This destruction is the Battle of Magog. The "peace and safety" part is the time of recovery. We find that Paul is assuring the Thessalonian believers that they will not have to go through that (I Thessalonians 5:9).

In Ezekiel 38:12, we find that Magog will come to "plunder and loot." There is mention of this in both Isaiah 17:14 and Jeremiah 30:16. In the Jeremiah portion, we find that God is giving us a very detailed report of the Battle of Magog and its aftermath, but from a different angle. It is very Israel centered; the rest of the world is rather inconsequential. We can know that this is the Magog battle because of Jeremiah 30:22: "So you will be my people, and I will be your God." This refers to Israel's repentance as a nation, as mentioned in Ezekiel 39:22. Remember, this is a once-in-forever event ("from that day forward")! So establishing that Jeremiah 30 is referring to the Battle of Magog, we can glean more facts about this battle. Can you see how "markers" work? This arises from the marker of Ezekiel 39:22: "From this day forward, the house of Israel will know that I am the Lord their God."

In Ezekiel 38:6,15, we find that the main army of Magog is from the "far north." We find this mentioned also in Ezekiel 39:2. The reference in Ezekiel 39:2 could read "uttermost north," and is translated that way in several translations. We will discuss the identity of this and the other nations involved in this battle in the book series. (You can probably take a pretty good guess just with this information and a fair world globe anyway.) This is a marker that brings us to another portion that discusses that Battle of Magog. This is found in Joel 2.

In Joel 2, we find a great army attacking Israel. They are likened to an army of locusts, but they are a human army. The likeness of locusts is in the totality of destruction that they cause; like locusts, they destroy everything in their path. We are told early in this passage that "the Day of the Lord is coming. It is close at hand." This is an important phrase, and we will see it used over and over in prophecy of the end times. Essentially, it means that God is about to intervene directly in the affairs of mankind, and most of the time, this refers to the tribulation period. This is a marker that will lead us to many truths about the world's future history. Joel here describes an overwhelming, unstoppable army that is marching against Israel at God's command. The first thing that we find that hints at this being the Magog army is its magnitude. It is the largest army ever, and there will never be any greater. It is without number. We find in Revelation an army of 200,000,000 coming from the east. I always thought that that was the greatest army ever, but God's Word never says that. This Magog army is the greatest! How do I know that this isn't the same army as the one mentioned in Revelation? The army in Joel comes from the north (Joel 2:20)! Aha! Another marker! As you read the two passages together, Joel 2 and Ezekiel 38–39, it becomes clear that the battles mentioned are the same. In Ezekiel 38–39, we find that God intervenes on behalf of the nation of Israel and destroys the army from the far north. We also find that from that day forward, Israel will know that God is the Lord their God. In Joel 2, we find that at the height of the battle, when all seems lost, Israel is called to repent as a nation; they do repent from the heart, and God intervenes. He destroys the "northern army." Also, this is a key marker; in Joel 2:27, we find, "Then you will know that I am in Israel, that I am the Lord your God, and there is no other; never again will my people be shamed." This battle and the one in Ezekiel can only be the same one! The repentance of Israel can only happen once, according to God's Word. The rendition found in Joel adds some very important details and some important markers.

I already mentioned the Jeremiah 30 portion, and we have found that this also has to be referring to the time of the Battle of Magog, due to the assurance that "So you will be my people and I will be your God." Then we can find many important markers in this portion too. We find in each of these three portions that, in each case, God intervenes to save Israel.

I am only tracing a very few markers found in these scriptures here to show you how it works. There are many more markers and many other scriptures that we will trace in this book series. In fact, there are many more markers just in the Ezekiel 38–39 passage that we haven't mentioned here. I just picked a few as an example of what this book series is attempting to accomplish. I could go on and on but will strive to be brief. (Sorry, I guess I'm too late on that one!)

Anyway, this became a daunting task, as you can see, but it was a very rewarding one as well. I was constantly struck with awe at the things God showed me from His Holy Word and by His Holy Spirit. Gradually, the loose ends began to come together, and a fairly clear picture began to emerge.

As you read this book series, pray for God's guidance. Rid yourself of preconceived ideas and let God's Word direct you. See what God has in His Word and let His Word be your guide. This book series is only a tool. But the Bible is God's living word! Truly, God is the only "expert" we need to claim. If you hear an "expert' make a claim about Scripture, ask yourself, "Does this agree with all of Scripture, or is it just an idea he or she has to prove his or her point?" If you seem to find one scripture contradicting another scripture, that is God's way of telling you that you are misunderstanding what you've read. God *never* contradicts Himself. God's Word *never* contradicts itself! Always bear that in mind.

Another thing to beware of in Bible study is the concept that all Scripture applies directly to us. This simply isn't true. This is an idea that has led to much confusion over the years. For example, Christ told His followers to obey the Law of Moses. But today, we find that we are free from the Law! So not every word of the Bible is written to you or me! Be careful to study in light of that fact. It means a little more work on your part, but it's worth it. (Otherwise we'd be sacrificing a bull right now! We are free from the Law!) In the future, we will find that the Law of Moses will be rightfully practiced again. I cover this later in this book series.

Another caution is not to read more into a verse than is intended. God is very faithful at explaining metaphorical verses. If He doesn't make it clear either from context or from an explanation of the verse that it is a metaphor, it probably isn't one. A verse where people do this to a great extent is Matthew 24:32, the fig tree verse. This is also mentioned in this book series. (I know exactly what the fig tree in the verse is. Read this book series and find out!)

Well, this is enough for the preface. Read this book series with a Bible in close reach and study in light of God's Word, not the word of some expert. If we were to get in a war of experts, we could never conclude it. Experts will tell you whatever you want to hear. Trust God's Word and the Holy Spirit to guide you.

INTRODUCTION

Why study prophecy? Paul said, "We don't want you to be ignorant" (1 Thessalonians 4:13), and "Therefore encourage each other with these words" (1 Thessalonians 4:18). Christ said, "Watch out that no one deceives you." (Matthew 24:4b).

So here we have Paul telling us that the reason for his informing us of end-time matters is essentially for our education and our encouragement, or comfort. I think that is very interesting, especially in light of Christ's reason, which is a very detailed warning.

First, I wish to make something perfectly clear. The whole Bible is God's Word! Equally inspired! From Genesis 1 through Revelation 22! We are told in 2 Timothy 3:16–17, "All scripture is God breathed and is useful for teaching, rebuking, correcting, and training in righteousness, so that the man of God may be thoroughly equipped for every good work." This means that every scripture is God breathed, whether it was penned by Moses, John, Obadiah, Paul, or any of the other Bible authors. Understanding that, any Bible writer writes with as much authority as Christ himself! (In its original language and text.) On this basis, we need to be faithful to find translations that are as close to the original text as possible. Also, no one translation is perfect. Therefore, I searched primarily through five translations, often seeking the meanings of the original words used to determine what is the closest to what is meant in each text. Also, we need to stick to translations, not paraphrases. Paraphrases are an interpretation of an interpretation, someone else's idea of what the author is trying to say, and then you're assuming that this person is correct. I will not even completely trust a translator, let alone a person who will interject his own thoughts into God's Word. In fact, God warns us to beware of those who interject their own thoughts into His word in Revelation 22:18–19: "I warn everyone who hears the words of the prophecy of this book: If anyone adds anything to them, God will add to him the plagues described in this book. And if anyone takes words away from this prophecy, God will take away from him his share of the tree of life and in the holy city, which are described in this book." Proverbs 30:6 says, "Do not add to His words, or He will rebuke you and call you a liar." Also, it says in 2 Peter 1:20–21, "Above all, you must understand that no prophecy of Scripture came about by the prophet's own interpretation. For prophecy never had its origin in the will of man, but men spoke from God as they were carried along by the Holy Spirit."

The portions of Scripture that will be studied in this book series were not conceived by the men that penned them but were written as God himself directed. In fact, Christ is called *the Word*. This means that whatever was written, was written by Christ's own inspiration and carries His full authority!

I will strive to give you a biblical, logical (God is always logical, just sometimes *we* don't have all the facts!) view of God's prophecy of the end times, which we are entering shortly. Any time you go into a Bible study, even this one, look for errors based on *God's Word*, not someone else's idea (even your pastor, he's human too!) or on what you've been taught for your whole life or even notes you find in a study Bible. I've been faithful to change my mind on many matters from what I've been taught because God's Word didn't support what I'd been taught! This is a principle that Luke teaches in

Acts 17:11: "Now the Bereans were of more noble character than the Thessalonians, for they received the message with great eagerness and examined the Scriptures every day to see if what Paul said was true." I beg you to be as noble as the Bereans. Receive this word eagerly and search the Scripture to see if what I tell you is supported by God's Word.

Now, understanding that the whole Bible is God's Word, the writings of Paul are as inspired as the writings quoting Christ, because God inspired both. But unfortunately, believers often put more emphasis on the gospels than on Paul's books because Christ is God in the flesh. God's Word is *all* God's Word. But to humor those who emphasize one portion over another, I will begin this book series with prophecies made in Christ's Olivet discourse and with prophecies throughout the Bible detailing and relating to His words.

Another thing we must understand is that many of the end-times prophecies are partially fulfilled or can even have multiple fulfillments. This doesn't mean that the prophecy is no longer valid for the future. In fact, often we find that God is giving us an historic event that the world will be able to relate to when it occurs in the future. An example is the Abomination of Desolation mentioned by Christ in Matthew 24:15. He mentions that Daniel prophesies it. In Daniel 8:13, we find that there was to be a desecration of the sanctuary, which was fulfilled by Antiochus Epiphanes in 171–164 BC Christ's mention of it was for Israel to watch for it as something that will happen in the future. The desecration by Antiochus Epiphanes was a "preview" of things to come, but Christ said that it will happen again in the end times and to watch for it. Daniel even alluded to the end-times event in Daniel 9:27, and this is what Christ was specifically referring to. This is an example of multiple fulfillments. The desecration of the temple by Antiochus was something that the Jews could look upon as a historic event and a view of things to come when it will be far worse. An example of partial fulfillment is the destruction of Babylon as mentioned in many portions of scripture, including Isaiah 21:9, Jeremiah 50–51, and many others. Alexander the Great captured Babylon (the city), and it went into decline and died out, fulfilling those prophecies about the destruction of Babylon. To this day, Babylon (the city) is uninhabited. This doesn't mean that the prophecy is completely fulfilled though. These portions also describe the destruction of Babylon the country (Iraq). That hasn't happened yet. It will! If you read the portions prophesying the destruction of Babylon, you'll see that there is much that is not yet fulfilled. This is a case of partial fulfillment. God doesn't do things half way. If the prophecy isn't completely fulfilled 100 percent, it isn't finished yet, and *it will be fulfilled exactly as God said it would be!* The unfulfilled parts will be completed in the future.

One difficulty that I've faced in writing this book series is that so many events of prophecy are dependant on each other. It is sometimes hard to separate the events for a clear progression of details. There will be much referring to material covered in other chapters, because the other chapters arise from events that happen earlier.

Also, the biggest error that many Christians make is to make God's Word into a coded message or to find a portion that doesn't make sense to a person's own mind and say that it is "metaphorical" or "symbolic." Granted, God does use metaphor and symbolism in His word, *but* He always makes it clear that it is a metaphor or a symbol, and he *always* explains it in scripture or context! Also in prophecies of end times, the person who is recording God's Word often describes things that he has no personal reference to by experience, so he describes the event or technology as best he can relate. In Revelation 11, we have some excellent examples of metaphor and description of technology beyond John's time. Revelation 11:7: (this portion is speaking of the two witnesses) "Now when they have finished their testimony, the beast that comes up from the abyss will attack them, and overpower and kill them. Their bodies will lie in the street of the great city, *which is figuratively called* (here we are being notified of a metaphor) Sodom and Egypt, *where also the Lord was crucified."* (And here we have the explanation! God isn't trying to fool us! He's trying to give us truth!) God tells us that he's speaking of Jerusalem. Why call it Sodom? Because of the abominable sins committed there. Why call it Egypt? Because of the idolatry and false worship committed there. These are the first things one would think of when hearing of these cities. Also in this chapter, we have a portion that people have misunderstood for centuries. Revelation 11:9 tells us, "For three and a half days, men from *every people, tribe, language, and nation* will gaze on their bodies and refuse them burial." "Now, how could people from all around the earth come and look at these fallen witnesses? God couldn't mean that people from all around the world would come and look at them! Why, it would take weeks or even months to travel that far!" These were some of the comments people made about this portion *before the advent of television and satellite transmission!* No, God meant exactly what he said! Men will look on their dead bodies for three and a half days! In Revelation 17, we have a portion where God uses symbolism. Revelation 17:3: "…There I saw a woman sitting on a scarlet beast that was covered with blasphemous names and had seven heads and ten horns." Revelation 17:7: "…I will explain to you the mystery of the woman and of the beast she rides, which has seven heads and ten horns." Revelation 17:9: "…The seven heads are seven hills on which the woman sits. They are also seven kings. Five have fallen, one is, the other has not yet come; but when he does come, he must remain for a little while." Revelation 17:18: "The woman you saw is the great city that rules over the kings of the earth." Here we have symbolism and the explanation. The seven heads are two things: a) seven kings. God tells us that this symbolic beast's seven heads are seven kings, (yes, it is somewhat cryptic, but it is speaking of seven literal kings) and b) we find that the heads are also seven hills (the word could also be translated *mounts*), yes seven literal hills. The woman is that great city that sits on the beast with seven heads (hills). The city of seven hills is and has been known for centuries as Rome! Of course, God is God; He could certainly raise up another city that sits on seven hills that exercises some kind of power over nations, but I think it's unlikely. The reason is the phrase in the context, "here is the mind with wisdom," and this implies that we can figure this out, even in John's time. That being the case, the only city that meets that definition then and now would be Rome. But I will not limit God! Please, student of God's Word, don't make God a liar and don't accuse Him of playing games! He has given us his Word to be understood. Granted, some portions are easier than others, but it is all true and should be taken literally unless He tells us otherwise!

CHAPTER 1

War with Damascus and Surrounding
Countries and Israel's Recovery
Matthew 24:4–8

We will start out with the words of our Savior, Jesus the Christ, as He spoke to us in Matthew 24:4–8. Here we will see that he is giving us, in a nutshell, a quick summary of events leading up to the time known as the tribulation period. Christ here refers to that time as "the beginning of birth pains" (NIV), or "the beginning of sorrows," (KJV).

> Jesus answered: "Watch out that no one deceives you. For many will come in my name, claiming, 'I am the Christ,' and will deceive many. You will hear of wars and rumors of wars, but see that you are not alarmed. Such things must happen, but the end is still to come. Nation will rise against nation, and kingdom against kingdom. There will be famines and earthquakes in various places. All these are the beginning of birth pains."
>
> Matthew 24:4–8

Here we have a quick summary of events leading up to the time known as the Tribulation. Notice that Christ states, "The end is still to come." This is not the birth, but only the beginning of labor.

Lest there is any misunderstanding, I do not believe that we are in the time of the beginning of labor yet. I suppose that I would call the time that we are in the "Braxton Hicks contractions" of prophecy. It makes you think that it's here, it's close, but this isn't it. We will discuss our present time in Chapter 5 of this book.

The rest of this chapter (and several others following this) will be expanding on the brief message that Christ has given us here. Supporting scriptures will fill in details.

In Revelation 6:1–8, I believe that God is giving us another summary of events of the beginning of birth pains. The parallels are uncanny. As we progress, we will examine these parallels.

I watched as the Lamb opened the first of the seven seals. Then I heard one of the four living creatures say in a voice like thunder, "Come!" I looked, and there before me was a white horse! Its rider held a bow, and he was given a crown, and he rode out as a conqueror bent on conquest. When the Lamb opened the second seal, I heard the second living creature say, "Come!" Then another horse came out, a fiery red one. Its rider was given power to take peace from the earth and to make men slay each other. To him was given a large sword. When the Lamb opened the third seal, I heard the third living creature say, "Come!" I looked, and there before me was a black horse! Its rider was holding a pair of scales in his hand. Then I heard what sounded like a voice among the four living creatures, saying, "A quart of wheat for a day's wages, and three quarts of barley for a day's wages, and do not damage the oil and the wine!" When the Lamb opened the fourth seal, I heard the voice of the fourth living creature say, "Come!" I looked, and there before me was a pale horse! Its rider was named Death, and Hades was following close behind him. They were given power over a fourth of the earth to kill by sword, famine and plague, and by the wild beasts of the earth.

Revelation 6:1–8

I believe that the Antichrist will be intimately associated with the battle of Damascus; whether arising from it or instigating it, this isn't sure (probably instigating it because we see him mentioned first when both are listed), but he will be there.

As we begin, we will examine events that will happen in "the beginning of birth pains" that our Lord told of in Matthew. One of the first events will be a battle between Israel and the Islamic countries surrounding Israel today. I will be referring to this as "the Damascus battle," because Damascus will be a key player in this event.

This portion will introduce Damascus and its pivotal role that it will play in prophetic events. It will describe the battle, some of the participants, and its immediate results.

> An oracle concerning Damascus: "See, Damascus will no longer be a city but will become a heap of ruins. The cities of Aroer will be deserted and left to flocks, which will lie down, with no one to make them afraid. The fortified city will disappear from Ephraim, and royal power from Damascus; the remnant of Aram will be like the glory of the Israelites," declares the Lord Almighty. "In that day the glory of Jacob will fade; the fat of his body will waste away. It will be as when a reaper gathers the standing grain and harvests the grain with his arm—as when a man gleans heads of grain in the Valley of Rephaim. Yet some gleanings will remain, as when an olive tree is beaten, leaving two or three olives on the topmost branches, four or five on the fruitful boughs," declares the Lord God of Israel. "In that day men will look to their Maker and turn their eyes to the Holy one of Israel. They will not look to the altars, the work of their hands, and they will have no regard for the Asherah poles and the

incense altars their fingers have made. In that day their strong cities, which they left because of the Israelites, will be like places abandoned to thickets and undergrowth. And all will be desolation. You have forgotten God your savior; you have not remembered the Rock, your fortress. Therefore, though you set out the finest plants and plant imported vines, though on the day you set them out, you make them grow, and on the morning when you plant them, you bring them to bud, yet the harvest will be as nothing in the day of disease and incurable pain."

Isaiah 17:1–11

We find in Isaiah 17:1 that Damascus is destroyed. It is a "heap of ruins." Today, at the time of this writing, Damascus prides itself on being the oldest perpetually inhabited city on earth. It has *never* been a heap of ruins or uninhabitable. But it is prophesied that it will "no longer be a city." Since Damascus is the oldest perpetually inhabited city, this verse is pivotal in prophesy. This is an indicator that points to a specific event. When it is mentioned that Damascus is destroyed, it can only be referring to this event. This is why I refer to this conflict as "the battle of Damascus," even though many other cities and countries are involved.

In Isaiah 17:2, we find that "The cities of Aroer will be deserted." This is in ancient Jordan. Actually, there were two cities in what we now call Jordan that were named Aroer. The name means *ruins*, and by the context, I believe that it is speaking of the condition of Syria after this battle rather than a group of cities, especially since Aroer is not a territory, but a city. There is also a place referred to as Aroer in the Gaza area. Interestingly, all these areas are mentioned in the context of the battle of Damascus, so what is being referred to here is really not important. They will all face destruction. This area will be deserted, a place for sheep to lie down in.

In Isaiah 17:3, we find that there will be much destruction. First, the "fortified city" or "fortress" (KJV) will disappear from Ephraim.

Ephraim is in central Israel, north of Jerusalem. Damascus will lose its governing power over Syria. And the "remnant of Aram" (present-day Syria) "will be like the glory of the Israelites." This is showing that Israel will be nearly destroyed in this battle. This is the Word of the "Lord Almighty."

Isaiah 17:4 verifies this destruction. "In that day the glory of Jacob will fade; the fat of his body will waste away." We find that Israel, the father of the nation known today as Israel, was originally named Jacob. When God speaks of Jacob, He is referring to Israel. It has been said that today, Israel has threatened the "Samson option" of defense. This is, that if Israel is threatened with certain destruction, it will unloose all of its military capability (presumed nuclear) rather than let anyone just walk over them. During the "Cold War" between the U. S. and the Soviet Union, this concept would be likened to the idea of "mutually assured destruction" or "Better dead than Red." This *appears* to be what happens here. It doesn't say that this is what occurs, but it isn't unlikely. I will not say that this is certain to occur, but it is a logical conjecture.

Isaiah 17:5 goes on with an illustration. It likens the destruction of Ephraim to a grain harvest. Even though the field is harvested, there is always a little bit that is overlooked.

Isaiah 17:6 continues the thought with a likeness of an olive harvest. No matter how thorough you may be, there'll be some left. Not every one will be destroyed, but it will be close!

Isaiah 17:7 and 8 makes an interesting statement. It says that "In that day men will look to their Maker and turn their eye to the Holy One of Israel." And Isaiah 17:8 elaborates on this thought by stating that they will not look to their idols, their false gods. By the wording, it would appear that this is a revival of mankind in general. It doesn't say *Israel*, it says, *men*, which would mean *mankind* and would include Jews. So we have *men* turning to *the Holy One of Israel*, which would be Christ. But in short order, they turn back again! We will find that humanity is deceived by the antichrist and turns their worship to him! They haven't changed their heart. They only turn their eyes to Him, not their hearts! Only when God changes their hearts and Israel rids itself of its idols with the help of God is there true lasting repentance as a nation. Isaiah 27:9 says, "By this, then, will Jacob's guilt be atoned for, and this will be the full fruitage of the removal of his sin: When he makes all the altar stones to be like chalk stones crushed to pieces, no Asherah poles or incense altars will be left standing." Only when the idols have been disposed of (and God will help with that!) will their repentance be complete. This isn't speaking of only the idols of the ancient world; it is speaking of anything that becomes a god to a person, anything that will keep a person from God. The significance for the Jews is that they haven't repented! So this is not the Day of Atonement; they have not, as a nation, received Christ, but they may begin to consider Him. It seems likely that they are instead sidetracked at this time by the antichrist. But they are *compelled* to repopulate the land and annex the lands of their attackers. We will see this later in this chapter.

Isaiah 17:9 reiterates the destruction of the enemies of Israel, "because of the Israelites."

Isaiah 17:10 then makes the heart-breaking statement that "You have forgotten God your Savior; you have not remembered the Rock, your fortress." This could very likely be the satanic intervention of the antichrist deceiving them away from the true Christ. They haven't had a change of heart. This also places this battle before the Battle of Magog in Ezekiel 38 and 39. Because, as we will see in chapter 3, at the Magog war, Israel does have a change of heart; they do repent! This repentance doesn't happen here. When it does, it will be a permanent condition, as we will see. Also, as you will see in Chapter 4 of this book, at this time, it is likely that there will be a "foolish shepherd" set over them: (Zechariah 11:15–17) the antichrist. Because of their not turning to God in truth, their crops will fail. This is interesting because this goes hand in hand with Matthew 24:7 and Revelation 6:6, which both speak of famine. Isaiah 17:11 continues the thought of their crops failing because of their unbelief.

In this next portion, we will find the participants in this battle listed. Here we will find a more detailed description of the battle itself. We will also find some reasons for the judgments being handed out by God. This portion will describe the destruction quite graphically, giving details that can best be related to modern warfare, making that possibility very likely.

> This is what the Lord says: "For three sins of Damascus, even for four, I will not turn back my wrath. Because she threshed Gilead with iron sledges having iron teeth, I will send fire upon the house of Hazael that will consume the fortresses of Ben-Hadad. I will break down the gate of Damascus; I will destroy the king who is in the Valley of Aven and the one who holds the scepter in Beth Eden. The people of Aram will go into exile to Kir," says the Lord. This is what the Lord says: "For three sins of Gaza, even for four, I will not turn back my wrath. Because she took captive whole communities and sold them to Edom, I will send fire upon the walls of Gaza that will consume her fortresses. I will destroy the king of Ashdod and the one who holds the scepter in Ashkelon. I will turn my hand against Ekron, till the last of the Philistines is dead," says the sovereign Lord. This is what the Lord says: "For three sins of Tyre, even for four, I will not turn back my wrath. Because she sold whole communities of captives to Edom, disregarding a treaty of brotherhood, I will send fire upon the walls of Tyre that will consume her fortresses." This is what the Lord says: "For three sins of Edom, even for four, I will not turn back my wrath. Because he pursued his brother with a sword, stifling all compassion, because his anger raged continually and his fury flamed unchecked, I will send fire upon Teman that will consume the fortresses of Bozrah." This is what the Lord says: "For three sins of Ammon, even for four, I will not turn back my wrath. Because he ripped open

the pregnant women of Gilead in order to extend his borders, I will send fire upon the walls of Rabbah that will consume her fortresses amid war cries on the day of battle, amid violent winds on a stormy day. Her king will go into exile, he and his officials together," says the Lord. This is what the Lord says: "For three sins of Moab, even for four, I will not turn back my wrath. Because he burned, as to lime, the bones of Edom's king, I will send fire upon Moab that will consume the fortresses of Kerioth. Moab will go down in great tumult amid war cries and the blast of the trumpet. I will destroy her ruler and kill all her officials with him," says the Lord.

Amos 1:3–2:3

In this portion, we have a very detailed description of the battle that will happen at the time of the destruction of Damascus. It begins with Damascus. It tells us for three sins of Damascus, even for four, God will turn His wrath upon it. Interestingly, since Israel's rebirth in 1948, Syria (whose capital is Damascus) has made war with Israel three times, once in 1948, once in 1967, and once in 1973. Now all of the countries mentioned in this portion are confederates of Syria (with the exceptions of Israel and Judah, of course), and all have been involved with hostility against Israel in recent times. Syria is still hostile to Israel and harbors terrorist organizations that attack them. It has been suggested that if Israel is attacked again by Syria, this could be the battle that is prophesied. Please understand that it could be speaking of past offences that each of these countries made; it doesn't have to be just in the last sixty years. The three recent attacks on Israel is just an interesting speculation. The reason that God is pouring out his wrath upon Damascus is that they attacked "Gilead." Gilead is the area just east of the Jordan River in the country presently called Jordan. This area was originally supposed to be occupied by the tribes of Manasseh and Gad. Hazael was the ancient Syrian king, thus the "House of Hazael" would be the country of Syria. Ben-Hadad was the king of the ancient country of Aram, which became Syria. God is making it clear that his judgment is going to be poured out upon the land of Syria. The valley (or plain) of Aven is also in southwestern Syria. To show the extent of God's judgment on Syria, Beth Eden is named. Beth Eden is in Syria but is well away from the Israeli border to the north and east. Another name for Syria is Aram. God is not being ambiguous here! Syria is going to be judged harshly. The people of Aram will go into exile in Kir. Kir is in central Assyria, which is in present-day Iraq. Today, it is no secret that Syria and Iraq are allies; although, with the American occupation of Iraq, it will be interesting to see how this all plays out.

There is also a reference to a "Kir" in Moab in Isaiah 15:1, but this reference just tells us that it is destroyed in a night. Since we will see that Moab is utterly destroyed in this same battle, and this reference (Isaiah 15–16 is another rendition of the judgment on Moab) is prophetic of end-time events, this is probably the same event. I feel it unlikely that this is where they would flee to. It appears that the full name of the town in Moab was Kir Hareseth.

Just recently, Israel gave up the Gaza strip. They were to abandon their houses and go elsewhere, which they did. I couldn't believe it! How could they give up land to their enemies? Then I went ahead with this study and found the judgment of Gaza. Israel *had* to give it up! Now prophecy can be fulfilled! I heard on the news that in the weeks following the release of this territory, there were something like forty-six missile attacks on Israel from within the Gaza strip! While it's tragic to see, it's also exciting to see things being set up for the fulfillment of prophecy! Notice that it speaks of Israelites being displaced by the hand of Gaza! I don't think that this was the displacement that was prophesied here, because the Israelis were not sold to Edom (southern Jordan). But God's Word says they will be sold to Edom. If it hasn't already happened (and I haven't seen where it has), it will happen. The displacement was just a prelude. All the cities mentioned here are in the Gaza strip and near each other. It says that God will not stop His attack until the last of the Philistines is dead! The Palestinians of today consider that they are the descendants of the ancient Philistines.

Next, we have the judgment on Tyre. They will be guilty of the same sin as Gaza. Tyre is in the country of Lebanon, on the coast of the Mediterranean Sea. Their judgment will also be the same. This prophecy on Tyre may have been already fulfilled to some extent with the conquest of Alexander the Great. He destroyed Tyre. Tyre is now a small town in southern Lebanon, not nearly the power center it was in ancient times. In fact, the modern Tyre isn't even in exactly the same place as ancient Tyre, just very near. This will be a definite battle zone.

Then there is the judgment on Edom. Edom is in present-day southern Jordan. This includes the city of Petra, which was carved into the rock walls. If you've seen the movie *Indiana Jones and the Last Crusade*, their quest took them to Petra, where the Holy Grail was found, according to this fictional tale. Some claim that this city of Petra will play a role later in prophecy. Frankly, there truly isn't much scriptural evidence for it. The book of Obadiah tells the judgment of Edom. Some of this judgment has already come to pass but not all. From Obadiah verse 10 onward, it is still future. In Obadiah verse 10, we find that they will be destroyed "forever" because of their violence against their "brother Jacob." Esau founded the area of Edom. He was the brother of Jacob, who became Israel. So because of their aggression against Israel, God will judge them. Also, it says that when they were not actively attacking them, Edom stood by while others did attack, even giving their approval. Edom, as a political entity, will not survive the "battle of Damascus." It even says in Obadiah verse 18, "There will be no survivors from the house of Esau." In fact, Obadiah verse 21 says, "Deliverers will go up on Mount Zion to govern the mountains of Esau." This will set things up for more fulfillment of prophecy with Israel in the wilderness.

Next, we find the judgment of Ammon. Ammon is in northern Jordan. Today there is a city called Amman that is in this region. It is the remnant of the country of Ammon and retains the name to this day (spelled only slightly differently). God here is judging them for their ruthless methods of expansion. Murdering pregnant women is the crime mentioned specifically here. Take note that it says that it will be a "stormy day." There will be a fire on the walls that will consume the fortresses and violent wind. Pardon my occasional journey into speculation, but consuming fire and violent wind on the day of battle sounds very much to me like a nuclear attack. While this is speculation, I certainly wouldn't rule this out. Then in Amos 2:1–3, we find the judgment on Moab. Moab is in central Jordan. Here we find that the judgment listed is for their ruthlessness in dealing with neighbors. Specifically, it says that they burned the bones of the king of Edom. For their sins, they will be destroyed.

It is interesting to note that these last three countries, Edom, Ammon, and Moab are all now the country Jordan. In early 2005, I found a news article that stated that the king of Jordan wanted to divide the country into three self-governing states. These states would roughly coincide with Edom, Ammon, and Moab! In every prophecy that mentioned these areas, it mentioned them separately yet together. I wonder if this is prophetically significant. It may be related to the rise of the antichrist, as we'll find in Chapter 4 of this book.

Now notice what it says in Amos 2:4–16. This is the judgment on Judah and Israel. This isn't a separate pronouncement; it is a continuation of the judgment on the countries involved in the battle of Damascus. It just happens to be God's judgment on Israel because, at this time, Israel is not a God-fearing country! They haven't repented. They stand in danger from the true God due to their rebellion. That is why Israel is virtually destroyed in this battle.

This is what the Lord says: "For three sins of Judah, even for four, I will not turn back my wrath. Because they have rejected the Law of the Lord and have not kept his decrees, because they have been led astray by false gods, the gods their ancestors followed, I will send fire upon Judah that will consume the fortresses of Jerusalem." This is what the Lord says: "For three sins of Israel, even for four, I will not turn back my wrath. They sell the righteous for silver, and the needy for a pair of sandals. They trample on the heads of the poor as upon the dust of the ground and deny justice to the oppressed. Father and son use the same girl and so profane my holy name. They lie down beside every altar on garments taken in pledge. In the house of their god they drink wine taken as fines. I destroyed the Amorite before them, though he was tall as the cedars and strong as the oaks. I destroyed his fruit above and his roots below. I brought you up out of Egypt, and I led you forty years in the desert to give you the land of the Amorites. I also raised up prophets from among your sons and Nazirites from among your young men. Is it not true, people of Israel?" declares the Lord. "But you made the Nazirites drink wine and commanded the prophets not to prophecy. Now then, I will crush you as a cart crushes when loaded with grain. The swift will not escape, the strong will not muster their strength, and the warrior will not save his life. The archer will not stand his ground, the fleet-footed soldier will not get away, and the horseman will not save his life. Even the bravest warriors will flee naked on that day," declares the Lord.

Amos 2:4–16

This gives a much more detailed account of the destruction poured out on Israel (and Judah) as mentioned in Isaiah 17. Israel will not come out of this unscathed. They will be mostly destroyed because of their sins. They will be treated the same as the pagan world around them. This is because, at this time, they are a mostly pagan country.

The next portion restates other scriptures, but it does also bring out some important facts not mentioned as clearly elsewhere. It mentions that this time will be like the time of a woman's labor pain. This may be referring to Christ's description of this time in Matthew 24.

In Jeremiah 49:23–27, we find the destruction of Damascus mentioned again.

> Concerning Damascus: "Hamath and Arpad are dismayed, for they have heard bad news. They are disheartened, troubled like the restless sea. Damascus has become feeble, she has turned to flee and panic has gripped her; anguish and pain has seized her, pain like that of a woman in labor. Why has the city of renown not been abandoned, the town in which I delight? Surely, all her young men will fall in the streets; all her soldiers will be silenced in that day," declares the Lord Almighty. "I will set fire to the walls of Damascus; it will consume the fortresses of Ben-Hadad."
>
> Jeremiah 49:23–27

Here we find that the destruction of Damascus is likened to pain of childbirth (Jeremiah 49:24). I find it interesting that Christ used the same comparison in Matthew 24:8 for the time just before the tribulation. Jeremiah 49:25 is taking the viewpoint of a citizen of Damascus. Why isn't the city evacuated? All her young men and soldiers will fall in the streets. Notice again the fire on the walls and the consuming of the fortresses. This gives credence to the possibility of modern (perhaps nuclear) warfare.

In the following portion, we will find that there will be an annexing of attacking territories after this battle. The territory mentioned here is in the Gaza strip. Israel will get it back!

In Zechariah 9:1–7, we find another account of the Damascus battle.

The word of the Lord is against the land of Hadrach and will rest upon Damascus—for the eyes of men and all the tribes of Israel are on the Lord—and upon Hamath too, which borders on it, and upon Tyre and Sidon, though they are very skillful. Tyre has built herself a stronghold; she has heaped up silver like dust, and gold like the dust of the streets. But the Lord will take away her possessions and destroy her power on the sea, and she will be consumed by fire. Ashkelon will see it and fear; Gaza will writhe in agony, and Ekron too, for her hope will wither. Gaza will lose her king and Ashkelon will be deserted. Foreigners will occupy Ashdod, and I will cut off the pride of the Philistines. I will take the blood from their mouths, the forbidden food from between their teeth. Those who are left will belong to our God and become leaders in Judah, and Ekron will become like the Jebusites.

Zechariah 9:1–7

The wording in the first verse can be confusing. By just reading this, it would give the impression that everyone is following the Lord. This obviously isn't so! An alternative reading of this portion is, "The word of the Lord is against the land of Hadrach and will rest upon Damascus—For the eye of the Lord is on all mankind, as well as on the tribes of Israel." The Amplified Bible states it this way: "…for the Lord has an eye upon mankind as upon the tribes of Israel." This is much more consistent with other scripture.

The remainder of the chapter, after Zechariah 9:7, goes on to cover the rest of the time from the rise of Alexander the Great and going into the millennial reign of Christ. It is telling us in these first seven verses that Damascus and the other countries that are involved in this battle will be beaten and will be plundered. For instance, Tyre was destroyed by Alexander the great and is now only a shadow of its former self, as mentioned earlier. It could be speaking of this destruction here, as it was future prophecy at this point. It could also be speaking of the destruction of this area in the end times. There will be battles fought in this area. This portion may be one of those that are partially fulfilled, not totally, as we find in the prophecy against Damascus and as the Amplified Bible points out in Zechariah 9:7: "…and Ekron will be like the Jebusites (who at last were merged and lost their identity with Israel)." 2 Chronicles 8:7–8 tells us that when Israel conquered the Jebusites they "had not destroyed" them, but "these Solomon conscripted for his slave labor force, as it is to this day." Also note that the ones who are left in these countries will belong to God and will become leaders in Judah. This seems to suggest that God will protect His own people (it is His nature!), that they will be leaders in Israel, and that *Israel will annex* territories after the battle. Specifically here, they will annex the territory of the Gaza strip. The book of Obadiah supports this scenario, only with the annexation of Edom (southern Jordan).

Obadiah contains one theme: the judgment on Edom (modern day southern Jordan). Edom will be attacked by a coalition. Obadiah verse 3 is probably speaking of Petra, which is in southern Edom: "you who live in the clefts of the rocks." Edom will be important, but I don't see anything in Scripture that says that Petra specifically is important. I mention this because there are many saying that Petra is important.

This coalition will be made up of those who appear to be friends of Edom, according to Obadiah verse 7. Obadiah gives much greater detail of this judgment than Amos. It mentions that the Day of the Lord is near for all nations at this point. It says in Obadiah verse 18, "The house of Jacob will be a fire…and the house of Esau (Edom) will be stubble." This gives the appearance that Edom will be destroyed by Israel in this battle. It says in Obadiah verse 19, "People from Negev will occupy the mountains of Esau, and the people from the foothills will possess the land of the Philistines. They will occupy the fields of Ephriam and Samaria, and Benjamin will possess Gilead." Obadiah verse 20: "This company of Israelite exiles who are in Canaan will possess the land as far as Zarephath;

the exiles from Jerusalem who are in Sepharad will possess the towns of the Negev." Obadiah verse 21 says, "Deliverers will go up on Mount Zion to *govern the mountains of Esau.* And the kingdom will be the Lord's. This portion speaks of Israel annexing much land after the battle of Damascus. This includes the land of Edom. This will prove important later, as mentioned.

In Amos 9:11–12, we find an interesting portion telling us, in a nutshell, the message of Obadiah. God tells us that Israel will be destroyed, rebuilt, and that they will annex Edom. We are told in this passage that this is the work of the Lord.

Amos 9:11–12: "In that day I will restore David's fallen tent. I will repair its broken places, restore its ruins, and build it as it used to be, so that they may possess the remnant of Edom and all the nations that bear my name, declares the Lord, who will do these things."

This is an excellent support passage for Obadiah. This explains how Israel can be called back to their homeland and still flee to the wilderness of Edom without ever having to leave Israel. Israel is much larger after the battle of Damascus.

An excellent passage dealing with the battle of Damascus and the annexation of territory afterward is found in Micah 5:5b-15. Here, we will find mention of one of the participants of this battle that is mentioned only in a very few portions in relation to this battle. This is the country of Assyria (modern-day Iraq). This portion explains why Assyria is not mentioned in relation to the Battle of Magog; it is already in Israeli possession. This may also have influence on the Battle of Magog as the hook in the jaws, (the inducement to attack, Ezekiel 38:4) as we will see in the next chapter of this book. Israel will own Iraq's oil fields!

> "…When the Assyrian invades our land and marches through
> our fortresses, we will raise against him seven shepherds, even
> eight leaders of men. They will rule the land of Assyria with

the sword, the land of Nimrod with drawn sword. He will deliver us from the Assyrian when he invades our land and marches into our borders. *The remnant of Jacob will be in the midst of many peoples like dew from the Lord,* like showers on the grass, which do not wait for man or linger for mankind. *The remnant of Jacob will be among the nations, in the midst of many peoples,* like a lion among the beasts of the forest, like a young lion among flocks of sheep, which mauls and mangles as it goes, and no one can rescue. *Your* hand will be lifted up in triumph over *your* enemies, and your foes will be destroyed. In that day," declares the Lord, "I will destroy *your* horses from among you and demolish *your* chariots. I will destroy the cities of *your* land and tear down *your* strongholds. I will destroy *your* witchcraft and *you* will no longer cast spells. I will destroy *your* carved images and *your* sacred stones from among *you*; *you* will no longer bow down to the work of *your* hands. I will uproot from among *you your* Asherah poles and demolish *your* cities. I will take vengeance in anger and wrath upon the nations that have not obeyed me."

Micah 5:5b-15

This is a very important portion dealing with the time of the battle of Damascus. First, in Micah 5:3–5a, it is dealing with the mission of Christ as the Messiah of Israel in the tribulation time through the millennium. Then it goes into background, specifically the battle of Damascus and its bearing on end-times events. In the last part of Micah 5:5 (unfortunate division of verses, also proof that while the text is inspired, the division of verses isn't!), it begins speaking of the invasion of the Assyrian (Iraqi) army. We will find that Assyria's participation in this battle is mentioned in Psalm 83 as well. We find here that there will be "seven, even eight" leaders raised to fight this invasion. We are told here that they will rule the land of Assyria with a sword. So here we have the annexation of Iraq after this battle. Then we are told a very pertinent piece of information: the remnant of Jacob (Israel) will be in the midst of many peoples and among many nations. This is important because it tells us that Israel hasn't re-gathered from throughout the world yet. It also brings out the point that the remnant that is found through-out the world is a force to be reckoned with. After this battle with Damascus (Syria) and other surrounding countries, there is a great re-gathering and rebuilding. They come from all over the earth to repopulate the land of Israel and annex the territories of their attackers. This is what we find happening here in Micah. They are invaded and end up ruling Assyria with a sword. This explains why Iraq will not be included in the list of nations attacking Israel in the Battle of Magog. (But we will find that Iraq is one of the nations being attacked in the Battle of Magog.) This isn't a bad comeback for a nation that was only recently virtually destroyed in the battle of Damascus! There is only one simple explanation for this remark-able recovery. No other country on earth has such a vast reserve of people living throughout the world as does Israel. Today there are more Jews living outside Israel than in Israel. (This is especially true in the US and Russia.) This information can be found in many sites on the internet. With this great population of people available, they will be able to rebuild Israel and annex their attacker's lands! No other nation could do this. The stage is set!

Next we are told that "your" hand will be lifted in triumph over "your" enemies. "Your" and "You" throughout this portion is speak-ing of Israel. We will find in the next battle, it is God who will be triumphant over Israel's enemies, but here, Israel is triumphant, even though barely so. Then we will also find judgment on Israel from God, because they haven't repented from their sins. God will destroy their horses and chariots, cities and strongholds, witchcraft and idols. This is why their apparent repentance isn't effective, as we found in Isaiah 17. They didn't repent from the heart; they were forced from their idols by the hand of God. God had to do this so they couldn't accuse Him of not doing everything He could to save them from their own sin, to show them that they had to repent from the heart. Then God states in Micah 5:15, "I will take vengeance…upon the nations that have not obeyed me." He pours out His wrath on these gentile nations as well as Israel. None have obeyed God!

This portion describes the battle of Damascus very well. It also gives details that aren't found in other portions detailing the turning away from idols. They turn away because God destroys them. This portion is also the best at describing Iraq's involvement in this battle. This also gives a possible reason for the invasion of Magog, which is coming up in the next chapter of this book; Israel will own Iraq's oil fields! This may be the "hook in the Jaw," as already mentioned. Of course, this is only conjecture. We don't know for sure what the "hook in the jaw" is, because God doesn't tell us, but this is a possibility. Wow, big stuff!

Perhaps the best portion dealing with the annexation of enemy territory by Israel is found in Zephaniah 2:4–10. This portion lists many of the attacking nations and tells us that they will be taken over by Israel. The land the Philistines inhabited will be destroyed and annexed (verses 5–7). Moab (central Jordan) will also be destroyed and annexed by Israel. Jordan is today appearing to be the Islamic voice of reason, but this will change. Verse 9 states that "the survivors of *my nation* will inherit their land." God is looking at a time that is future in this chapter (Israel's repentance) but is looking back to this event as it leads up to their repentance (Zephaniah 2:1–3). So He refers to Israel as "my nation." Zephaniah 2:12 tells us that "Cushites" will be slain as well. This is looking ahead to the Battle of Magog. The "Cushites," or the Ethiopians, as they are known today, will be involved in the Battle of Magog. The reason this is important is that it mentions the destruction of Assyria with the attack on Cush. The mention of the destruction of Cush is significant because it leads us to the understanding that Zephaniah has gone from the battle of Damascus to the Battle of Magog. You will notice that there is a small break in the action with Zephaniah

2:10 and 11, and then he picks it up with the destruction of Cush in Zephaniah 2:12. Then he tells us of the destruction of Assyria (Iraq). We will find in Jeremiah 50 that Iraq is destroyed in the Magog battle in the next chapter of this book.

The next portion we will look at is dealing with coalitions attacking Israel. This sets the stage for modern day events that we see every day in the news! It's almost as if Asaph (the writer of this Psalm) was reading a present-day newspaper, as far as coalition warfare is concerned!

Let's look at Psalm 83. Psalms is not often considered a prophetic book, but there are some very important prophecies in Psalms. Psalm 22, for instance is a very accurate prophecy of Christ's death on the cross. Psalm 83 appears to be a prophecy of the Damascus battle. This is because the peoples involved are many of the same ones that are mentioned in other portions that deal with the Damascus battle. Also, this coalition and condition has never existed up to this time. It is still to be fulfilled. Also note that in the present-day situation, *all* of these nations could very easily work together to try to destroy Israel. They all have said within the last sixty years that they would like to see Israel destroyed. I will copy certain words in *italic* print to emphasize certain important points to consider.

> "O God, do not keep silent; be not quiet, O God, be not still. See how your enemies are astir, how your foes rear their heads. With cunning they *conspire* against your people; they *plot* against those you cherish. '*Come*,' they say, '*let us destroy them as a nation, that the nation of Israel be remembered no more.*' With one mind they plot together; *they form an alliance* against you—the tents of Edom and the Ishmaelites, of Moab and the Hagrites, Gebal, Ammon and Amalek, Philistia, with the *people* of Tyre. Even Assyria has joined them to lend strength to the *descendants of Lot. Selah* Do to them as you did to Midian, as you did to Sisera and Jabin at the river Kishon,

who perished at Endor and became like refuse on the ground. Make their nobles like Oreb and Zeeb, all their princes like Zebah and Zalmunna, who said, 'Let us take possession of the pasturelands of God.' Make them like tumbleweed, O my God, like chaff before the wind. *As fire consumes the forest or a flame sets the mountains ablaze*, so pursue them with *your tempest* and terrify them with *your storm*. Cover their faces with shame so that *men will seek your name*, O Lord. May they ever be ashamed and dismayed; may they perish in disgrace. Let them know that you, whose name is the Lord—that you alone are the Most High over all the earth."

Psalms 83:1–18

First, let's examine Psalm 83:3. God's enemies "conspire"; they "plot" together. Psalm 83:5 states that "they form an alliance." This is going to be a coalition, which is so popular today among nations. There are many coalitions in existence today representing common ideologies. The people mentioned here are all Islamic, a basic religious common ground. Recently, the leadership of Iran stated publicly that they wanted to destroy Israel from the face of the earth. Iran is not one of this group but will be involved in a similar fashion later (Chapter 2 of this book). But this sentiment has been stated by Islamic nations from the inception of Israel as a nation in 1948. Notice Psalm 83:4: "'Come,' they say, 'let us destroy them as a nation, that the nation of Israel be remembered no more.'" Then it names several nations until it gets to "the people of Tyre." Alexander the Great destroyed the city of Tyre before Christ, but *the people* could be referring to the descendants of the people of Tyre or the people who live in the region that Tyre existed in. Tyre today is in Lebanon, as I mentioned earlier. Also note that it speaks of "the descendants of Lot." This takes in Jordan but may include others that have settled elsewhere. Notice also that fire consumes them. This fire is likened to a forest fire or mountains ablaze. That's a big fire! I wouldn't rule out nuclear warfare. God's Word also likens it to a "tempest" or a "storm." I cannot say that this is definitely nuclear, but the description is apt. There was not nuclear warfare to compare it to at the time, of course, but the description would be like this mentioned here.

Isaiah 15–16 also mentions prophecies concerning Moab. The problem with these chapters is that it contains prophecies that are already fulfilled as well as prophecies yet to be fulfilled. There are no end-times prophecies here that are not covered elsewhere. Although, there is a statement in Isaiah 16:1 that is interesting. I will highlight certain parts that reinforce prophecies made elsewhere in scripture. "Send lambs as tribute to the *ruler* of the land, from Sela across the desert, to the mount of the *Daughter of Zion*." This points out that at this time, Israel (Zion) will be the ruler of the land. God is telling the exiles (fugitives, Isaiah 16:3, 4) of Moab (central Jordan) to send tribute to Jerusalem. This then supports the contention that Israel will annex these lands after the battle of Damascus. Isaiah 15:6–16:5 takes us from the battle of Damascus through to the reign of Christ as it pertains to Moab. It is a fact that Sela is another name for Petra. This is one of the weak portions that some use to support their contention that Israel flees to Petra.

In the next portion, we will find a very interesting passage that is coincident with the battle of Damascus, although not directly involved with the battle. I mention it because it occurs at the same time in prophecy, as I will try to prove. This portion deals with Egypt and is the reason that they aren't involved in any of the end-time battles as an aggressor. We'll find that they will be a victim in the next chapter, which will also help pinpoint the timing of this prophecy. Bear with me, please!

In Isaiah 19:1–15 is the oracle of Egypt.

> An oracle concerning Egypt: "See, the Lord rides on a swift cloud and is coming to Egypt. The idols of Egypt tremble before him, and the hearts of the Egyptians melt within

them. 'I will stir up Egyptian against Egyptian—brother will fight against brother, neighbor against neighbor, city against city, kingdom against kingdom. The Egyptians will lose heart, and I will bring their plans to nothing; they will consult the idols and the spirits of the dead, the mediums and the spiritists. I will hand the Egyptians over to power of a cruel master, and a fierce king will rule over them,' declares the Lord, the Lord Almighty. The waters of the river will dry up, and the riverbed will be parched and dry. The canals will stink; the streams of Egypt will dwindle and dry up. The reeds and rushes will wither, also the plants along the Nile, at the mouth of the river. Every sown field along the Nile will become parched, will blow away and be no more. The fishermen will groan and lament, all who cast hooks into the Nile; those who throw nets on the water will pine away. Those who work with combed flax will despair, the weavers of fine linen will lose hope. The workers in cloth will be dejected, and all the wage earners will be sick at heart. The officials of Zoan are nothing but fools; the wise counselors of pharaoh give senseless advice. How can you say to Pharaoh, 'I am one of the wise men, a disciple of the ancient kings?' Where are your wise men now? Let them show you and make known what the Lord Almighty has planned for Egypt. The officials of Zoan have become fools, the leaders of Memphis are deceived; the cornerstones of her peoples have led Egypt astray. The Lord has poured into them a spirit of dizziness; they make Egypt stagger in all that she does, as a drunkard staggers around in his vomit. There is nothing Egypt can do—head of tail, palm branch or reed."

Isaiah 19:1–15

I will end the quote there for now, as it is leading into the next chapter of this book. This portion doesn't directly speak of the battle of Damascus but does speak of a time that covers the same time period and more. We will find this to be true when we study the rest of this chapter in light of other portions. The fulfillment of this portion is in the beginning stages even now!

We find that the Egyptians are fearful. They know that they are in trouble. Their idols are no help. We find that God will stir up discontent among the Egyptians: Egyptian against Egyptian, brother against brother, neighbor against neighbor, city against city, and kingdom against kingdom. This seems to suggest terrorist activity and civil war. We all know that there has been much terrorist activity in this region, even some specifically in Egypt. Civil war hasn't broken out yet. Who knows when, but it will happen when there is enough unrest. The portion tells us that there will be a "cruel master" and a "fierce king" that God will put over them. This may be speaking of the antichrist but could be anybody who will come to power in Egypt. Again, this hasn't happened yet. With the turmoil in the Middle East, this could happen with very little notice. These first few verses speak of the political situation in Egypt. Next we will find the environmental situation. This is very interesting in light of recent events.

The water of "the river" will dry up. This is the Nile, as we will find in a few verses. Wow! The Nile will dry up? Now, that doesn't sound possible! But some very surprising things have happened in the last 100 years that make it more likely. For instance, the nations upstream of Egypt (Sudan and Ethiopia) have growing populations with increased agricultural and human needs. For many years, Egypt has had a treaty with these and other Nile-river-basin countries on water usage. Essentially, the treaty said that they were to use only so much water or Egypt will take military action to defend their use of the water. Sudan (and Libya, for that matter) has begun an aggressive armament program in recent years and has gotten to the stage that they are strong enough that they could tell Egypt they aren't going to honor their water treaties. Egypt no longer feels secure that they could successfully invade these countries. This is happening! To some extent, some of these countries have begun to ignore the treaties they have signed and have begun using more water than they are allowed. This is just one small problem. Also, there has been a climate change in North Africa that has caused the Nile to receive about forty percent less rain into the Nile River basin.

Egypt has built two dams in recent history, first in the early 1900s, the Aswan Dam, and later, the Aswan High Dam, forming Lake Nasser. This lake, according to some reports, is pressing on the land enough that it is actually reversing the flow of the aquifer feeding Egypt. Libya has been drilling wells into the aquifer that feeds water to Egypt, using large amounts of water and reducing the water available to Egypt. The sediment that fertilizes Egypt's farmland is precipitating out of the water into the bed of the lake, starving the farmland of nutrients that the farmers have depended on for millennia. The water that is trapped in this lake experiences strong evaporation, causing salinization of the water that is intended for irrigation. This causes crops to fail. The water that flows out of the lake is so lacking in silt that, instead of depositing it, the water picks it up, draining the land of its topsoil and further damaging the farming. Also, the lake is so big that it is actually changing the climate of the area, and no one knows exactly what the outcome of this will be—except God! God does tell us that it won't be good. The salinization of the lake has damaged Egypt's fishing industry, causing greatly depleted fish harvests. One of the intentions of developers was to help the fishing industry. The reverse has been true. When they built the dams, they wished to save as many of the Egyptian statues of idols as they could, so they moved them to higher ground. The problem is that because of the drainage of the land around some of these temples—Karnack, for example (Karnack is the largest temple in Egypt. It contains all the idols that ancient Egypt used to worship.)—salt is building up on the temples and statues, causing erosion of the sandstone that was used to build them. They are crumbling where they stand.

I find the wording of the King James translation interesting here in Isaiah 19:10: "And they will be broken in the purposes thereof, all that make sluices *and* ponds for fish." (Sluices are dams.) The Amplified Bible states it: "(Those who are) the pillars *and* foundations of Egypt will be crushed, and all those who work for hire *or* who build dams will be grieved." There seems to be a double meaning to the word translated as *wage earners* in the NIV. It also seems to suggest that they are working on dams. This is one of the problems in translating from one language to another, especially coming from an ancient language. The ancient Hebrew language here had nuances that could be interpreted to mean different things. One translator pursued one meaning and another pursued the other. The original meaning was both! According to *Strong's Exhaustive Concordance*, the word means *wage, reward,* and *sluices*. It means someone who gets paid for making dams! How very interesting! We are seeing the beginning of prophetical fulfillment, the preparation for the fulfillment of prophecy, and it is irreversible. The rest of this portion that I have quoted here tells us that the leadership of Egypt will not be able to stop events. It is out of their control. I will show why this is coincident with the Damascus battle and rebuilding time in the next chapter.

We find in Ezekiel 29:1–16 a portion of scripture that gives us another prophecy with multiple fulfillments. Nebuchadnezzar invaded Egypt and did carry off many of its people. From that time on, Egypt has never been the same world power that it was in the past. This will probably be a preview of the judgment that will be poured out on them in the future and has already begun.

In fact there is a lot of information in Ezekiel 30 as well. This is future. In Ezekiel 30:1–19 there is a portion that parallels the battle of Damascus events. In the Ezekiel 29 portion we find that an area of Egypt from Migdol (near the Mediterranean Sea) to Aswan (the dams previously mentioned) will be devastated and uninhabited for forty years. This is definitely a future event. Never has so large a portion of Egypt been rendered uninhabitable. Notice that neither man nor beast will set foot in it for forty years! To me, again, this sounds nuclear. Chapter 30 gives details of this battle. So it appears that while much of Egypt will waste away, portions of it will be violently attacked! This would certainly add to their confusion and the general conundrum that is described in Isaiah 19.

This next portion will bring us full circle in dealing with prophecy. It is Christ's words as He revealed them to the apostle John on the Isle of Patmos, where he was banished for his testimony of Christ. It coincides with Christ's words in Matthew (and Luke) very well. It gives more detail of conditions leading up to (and including) the time of tribulation. This portion introduces the "four horsemen of the Apocalypse" and their roles in prophecy.

Revelation 6:1–8—I realize that this portion is often considered a seven-years-tribulation portion; in fact, I thought this just as little as a year before this writing. Much study of the subject has subsequently changed my mind. This is a beginning-of-sorrows or beginning-of-birth-pains portion, a time leading to the seven years of tribulation. It parallels the portion in Matthew 24:4–8 (which, last year, I would also have included in the tribulation) quite well. I will explain in the next chapter why this isn't part of the seven years of tribulation but only a time leading into it.

> I watched as the Lamb opened the first of the seven seals. Then I heard one of the four living creatures say in a voice like thunder, "Come!" I looked, and there before me was a white horse! Its rider held a bow, and he was given a crown, and he rode out as a conqueror bent on conquest. When the Lamb opened the second seal, I heard the second living creature say, "Come!" Then another horse came out, a fiery red one. Its rider was given power to take peace from the earth and make men slay each other. To him was given a large sword. When the Lamb opened the third seal, I heard the third living creature say, "Come!" I looked and there before

me was a black horse! Its rider was holding a pair of scales in his hand. Then I heard what sounded like a voice among the four living creatures, saying, "A quart of wheat for a day's wages, and three quarts of barley for a day's wages, and do not damage the oil and the wine!" When the Lamb opened the fourth seal, I heard the voice of the fourth living creature say, "Come!" I looked, and there before me was a pale horse! Its rider was named Death, and Hades was following close behind him. They were given power over a fourth of the earth to kill by sword, famine, and plague, and by wild beasts of the earth.

Revelation 6:1–8

In the Matthew 24:4–8 portion, we find first that there will be many who will come in Christ's name, claiming indeed to be Him. Christ warns them not to be deceived. The first thing Christ warns them of are false Christs. The first thing that we find in Revelation 6 is a rider going out on a white horse, which speaks of royalty. He goes out armed, capable of war, and bent on conquering. He is given a crown. This implies that he hasn't absolute authority. If he were God, he wouldn't have to be given anything; it would be his already. So he is allowed to have the role of world leader. He goes out conquering. Whether he conquers through war initially or through diplomatic persuasion may be irrelevant. I personally feel that he uses diplomatic persuasion and some warfare to intimidate and manipulate. This is because peace isn't taken from the earth until the next rider comes on the scene. This first rider is most likely the antichrist. In every description we have of him, we find that he is very charismatic, very persuasive in his speech. Perhaps a modern-day model of him would be Adolph Hitler. He was a genius speechmaker. He persuaded more than one country just to lay down their arms and join with him. He persuaded Great Britain to appease him until he had gotten much power, so much so that he felt he was in a good position to take over the world! This seems to parallel the activities of the antichrist in Revelation 6:2. Hitler was not the antichrist, but he was an antichrist! He wanted to start the thousand-year Reich. This was a reference to the thousand-year reign of Christ. But the real antichrist will be much more powerful and much more dangerous. Hitler was dangerous enough, but he will be small stuff compared to the real deal. It seems likely that the antichrist will come to power and build his power base, and then we will find the second rider, also the antichrist but in a different role. He will "take peace from the earth." He will probably reward those who betray and murder believers who come to Christ after the Damascus battle. We will spend an entire chapter devoted to the person and activities of the antichrist in Chapter 4 of this book. The Matthew 24 portion mentions "wars." This would certainly include the battle of Damascus (and others, which we will discuss in the next chapter), which Christ mentions after the introduction of the false Christs who deceive many. That's happening today, but with the presence of the true antichrist on the scene, it will be much worse. He will probably be the big one among many. Then we find that Christ warns of famines and earthquakes. In Revelation 6, we find the next thing mentioned is a scarcity of food (this is referred to in Isaiah 17:10–11). The parallels are too strong to be speaking of two different events. In fact, I believe that Revelation 6 and Matthew 24 are speaking of the same thing, just giving different details.

In the next portions, we will find small verses that should be mentioned for their bearing on the battle. They will fill in bits of detail or nuances that may not be expressed as clearly in other portions.

In Isaiah 26:15, we find another mention of Israel's annexation of the attacking lands that merits mention here. "You have enlarged the nation, O Lord; you have enlarged the nation. You have gained glory for yourself; you have extended all the borders of the land." Isaiah 27:7 also mentions the battle of Damascus. It says, "Has the

Lord struck her as he struck down those who struck her? Has she been killed as those were killed who killed her?" We will find in the following context that it is speaking of the Damascus battle, because the Day of Atonement, which we will study more in Chapter 3 of this book, follows after the rebuilding and during the Magog battle. These events haven't happened here.

In the next portion, we will examine the regathering of Israel to their land after they were punished. It covers the Damascus battle and the regathering afterward beautifully! It covers the time of the battle of Damascus in a nutshell very well! Not only this, but it also leads into events that will be covered in the next chapter rather beautifully.

Hosea 11 speaks of Israel's judgment by God and their re-gathering.

> "When Israel was a child, I loved him, and out of Egypt I called my son. But the more I called Israel, the further they went from me. They sacrificed to Baals and they burned incense to images. It was I who taught Ephraim to walk, taking them by the arms; *but they did not realize it was I who healed them.* I led them with cords of human kindness, with ties of love; I lifted the yoke from their neck and bent down to feed them. Will they not return to Egypt and will not Assyria rule over them *because they refuse to repent? Swords will flash in their cities, will destroy the bars of their gates and put an end to their plans. My people are determined to turn from me. Even if they call to the Most High,* he will by no means exalt them. How can I give you up, Ephraim? How can I hand you over, Israel? How can I treat you like Admah? How can I make you like Zeboiim? My heart is changed within me; all my compassion is aroused. I will not carry out my fierce anger, nor will I turn and devastate Ephraim. For I am God, and not man—the Holy One among you. I will not come in wrath. They will follow the Lord: he will roar like a lion. When he roars, *his children will come trembling from the west.* They

will come trembling like birds from Egypt, like doves from Assyria. I will settle them in their homes," declares the Lord. *Ephraim has surrounded me with lies, the house of Israel with deceit. And Judah is unruly against God, even against the faithful Holy One.*

Hosea 11:1–12

This is a very interesting passage. This is dealing with the Damascus battle and the recovery, but it also introduces a very important event in future Israeli history: their Rosh Hashanah! This will be an important part of the next chapter of this book, but it is also important here to show the blend of events from the Damascus battle to the Magog battle and eventually to their *Yom Kippur*, their Day of Atonement! We find this to be true, because throughout the passage, we find that they haven't repented! Their Day of Atonement hasn't happened yet, but they are regathered home! First, we find that they strayed from God. They didn't realize who their God was (Hosea 11:3). They will be scattered to other nations (Hosea 11:5). This scattering was fulfilled in 70 AD, and they only had a nation to go to since 1948. Even though they have a nation today, they are still mostly scattered throughout the world. There will be a battle in their cities (please note that this is mentioned *after* they are scattered!). This battle is most likely speaking of the Damascus battle, because this is pivotal in God's plan for Israel. Their plans are ruined! All the battles since 1948 have promoted Israel as a nation, except they haven't turned to God. This one ruins their plans; they are virtually destroyed as a nation, but they still don't turn to God (Hosea 11:7, 12). Notice in Hosea 11:7 that "Even if they call to the Most High, he will by no means exalt them"! This refers to Isaiah 17:7–8,10. One thing they do follow the Lord in though is when he roars, they will follow him out of the nations where they are scattered (Hosea 11:10–11). This, I believe, is a reference to Rosh Hashanah. This is because here they begin to obey God. They come home *trembling*; something has shaken them to their core. We will find out what in the next chapter of this book. An interesting note: the first place where they come trembling (yet unrepentant!) is "*the west*"! That could be a thinly veiled reference to the western hemisphere. We in the USA are referred to as "the west" throughout the world. There is a greater population of Jews in the rest of the world than live in Israel at the time of this writing. The largest concentration of Jews lives in the US! I wouldn't argue against this possibility. This portion is speaking about the destruction of Israel, as mentioned in Isaiah 17 and Amos 2, and it also speaks of the recovery of Israel. This portion also introduces the Rosh Hashanah, the Feast of Trumpets, and their call to repentance as a nation, for which they re-gather home. There are more references to this elsewhere in Scripture.

In Ezekiel 34–37, we have an account of the battle of Damascus. Although it doesn't speak of Damascus, it does speak of many of the other countries involved in this battle, as mentioned in other portions. Then it speaks of the regathering of God's people (the vision of dry bones). Please read this for yourself; I will not try to copy it all here. The re-gathering mentioned throughout Scripture is *not the one that happened in 1948*! That one was just a seed, a place for Israel to go to when they are called. They will be virtually destroyed, and then the real regathering will occur, which will be their Rosh Hashanah, which we will find more about in the next chapter. God is much more interested in their regathering to Him than to the land of Israel. We find this to be true because there are many more verses referring to their returning to Him than returning to their land, and the portion in Ezekiel is more focused on their return to Him. The only very clear portion in Ezekiel that refers to their rebuilding of their country is Ezekiel 38:8: Magog will attack "a land that has recovered from war, whose people were gathered from many nations to the mountains of Israel..." This is their physical gathering, not their spiritual gathering, as found in Ezekiel 39:22. This will be covered in more depth in the next two chapters.

Another portion that is very interesting in dealing with the battle of Damascus is Ezekiel 33:1–20. While this isn't specifically dealing with the Damascus battle, it does set the rules that will be in effect for that time. It sets a hypothetical event before the people of Israel. Their country is about to be invaded, so they pick a man to be their watchman. If he sounds the trumpet and warns them of the impending battle and they do nothing about it, they are to blame for their own death, but if the watchman doesn't warn them, they are still going to die, and the watchman is held accountable. Then it says that the watchman is to warn Israel of sin. If he does and they don't repent, they will be judged for their sin; if he doesn't warn them, they are still guilty and will die, but the watchman is held responsible for their death and will be judged. This will be the way things will go at the battle of Damascus. They will pick a "watchman." We will find that he will be the antichrist. He doesn't warn them, and they are killed because of their sin (Isaiah 27:7). God orders the sounding of the trumpet, but it is not sounded. Many die in their sin. Then there is the restoration of Israel to their land after the battle of Damascus in Isaiah 36–37, which will be their Rosh Hashanah! We see this woven into prophecy for Israel throughout these portions. The battle of Damascus is directly leading them into Rosh Hashanah. But as I said, the next chapter of this book will deal more thoroughly with Rosh Hashanah.

An interesting passage that parallels the events of the end times is Isaiah 9:8–10:19 (Please read this for yourself). At first, I thought it was end times, but certain things didn't fit with future prophecy. Then upon deeper study, I found that it is already fulfilled in the time of Ezra. While this is already fulfilled, I do believe that it is a picture of future events, a type of the end-times judgments found in Scripture. In fact, there is a theory that "the Assyrian" mentioned frequently in Isaiah 10 is the antichrist. This would be unlikely, because we find in Psalm 83 that Assyria aids the attackers of Israel in the battle of Damascus, but he is shepherding Israel (Zechariah

11:15–17). If his people attacked Israel, it seems strange that he would quickly be shepherding them. This is why I had a problem considering this to be a true end-times portion, although it does draw strong insights into events that are still future and could be at least a model of things to come. It shows a remnant's repentance in the face of disaster, and this is what will happen in the Battle of Magog. The "remnant" is a very populated nation of Israel (Ezekiel 38:8), but God spares them because of their repentance. The circumstance in Ezra's time was that they were massacred, and the remnant repented and God defended them by sending his death angel to kill the Assyrians. This angel killed over 180,000 Assyrians. Also, as already noted, Micah 5 tells us that Assyria is already annexed by Israel at the time after the Damascus battle. So after the Damascus battle, Assyria (Iraq) is out of the picture.

The portions that we have covered in this chapter are showing us an important event that is largely ignored in prophecy yet is very important. It is a time of preparation for very important spiritual events to follow. It is a time that will set up governments and conditions that will bring about the seven years of tribulation!

Now to recap what we've covered in this first chapter: We find Christ talking to his disciples about what would happen at the "end of the age." Here we find Christ introducing a time He called "the beginning of birth pains." The KJV refers to it as "the beginning of sorrows." Until recently, I always thought that the beginning of birth pains was the start of the "seven years of tribulation." But things didn't add up, as we'll find as we study God's Word. Please bear with me on this. My first reaction would be to automatically reject this notion, because I was always taught that all end-times prophecies start at the beginning of the seven years of tribulation. I needed to change my mind. God doesn't do things the way we expect just because we expect him to do it that way! Also, quite frankly, the way it is actually described in Scripture is much more understandable and logical, especially in light of recent world events and conditions.

Christ speaks of false Christs. This is nothing new to us, even now, even though we are not yet in the beginning of birth pains. It will become very pronounced. These false Christs will even be able, by the power of Satan, to perform miracles! Nothing like the liars we have had recently, such as Moon, David Koresh, Jim Jones, and many others. Christ speaks of wars and rumors of wars. We are not strangers to wars. In the previous century, we've had two world wars, the Korean "conflict" (ask anyone who was there, it was a war), the Vietnam War, the Gulf War, and specific to Israel, the conflict in 1948, when the modern nation of Israel was born, the Six Day War in 1967, the Yom Kippur war in 1973, and many other conflicts in the world. These will all pale when hostilities start during the beginning of birth pains. The descriptions of the battles then are devastating. The descriptions are very reminiscent of nuclear war and may actually be. I will not say that nuclear war is certain, because Scripture doesn't specifically mention nuclear weapons, but the description does certainly make the possibility plausible. I will repeat this frequently, lest someone claims that I said there will definitely be nuclear weapons. I cannot claim that, but it is likely. First we find mention of the destruction of Damascus. Damascus prides itself as "the oldest perpetually inhabited city on earth." And according to any records available at this time, that is probably true. So the prophecies of Damascus's destruction are future. We find in Isaiah 17 a battle between Syria and Israel. Both countries are nearly mutually destroyed. Damascus, Syria's capital city, is a heap of ruins, uninhabitable. Israel is, for all intents, also destroyed. The portion says that there are only a few left, like the grain left in the field after the field has been harvested or like the olives left on the uppermost branches that didn't fall when the tree was beaten to knock the olives down. Now, right after this time, Jews will be returning to Israel to make it their home. We find in other portions, i.e. Amos 1–2, another account of this battle and find that there are many more nations involved: Jordan, Gaza (recently given up by Israel, so this prophecy could be fulfilled, even though they don't realize it at this time), Lebanon, and in other portions, the Philistines (Palestine may soon be a country of their own but not necessarily, because the Bible refers to the Philistines as dwelling in cities of other countries, for example, in Gaza, in Amos, and with Tyre in Psalms.), Assyria (Iraq today) in a supporting role, and Egypt, which during this conflict is not attacked but is withering on the vine (already begun!). All of these countries are suffering. All except Egypt are nearly wiped out, but Israel has one thing up its sleeve that no other country has. They have a storehouse of settlers that can move into Israel, and for that matter, they can move into the attacking countries and annex them as well, and they will. These are the Jews that live in countries all over the world. Today, there are more Jews living throughout the world than in Israel! Many of these will recognize an opportunity and take it, making Israel even more powerful than it is today, or ever, for that matter! We find in several scriptures that Israel annexes much of their attackers' lands after this battle. No other country has this capability! We find that God allows the destruction that is poured out on Israel because of their sin (of rejecting Christ) to bring them to repentance. The destruction poured out upon the gentile nations is because of their ungodliness and their attack on His people. God will punish greatly the nations who hurt his people! Do not think that we should ever stand against Israel. They are and always will be his chosen people, and He will not allow nations to go unpunished who hurt His people. The aim of the attacking countries is to wipe out Israel so that they will not be remembered any more (Psalm 83). The president of Iran and other powerful terrorist leaders in Syria and elsewhere recently voiced this aim. The outcome of this battle will be the destruction of all these countries that are fighting. Jews from around the world rebuild Israel and make it bigger and more powerful than ever and give them a sense of security that they have never enjoyed since it became a modern nation. During the annexation phase of Israel's recovery, not all Jews come back to Israel though. We will find in the next chapter when all the Jews will return to Israel. (A hint: it's just before the Battle of Magog!)

In the next chapter, we will find the reason that we placed the battle of Damascus here in future history.

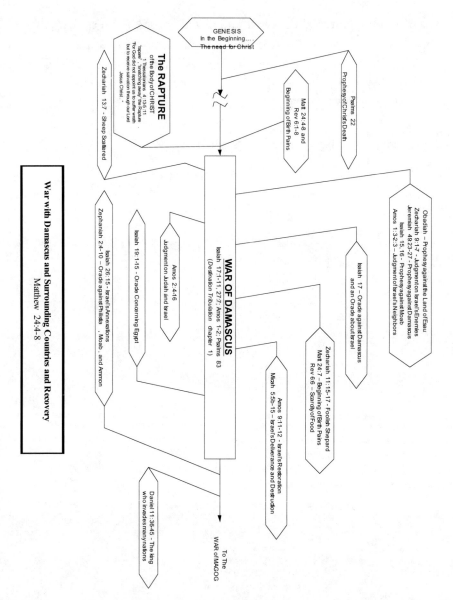

War of Damascus Event Line

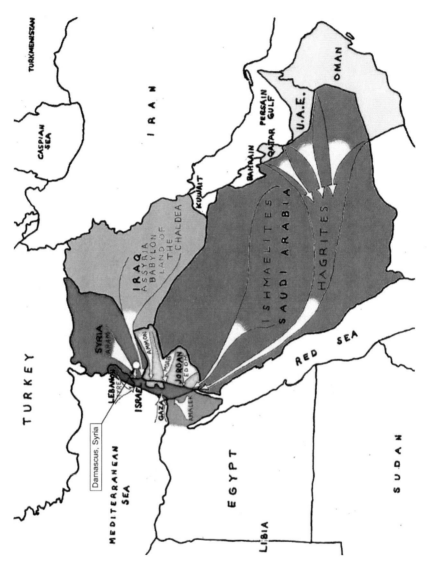

Pre-War with Damascus and Surrounding Countries Map

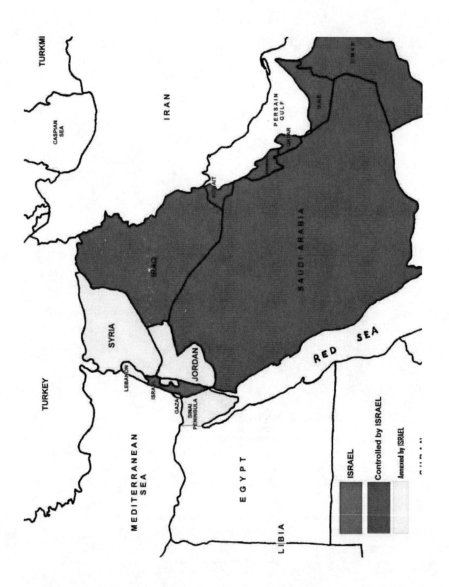

Post-War with Damascus and Surrounding Countries Map

CHAPTER 2

War of Magog - Rosh Hashanah
Matthew 24:4–8

In Ezekiel 38–39, we find a very interesting portion known as "the Battle of Magog." This battle is only referred to as the Battle of Magog here in Ezekiel. Now before you get all upset and cite the portion in Revelation 20:7–15, that is a different battle, as I will prove by scriptures later in this chapter and in the next volume. We will see that this battle is mentioned repeatedly in other portions of Scripture but not by the name "Magog."

> The word of the Lord came to me: "Son of man, set your face against Gog, of the land of Magog, the chief prince of Meshech and Tubal; prophesy against him and say: 'This is what the Sovereign Lord says: "I am against you, O Gog, chief prince of Meshech and Tubal. I will turn you around, put hooks in your jaws and bring you out with your whole army-your horses, your horsemen fully armed, and a great horde with large and small shields, all of them brandishing their swords. Persia, Cush and Put will be with them, all with shields and helmets, also Gomer with all its troops, and Beth Togarmah from the far north with all its troops-the many nations with you. Get ready; be prepared, you and all the

hordes gathered about you, and take command of them. After many days you will be called to arms. In future years you will invade a land that has *recovered from war, whose people were gathered from many nations to the mountains of Israel*, which had long been desolate. *They had been brought out from the nations, and now all of them live in safety.* You and all your troops and the many nations with you will go up, advancing like a storm; you will be like a cloud covering the land." This is what the Sovereign Lord says: "On that day thoughts will come into your mind and you will devise an evil scheme. You will say, 'I will invade a land of unwalled villages; I will attack a peaceful and unsuspecting people-all of them living without walls and without gates and bars. I will plunder and loot and turn my hand against *the resettled ruins and the people gathered from the nations*, rich in livestock and goods, living at the center of the land.' Sheba and Dedan and the merchants of Tarshish and all her villages will say to you, 'Have you come to plunder? Have you gathered your hordes to loot, to carry off silver and gold, to take away livestock and goods and to seize much plunder?' Therefore, son of man, prophesy and say to Gog: 'This is what the Sovereign Lord says: "In that day, when my people Israel are living in safety, will you not take notice of it? *You will come from your place in the far north*, you and many nations with you, all of them riding on horses, a great horde, a mighty army. You will advance against my people Israel like a cloud that covers the land. In days to come, O Gog, I will bring you against my land, so that the nations may know me when I show myself holy through you before their eyes." This is what the Sovereign Lord says: "Are you not the one I spoke of in former days by my servants the prophets of Israel? At the time they prophesied for years that I would bring you against them. This is what will happen in that day: When Gog attacks the land of Israel, my hot anger will be aroused," declares the Sovereign Lord. "In my zeal and fiery wrath I declare that at that time there shall be a great earthquake in the land of Israel. The fish of the sea, the birds of the air, the beasts of the field, every creature that moves along the ground, and all the people on the face of the earth will tremble at my presence. The mountains will be overturned, the cliffs will crumble, *and every wall will fall to the ground*. I will summon a sword against Gog on all my mountains," declares the Sovereign Lord. "Every man's sword will be against his brother. I will execute judgment upon him with plague and bloodshed; I will pour down torrents of rain, hailstones and burning sulfur on him and on his troops and on the many nations with him. And so I will show my greatness and my holiness, and I will make myself known in the sight of many nations. Then they will know that I am the Lord."

Ezekiel 38:1–23

Son of man, prophesy against Gog and say: "This is what the Sovereign Lord says: 'I am against you, O Gog, chief prince of Meshech and Tubal. I will turn you around and drag you along. I will bring you *from the far north* and send you against the mountains of Israel. Then I will strike your bow from your left hand and make your arrows drop from your right hand. On the mountains of Israel you will fall, you and all your troops and the nations with you. I will give you as food to all kinds of carrion birds and to the wild animals. You will fall in the open field, for I have spoken,' declares the Sovereign Lord. 'I will send fire on Magog and on those who live in safety in the coastlands, and they will know that I am the Lord. I will make known my holy name among my people Israel. I will no longer let my holy name be profaned, and the nations will know that I the Lord am the holy one in Israel. It is coming! It will surely take place,' declares the Sovereign Lord. 'This is the day I have spoken of. Then those who live in the towns of Israel will go out and *use the weapons for fuel and burn them up*—the small and large shields, the bows and arrows, the war clubs and spears. *For seven years they will use them for fuel*. They will not need to gather wood from the fields or cut it from the forests, because they will use the weapons for fuel. *And they will plunder those who plundered them and loot those who looted them*,' declares the Sovereign

Lord. 'On that day I will give Gog a burial place in Israel, in the valley of those who travel east toward the sea. It will block the way of travelers, because Gog and all his hordes will be buried there. So it will be called the Valley of Hamon Gog. For seven months the house of Israel will be burying them in order to cleanse the land. All the people of the land will bury them, and the day I am glorified will be a memorable day for them,' declares the Sovereign Lord. *'Men will be regularly employed to cleanse the land. Some will go throughout the land and, in addition to them, others will bury those that remain on the ground. At the end of the seven months they will begin their search. As they go through the land and one of them sees a human bone, he will set up a marker beside it until the gravediggers have buried it in the Valley of Hamon Gog.* (Also a town called Hamonah will be there.) And so they will cleanse the land.' Son of man, this is what the Sovereign Lord says: 'Call out to every kind of bird and all the wild animals: Assemble and come together from all around to the sacrifice I am preparing for you, the great sacrifice on the mountains of Israel. There you will eat flesh and drink blood. You will eat the flesh of mighty men and drink the blood of princes of the earth as if they were rams and lambs, goats and bulls-all of them fattened animals from Bashan. At the sacrifice I am preparing for you, you will eat fat until you are glutted and drink blood until you are drunk. At my table you will eat your fill of horses and riders, mighty men and soldiers of every kind,' declares the Sovereign Lord. 'I will display my glory among the nations, and all the nations will see the punishment I inflict and the hand I lay upon them. *From that day forward the house of Israel will know that I am the Lord their God.* And the nations will know that the people of Israel went into exile for their sin, because they were unfaithful to me. *So I hid my face from them and handed them over to their enemies, and they all fell by the sword. I dealt with them according to their uncleanness and their offenses, and I hid my face from them.'* Therefore this is what the Sovereign Lord says: 'I will now bring Jacob back from captivity and will have compassion on all the people of Israel, and I will be zealous for my holy name. *They will forget their shame and all the unfaithfulness they showed toward me when they lived in safety in their land with no one to make them afraid.* When I have brought them back from the nations and have gathered them from the countries of their enemies, I will show myself holy through them in the sight of many nations. *Then they will know that I am the Lord their God,* for though I sent them into exile among the nations, *I will gather them to their own land, not leaving any behind. I will no longer hide my face from them, for I will pour out my spirit on the house of Israel,* declares the Sovereign Lord.'"

Ezekiel 39:1–29

I typed certain key portions in *italics* print to draw attention to them. These portions contain information that is important to understanding the placement of this event and other pivotal events in prophesy. I will address these portions in the order that we arrive at them.

First we find that a certain person, Gog, is addressed here. Whoever Gog is, he is the leader of a nation. The nation that he is leader of is called Magog. This portion also refers to certain other nations: Meshech, Tubal, Persia, Cush, Put, Gomer, and Beth Togarmah. There is much speculation as to the identity of not only Gog but also the identity of these nations.

The reference to Gog seems to be a title more than a specific name. We find this because there is a reference to Gog and Magog in Revelation 20:7–9. This reference is about one thousand years *after* the Gog and Magog of Ezekiel. The reason I say this is because of a couple of things in Scripture that make this clear: a) In Ezekiel 39: 22, we find that the battle is over and God has intervened on behalf of the nation of Israel, and "*From that day forward the house of Israel will know that I am the Lord their God.*" In Revelation, we find that Christ has been reigning *on the earth for one thousand years* (Revelation 20, Zechariah 14:4–9). In Ezekiel, the Battle of Magog causes the Israelites to come to the knowledge of just who their God is, but in Revelation, they will already know that Christ is their God; He will be with them on earth ruling them as king! So, the Battles of Gog and Magog must be separated by at least one thousand years. b). Also in Ezekiel, we find that they clean up the mess for seven years after the battle is over (Ezekiel 39:9); they spend seven months just burying the dead (Ezekiel 39:12)! After the battle in Revelation 20, we find Satan's final judgment, the final judgment of the unsaved, and then in Revelation 21, the new heaven and new earth. There will not be any need for the clean up mentioned in Ezekiel if they are speaking of the same battle, so clearly, there are two separate Gog-Magog battles. Now, since the name *Gog* is used for an individual over a thousand years apart, it would have to be a title, or it could be another name for a leader possessed by Satan (because Gog will be buried at Hamon Gog as mentioned in Ezekiel 39:11), which is entirely possible! Also, as to the identity of Gog, it appears that there are only two references in Scripture to the name *Gog*. In Joel, we find another portion that speaks of the Magog battle. I will prove this momentarily. It speaks of a mighty army advancing on Israel. Israel is forced to repent or be annihilated (Joel 2:12–14). Then in Joel 2:25, it says, "I will repay you for the years the *locusts* have eaten—the great locust and the young locust, the other locusts and the locust swarm—my *great army* that I sent among you." Here, it likens the great northern army (Joel 2:20) and other armies that will ravage Israel in the near future to swarms of locusts. These "locusts" are indeed human! Real locusts don't use fire, Joel 2:3, 5 and don't sound like chariots! Also Joel 2:27 is clearly the same event as Ezekiel 39:22. This king then will be the satanic leader of an ungodly country. When the antichrist takes credit for destroying Magog (Revelation 13:4), the whole world, with the exception of Israel, will worship the antichrist as god.

There is also an opinion that Gog is the antichrist. This is impossible, because we find that at the end of this battle, Gog is killed and buried at "Hamon Gog." We find in Revelation 19:20 that the antichrist (the beast) and the false prophet are thrown alive into the lake of fire. Also, we find the antichrist fighting against the army of the north in Daniel 11:40–45. Gog is not the antichrist.

Now we will investigate the identity of Magog. There are many suggestions about the identity of Magog as well. One thing is clear: it is a land in the north of Israel. I have read theories suggesting it could be from Syria to Russia to Great Britain, even to the USA. The USA is suggested because descendants of all these people have migrated to the US throughout its short history. I don't believe that this has any merit.

In fact, I feel that it is important to make certain conclusions about what is acceptable to consider. Ezekiel was referring to people who lived in specific regions of the world at the time. I believe that the people living in those areas today would be the most likely aggressors in this future conflict; if you try to follow the migrations of the people who lived there and tag it to some future country, you end up with ridiculous theories like some of those addressed above. Ezekiel was addressing people who lived in specific areas, and it was clear to the people living at the time. Of course, borders have changed, but the historic areas that they lived in haven't. Many historians, including Josephus, have identified Magog as the area of modern-day Russia. Josephus states this in his Book 1, Chapter 4. He tells us, "The Scythians were called Magogites by the Greeks. The Scythians populated Russia. In fact, Arab writers state in the Arabic language that the Great Wall of China is known as the Wall of 'Al Magog.' It was built to keep out the armies that were invading from 'Magog.'"

By the way, the NASB translates Ezekiel 38:3 as: "and say, 'thus says the Lord God, "Behold, I am against you, O prince of Rosh, Meshech, and Tubal..." In most applications, the NASB is my favorite translation, but not in this case. The word translated *Rosh*, a noun in this case, is translated over 400 times as an adjective, specifically *Chief*. Only here is it translated as a noun. I have to wonder, why just here? Some say that it strengthens the case of Russia as being the country from the "far north." I suppose it does, but if that were the only criteria, I would have to reject it. The case for it being Russia is strong enough already anyway. So I will not include this "nation" in the discussion, as it is unnecessary.

Now rather than belabor the point any longer, let's just let Scripture decide the identity of Magog. Ezekiel 38:15 says, "You will come from your place in the *far north*, you and many nations with you, all of them riding on horses, a great horde, a mighty army." Now let's start in Israel and walk north. (You'll likely be arrested or shot at some point in your travels, so let's just do it figuratively!) After you cross out of the border of Israel, you'll go either into Lebanon or Syria, depending where you exit Israel; it really doesn't matter. If you go into Lebanon, you will then pass into Syria anyway. Sorry, Syria doesn't qualify as "far north." It's too near. There is a note in my Scofield study Bible that it could be translated *uttermost*. NASB translates it *remote* (Ezekiel 38:15), and *remotest* in Ezekiel 39:2. The Amplified Bible translates it *uttermost*. Also, Syria has been destroyed in the battle of Damascus anyway! Then you will pass into Turkey. Turkey is pretty far north, but we'll find that Turkey is very well referred to in relation to the countries accompanying Magog. You then get to the Black Sea. Keep going north. Next, you enter the Ukraine. This too is apparently mentioned in the nations accompanying Magog. Furthermore, the Ukraine, while it is very north, isn't *remotest* or *uttermost* north. It could be mentioned as Gomer and Beth Togarmah, because they inhabited this area, and so did Magog, along with most of present day Russia. Keep going north until you run out of "north." Look back, and the last nation that you have crossed is Russia! Russia is indeed "far north"! Russia has a history for aggressive invasion over many centuries, and they are presently not friendly to Israel. Also, we are talking about an army "beyond number" in Joel 2:11, which we will see is this same army. There are references in other books in the Bible as to the "Army of the North" referring to this nation. We will look into all of these in time.

Before I go any further, I believe it is important that we understand a little about the ancient Hebrew language. There is a word found frequently in prophetic scriptures that people have been questioning since the advent of mechanized warfare. This word is *horse*. People have been discussing the role horses will play in future warfare, even suggesting that any prophesied conflict must be many years away because all the scriptures mention the participation of large numbers of horses. I've heard more than one speaker from the time of my childhood suggest, "It would take years to build a cavalry that large!" Indeed it would! The only thing here is that to fulfill scripture completely, there doesn't need to be even one horse present! Let's examine the word translated *horse*. In the Strong's Concordance lexicon of Hebrew words, we find number 5483 (which is the reference number for the word translated *horse*), *soos*; from an unused root meaning to *skip*; a *horse* (as leaping); also a *swallow* (from its rapid flight): crane, horse (back, -hoof). So we find that the word translated *horse* can also be translated *swallow* or *crane*. The idea here is of its leaping or *flying*! This can be any fast moving vehicle, which may be perceived to jump, including tanks and aircraft! Now in these portions, we also find a word translated *horsemen*. This has a similar misunderstanding from translation into English. For this, we find number 6571, *parash*, from 6567; a *steed* (as *stretched* out to a vehicle, not single nor mounting, compare 5483); also (by implication) a *driver* (in a chariot), i.e. (collect.) cavalry: horseman. So *horsemen* could certainly mean a driver or pilot! In fact, it doesn't mean someone mounted on horseback! If you go to the original language, you no longer have a problem with modern warfare. The words for shields and swords are also rather general in their original meaning. They are speaking of protective armor and weapons or tools for cutting. There will be leapers with their drivers or pilots and armor plate and weapons involved in this war!

Okay, that out of the way, let's discuss the other countries involved in this conflict. The first one is Meshech. It is mentioned with Tubal. The best information on the identity of these people are that they were neighbors and lived around the area of (mostly south of) the Black and Caspian Seas. The area covered by them is today Turkey, southern Russia, and Northern Iran. Please notice that today they are mostly Islamic. Next we find Persia. This is fairly easy to identify. This would be the area known today as Iran (not too much of a stretch there). It may also include a small portion of Iraq. Again, they are mostly Islamic. Cush is the next one mentioned. This is the upper-Nile region covered today by Ethiopia and Sudan. These countries are also Islamic. (I'm beginning to see a trend here!) Put is modern Libya. This is also Islamic. Next we find Gomer (the nation!) and Beth Togarmah. Gomer and Beth Togarmah were neighbors again and inhabited the southern steppes of Russia, which could include the Ukraine, and extend down into northern Turkey. These are becoming Islamic rapidly. It isn't difficult today to see what is happening here. These countries that are all supported by Magog are all strongly Islamic and so have a basic hatred for Israel. Russia supports *all* of these countries militarily! So it is likely that these Islamic countries will be upset that Israel destroyed all the Islamic countries tightly surrounding them in the Damascus battle and then rebuilt the nation with Jews from around the world. They decide to once and for all destroy Israel from the face of the earth! Russia supports these countries, and Russia is not a friend to Israel anyway, so they give their wholehearted support to them with troops and arms. This is speculation, but it is a likely scenario. That could be the "hook" that draws Magog into the battle. But if you read Ezekiel 38:4 carefully, you will notice that it says "hooks"—more than one hook. Perhaps another "hook" is that Israel now is governing Assyria—Iraq! They now own the great Iraqi oil fields! Now there is a great hook in the jaws of Russia and their allies. We aren't given a specific reason for the invasion, but it seems to be twofold: first to plunder (perhaps oil, perhaps goods that we are unaware of at this time), second to destroy them. This would be the reason for the Islamic nations involvement. Specific reasons would at this time just be speculation, but as it stands at this time, this wouldn't be a bad bet.

Now we come across a portion that helps us identify the timing of the battle of Damascus. "...In future years you will invade a land that has *recovered from war, whose people were gathered from many nations to the mountains of Israel.*" (Ezekiel 38:8b) The people of Israel have recovered from war and gathered from many nations! It goes on to say that they are living in safety! This is not speaking about now. Yes, they have had many wars, but none to compare to the war with Damascus! Also, the re-gathering that Israel has experienced so far will pale in comparison to the one that will happen during the recovery. It is said that the antichrist will be a "man of peace" (we will study this more in Chapter 4 of this book). There will be a time of great peace during this recovery time. I believe that he will be "shepherding" Israel at this time. We'll cover this more in Chapter 4 of this book. Other verses that mention the battle of Damascus are Ezekiel 38 verses 11 and 12. It mentions that the invaders go against "a *peaceful* and *unsuspecting people*" and "...the resettled ruins and the people gathered from the nations." Again we have reference to the regathering and the war that precipitated it. Also, Israel hasn't been what you would call "unsuspecting" since they became a nation in 1948! This Battle of Magog is *after* a great battle and rebuilding. This war that they have recovered from can only be the battle of Damascus. This is because the nations that are mentioned in the Battle of Magog do not include the nations listed in the battle of Damascus. Syria, Libya, Iraq (at least as an aggressor), Palestine, etcetera, are very curiously absent here, but all are mentioned in conjunction with the battle of Damascus as being destroyed or ruled by Israel. The obvious conclusion is that the reason they aren't mentioned as participants in the Battle of Magog is that they are destroyed or owned by Israel. This is also a great portion for the rebuilding of Israel after the Damascus battle. There are many portions that deal with Israel coming home in droves in obedience to God's call at their time of Rosh Hashanah, which will happen at this time, but this rebuilding will happen prior to Rosh Hashanah. We can know this from several points mentioned in this portion. First, they came from every nation to rebuild Israel and live in peace. Today, the people are trying to build a nation, but they don't have any notions that they are going to live in peace in the foreseeable future. They hope to have a peaceable settlement in their future, but they realize that it is something they have to build for. So this hasn't happened yet! We find that they are recovered from war (of Damascus) and are living at peace. This can't be now or in the tribulation time, because at no time are God's people "at peace" during the tribulation. They are being put to death for their faith in Christ, as we find in Matthew 24. Also, we will find that during the tribulation time, God is pouring His wrath out upon the "nations," the Gentiles. This is because, by the time of the tribulation period, Israel has repented, as we will see clearly in Chapter 3 of this book. God is pouring His wrath out on Israel here to bring them to repentance, as we will find shortly. So the time that God is referring to here is between now (at the writing of this book series) and the time of the tribulation, in fact it is between the battle of Damascus and the time of the tribulation. We will find in other portions that God uses the Battle of Magog to bring Israel to repentance. In this way they are prepared, by God to enter the time of tribulation with His divine protection, but even with God's protection, God's Word tells us that many will die for the name of

Christ, as we will find in Matthew 24:9, Revelation 12:11, 13:7, etc (we will study this in more depth in Chapter 3 of volume 2).

So this time is prior to the tribulation time and during the time of "birth pains," as mentioned in Matthew 24. It seems to fit the picture that is presented as the time of birth pains perfectly. This time seems to agree with the seven seals of Revelation. We will discuss this in more detail later in this chapter. Second, Israel is unsuspecting (Ezekiel 38:11). Israel will be suspecting at Rosh Hashanah. They will know that something is up (Joel 2). So this rebuilding is before Rosh Hashanah and after the battle of Damascus!

We find that there are countries that give a halfhearted protest to this invasion. There is much speculation as to the identity of some of them. Sheba and Dedan are found in Saudi Arabia. Saudi Arabia doesn't attack Israel. The merchants of Tarshish and all her villages are not as easily identified. I don't know that it is really that important, but I'll mention a theory that I have heard more than once: Tarshish is Spain. Jonah fled to Tarshish, or tried to, when he did not want to do what God told him to do. As I understand it, Tarshish sent ships to England for tin for their bronze working. So England would be a merchant of Tarshish. The villages of the merchants of Tarshish would be the English-speaking world colonized by England. That would include the US, Canada, Australia, etc. I think that is a possibility, but it is a stretch. I wouldn't suggest that we could say that this is what this portion is telling us. It would fit our present political climate, but this could change, and it will, in accordance to God's Word. The whole world will forsake Israel at some point in the future (we'll discuss this more in Chapter 3 of this book).

There is an important portion of Scripture that applies to the situation as found here. This is Zechariah 13:8–9: "'In the whole land,' declares the Lord, 'two-thirds will be struck down and perish; yet one-third will be left in it. This third will I bring into the fire; I will refine them like silver and test them like gold. They will call on my name and I will answer them; I will say, 'They are my people,' and they will say, 'The Lord is our God.'"

As I was studying this portion, I at first thought that this was a portion dealing with conditions during the tribulation period. Indeed, it will be very bad at that time, but specifically, this is talking about the Battle of Magog. The reason I thought it was tribulation was that it came after Zechariah's mention of the Jewish national repentance. Then as I studied it, I carefully read Zechariah 13:7: "Awake, O sword, against my shepherd, and the sheep will be *scattered*, and I will *turn my hand against the little ones*." This speaks, prophetically, of Christ's death on the cross and the scattering of the Jewish people throughout the earth. It then goes on to a recap of end-time events, beginning with a mention of the Battle of Magog. In this battle, we learn that two thirds of the Jewish population will be killed! This is the only portion that addresses the number of Jewish casualties. It will be horrible! Please notice that *after* this massacre, God tells us, "I will say, 'they are my people,' and they will say, 'The Lord is our God.'" This is how it will be at the time of the Battle of Magog. They will turn to Christ, and then God will intervene on their behalf and destroy Magog (as we will see). Now the thing that finally convinced me that this is battle-of-Magog scripture instead of the tribulation is Zechariah 14:1: "A day of the Lord *is coming*." So the Day of the Lord hasn't happened when they are dying. It quickly follows, in fact, immediately after they come to Christ. The Day of the Lord is the tribulation (we will cover this in Chapter 1 of volume 2).

So we have the Battle of Magog destroying two thirds of the Jewish population, but through this, they come to Christ and repent (as we will see in Chapter 3 of this book).

Now we find the invasion forces coming from the far north (Russia). Please note that some of the invasion forces come from the south as well (Put and Cush). God's reason as stated here for the invasion is that the world will know Him. God's reaction to this invasion is "hot anger." He tells us that there will be a "great earth-quake in the land of Israel." All animals will tremble at his presence. It also says that *all the people on the face of the earth* will tremble" at His presence! This isn't just a local event! Everyone on earth will feel this earthquake! Mountains will be overturned, cliffs will crumble, and (this is important!) every wall will fall to the ground (at least in Jerusalem)! This will tell us the timing of an important event. Everyone is hearing about the impending rebuilding of the Temple in Jerusalem. It isn't going to happen until certain other things happen first. If it happened before the Battle of Magog, it would only be destroyed in the earthquake! Also, there is a sizable Islamic resistance to its construction. The Dome of the Rock sits on the Temple site. One of the very important reasons that it isn't being built today is that it would cause a very destructive war. Now at the Battle of Magog, the Islamic world (at least most of it) will attack Israel and be destroyed by God's hand. This eliminates two of the hurdles to the temple's construction. First, the Islamic resis-tance will be eliminated, and second, the Dome of the Rock will be destroyed (every wall will fall)! During the cleanup from the earthquake, they will be able to move the rubble aside and build the temple as described in Ezekiel 40–47. We find that there will be mass confusion caused by this earthquake. "Every man's sword will be against his brother," (Ezekiel 38:21). There will be great natural disturbances: torrential rain, hail, and "burning sulfur" This sounds volcanic and probably is; earthquakes often accompany vol-canoes. This may be the eruption of a "super volcano" that we have heard about so much lately, although I would doubt that it would be Yellowstone, because Yellowstone is in the USA, and this "earth-quake" is in Israel. For all we know, Yellowstone may have already blown by then! Although when we read the full description of this disaster, it may involve more than one super volcano! Now people will know who God really is, but they still won't repent! How fool-ish! In the beginning of the next chapter, we have mention of the "far north" country again. It tells us that their "bows and arrows" will be taken from their control. This is again a case of words that don't necessarily mean what we think of as bows and arrows. Bows are *launchers*, and arrows are any launched *missile*. Again, there is no problem with modern warfare. It tells us that the attacking armies will fall on the mountains of Israel. If you are studying this in the KJV (King James Version), you will notice that it tells us that one sixth of the attacking army will survive. This only appears in this version. The KJV was translated from a later text than most other translations, and in the earlier texts, it doesn't mention survivors. It also tells us that God will send "fire" on Magog (the country) and on "those who live in safety in the coastlands," or some translate it *isles*. This is rather cryptic in light of all the rest of the nations being so clearly named. This *may* be referring to nations that were unknown to Ezekiel and his people. We really don't know! Anything would be speculation, but God will judge these nations, and they will know who God is! There may be a hint as found in Jeremiah 30:11, where God tells us that He will destroy all the nations where He has scattered Israel! This may be the beginning of that! But their heart is hardened. God's reason for intervening on Israel's behalf is so that His Holy name will not be profaned any longer. We will find in other portions that it isn't for Israel, but it is for God.

Next, we find something that will be a key in understanding many other portions of Scripture. Israel will use their attackers' weapons as fuel and burn them; they won't need to cut forests for seven years. Then we are told that they will "Plunder those who plundered them and loot those who looted them." First, we'll address the burning of weapons. Today, Russia is building vehicles of warfare from a new substance known as lignostone. This was developed for use as a fuel prepared from compressed wood, but Russian scientists studied this substance and found that it exhibited some rather unique properties. It is light, pliable, strong as steel, and has stealth properties. It doesn't reflect radar well. So Russia is using this material in many of their military weapons and vehicles! It burns at a very high temperature, so it can be used as a fuel for fire. The fact that much of their military machines will be made from this material casts new light on the portion that Israel will not need to cut wood for seven years. Also, the seven-year period *may* be important. These weapons will be ubiquitous in the land of Israel. They will be everywhere! So that will likely sustain them throughout the entire seven-year tribulation period. Then note in this portion the phrase, "plunder those who plundered them and loot those who looted them." We will find this event mentioned in other portions, which we will discuss later in this chapter.

Next, please note that Israel will be cleansing the land of the dead from this battle for seven months. The burial is very interesting. They hire professionals to bury and search for the dead. They won't even go out searching for seven months; they will only *begin* then. Then they will employ great caution in dealing with the dead. When someone sees a bone they are to place a marker by it so the professionals can dispose it of it! This really makes me think of weapons of mass destruction, chemical, biological, or nuclear. All would require great care in disposal.

The next event in this portion will be one of the most important events in the entire history of Israel, past and future! "*From that day forward the house of Israel will know that I am the Lord their God.*" This is their Day of Atonement, their Yom Kippur! This is a central theme in end-times prophecy, and it is near! We will study this in much more depth in Chapter 3 of this book.

In the rest of this portion, God gives us a recap of the events and their significance.

In this next portion, we will show a progression of events in a more or less chronological order. This will give us a feel for how events will occur in future history. I find it very relevant that this order is found in the book of Ezekiel, giving us the events in a logical progression to help us understand God's plan.

Ezekiel 25–32 seems to be in chronological order for the most part (there may be excursions ahead and back in the chapters, but the events in the chapters seem to follow a logical, chronological order), so there is reference to the battle of Damascus (some of the participants are mentioned, even though Damascus isn't) (Ezekiel 25–28). Then there is the regathering of Israel (Ezekiel 28). In fact, the last two verses of Ezekiel 28 give us the events of the Battle of Magog in a nutshell (one of the excursions into the future). Then it goes into the judgment on Egypt, which actually extends over more than one event. I covered the "withering of Egypt" in the last chapter. We find here and in Daniel 11 that Egypt's problems are only beginning with this decline. Its withering begins at roughly the same time as the battle of Damascus, and in fact has already begun, but it will be destroyed during the Battle of Magog. We will find that it isn't exactly a participant, but it gets in the way of the armies of Libya, Sudan, and Ethiopia. The description of the battle in Joel will give us a good understanding of why Egypt is destroyed during this battle. We will discuss this event in more detail when we get to Daniel later in this chapter. But we find that the judgment on Egypt will be drawn out over the entire time from before the battle of Damascus to the end of Magog. The destruction of Egypt begins in Ezekiel 29. This portion covers some of the events of Isaiah 19. Then it goes on with the further destruction as Egypt is destroyed in the Battle of Magog, as told in Ezekiel chapters 30–32. Ezekiel 33 seems to be going back as a warning, to Israel in particular. As mentioned in the previous chapter of this book, Ezekiel 33:1–20 gives the hypothetical event, which will be completely fulfilled in the near future, beginning at the battle of Damascus. Ezekiel 33:21–32 gives a background of the failings of Israel in general. Then it says in Ezekiel 33:33, "*When this time comes to pass—for behold, it will come!*—then shall they know, understand, and realize that a prophet has been among them." This is the warning of the fulfillment! Ezekiel 34 deals more with the faithless shepherds of

Israel and their judgments. It goes back to the leaders of Israel, back to Ezekiel's day right on through to the antichrist. Ezekiel 35 picks up again with the results of the battle of Damascus as it pertains to Edom. We will find this to be important during the actual "tribulation period." Ezekiel 36–37 deals with Rosh Hashanah and will be covered in greater detail later in this chapter. Then we have the Battle of Magog in chapters 38–39 (with Yom Kippur, as we will find in the next chapter of this book), and then we have the rebuilding of the temple and a very detailed description of how it is to be done. This can only be done when Islam is virtually destroyed and the Dome of the Rock is gone. (But more about this in Chapter 2 of volume 2.) This order found in Ezekiel is no mistake. This is how it must go!

In the next portion, we will find a very dramatic and detailed description of the Battle of Magog, its outcome and effect. This portion will show God's intention for Israel and the effect it will have on Israel and the world.

> *Blow the trumpet in Zion*; sound the alarm on my holy hill. Let all who live in the land tremble, *for the day of the Lord is coming*. It is close at hand—a day of darkness and gloom, a day of blackness. Like dawn spreading across the mountains *a large and mighty army comes, such as never was of old nor ever will be in ages to come.* Before them fire devours, behind them a flame blazes. Before them the land is like the garden of Eden, behind them, a desert waste-nothing escapes them. They have the appearance of horses; they gallop along like cavalry. With noise like that of chariots *they leap over mountaintops*, like a crackling fire consuming stubble, like a mighty army drawn up for battle. At the sight of them nations are in anguish; every face turns pale. They charge like warriors; they scale walls like soldiers. They all march in line, not swerving from their course. They do not jostle each other; each marches straight ahead. They plunge through defenses without breaking ranks. They rush upon the city; they run

along the wall. They climb into the houses; like thieves they enter through the windows. Before them the earth shakes, the sky trembles, the sun and moon are darkened, and the stars no longer shine. The Lord thunders at the head of his army; his forces are beyond number, and mighty are those who obey his command. *The day of the Lord* is great; it is dreadful. Who can endure it? "Even now," declares the Lord, "*return to me with all your heart, with fasting and weeping and mourning." Rend your heart and not your garments. Return to the Lord your God,* for he is gracious and compassionate, slow to anger and abounding in love, *and relents from sending calamity. Who Knows? He may turn and have pity and leave behind a blessing—grain offerings and drink offerings for the Lord your God. Blow the trumpet in Zion, declare a holy fast, call a sacred assembly. Gather the people, consecrate the assembly; bring together the elders, gather the children, those nursing at the breast. Let the bridegroom leave his room and the bride her chamber. Let the priests, who minister before the Lord, weep between the temple porch and the altar. Let them say, "Spare your people, O Lord. Do not make your inheritance an object of scorn, a byword among the nations. Why should they say among the peoples, Where is their God?" Then the Lord will be jealous for his land and take pity on his people.* The Lord will reply to them: "I am sending you grain, new wine, and oil, enough to satisfy you fully; *never again* will I make you an object of scorn to the nations. *I will drive the northern army far from you,* pushing it into a parched and barren land, with its front columns going into the eastern sea and those in the rear into the western sea. And its stench will go up; its smell will rise." Surely he has done great things. Be not afraid, O land; be glad and rejoice. Surely the Lord has done great things. Be not afraid, O wild animals, for the open pastures are become green. The trees are bearing their fruit; the fig tree and the vine yield their riches. Be glad, O people of Zion, rejoice in the Lord your God, for he has given you the autumn rains in righteousness. He sends you abundant showers, both autumn and spring rains, as before. The threshing floors will be filled with grain; the vats will overflow with new wine and oil. "I will repay you for the years the locusts have eaten—the great locust and the young locust, the other locust and the locust swarm—*my great army that I sent among you.* You will have plenty to eat, until you are full, and *you will praise the name of the Lord your God,* who has worked wonders for you; *never again* will *my people* be shamed. *Then you will know that I am in Israel, that I am the Lord your God, and that there is no other; never again will my people be shamed.*"

Joel 2:1–27

What a powerful portion of scriptural prophecy! It starts out with "Blow the trumpet in Zion." I believe that this is very significant in future Jewish and world history. The first of the Jewish autumn feasts is the Feast of Trumpets, also known as Rosh Hashanah. It is celebrated by sounding trumpets. Trumpets were sounded in ancient Israel for two reasons: First, they were sounded to warn of impending war, to prepare for battle. Second, they were sounded for a solemn assembly, when a gathering of people was needed to meet before the Lord. Here we find that it is appropriate for both instances. War is impending; there is no hope of survival short of divine intervention, and the people need to meet before the Lord to examine themselves as a nation, repent, and beg for divine intervention on their behalf. We are told in Joel 2:1, "The Day of the Lord is coming." This is a very interesting phrase. When you see the phrase, "The Day of the Lord," it signifies that the Lord is going to intervene directly in the affairs of mankind. There will be no guessing that something is up; it will be obvious! Things will not be following a naturally predictable course. Events will be unprecedented, never before witnessed by mankind. In Joel 2:2, we find that it isn't going to be a walk in the park; it's going to be bad. I never cease to marvel at the comments I hear from people as I talk with them about the end times. Many of them say, "Wouldn't it be exciting to see that, to go through that time?"

89

I answer, "I suppose it would be exciting to go through a fatal car accident too, but someone you love, or yourself, will die in it. I guess it would be exciting to go through that, but I surely wouldn't want to." But my feelings aren't going to alter God's plan. We need to see what God has prepared for us, depending on where we are in prophetic time. Some of you reading this may not have to experience these things; some will. It depends on your relationship with Christ and where you are in God's timeline. We'll discuss this later, especially in Chapter 5 of this book.

We are told in this portion that "a mighty army comes, such as never was of old nor ever will be ..." This confused me when I first read it, because we are told that at Armageddon, there will be an army of two hundred million soldiers (Revelation 9:14–18, 16:12)! That will be an awesome army! In fact, we are told that one third of the world's population will be killed by this army! This led me, for a long time, to believe that this army was the same one. The armies of Joel 2 and Revelation 9 and 16 must be the same. But there are problems with that view. First, we are told that the armies at Armageddon are from the east. In fact, today, China has an army of two hundred million people; they have had one this large for many years now! The stage is set! But this army isn't from the east! It's from the north! We aren't told the number of soldiers in this army, but that may be irrelevant. It probably isn't the number of soldiers that it fields as much as it is the military might it possesses. We are told that the Magog army is innumerable, more than can be counted, so collectively, it may be even bigger than the army from the east (Joel 2:11). Also, when the Magog battle ends, much of the world's technology may be rendered unusable. This is because "every wall will fall." This will destroy much in the way of technological weaponry. It has been said, "I don't know what weapons World War Three will be fought with, but World War Four will be fought with sticks and stones." I don't know that I would go quite that far, but the idea is probably not too removed from reality. Power grids may not be put back in commission ever, let alone in just seven years. How long would it take to completely rebuild the infrastructure that we take for granted today? I would wager that it would take more than seven years, and during this time, the world will be lashed by God's wrath. It is likely that the Armageddon armies will fight with more conventional weapons. There is every reason to believe that the Magog army will be entirely nuclear. It mentions that, "before them a fire devours, behind them a flame blazes. Before them the land is like the garden of Eden, behind them, a desert waste—nothing escapes them." The description is very detailed and chilling. Again, I can't say with certainty that it will be nuclear, because the Bible doesn't say "nuclear," but the description is very fitting and likely. In today's technology, there isn't anything that man controls that could be this devastating that isn't nuclear. I say "that man controls" because this is a human army that God is using to bring judgment and repentance to Israel. When God intervenes, there will be other means of destruction involved, as we will see. Another verse that leads me to believe that modern warfare is involved is Joel 2:5. "With noise *like* that of chariots they *leap over mountaintops...* " Please notice that Ezekiel uses the word "like" a lot. This is significant. This is not implying that chariots are used, just that it sounds like chariots. These words are comparing, not defining. So in these instances, we have a description of what it is like, not what it is. So we can say that it appears to be modern warfare, likely even nuclear, but God's Word doesn't specify that it is indeed modern warfare. This is brought out by the fact that "At the sight of them nations are in anguish ..." A nuclear attack will put nations in anguish. Also note Joel 2:10: "Before them the earth shakes, the sky trembles, the sun and moon are darkened, and the stars no longer shine." You can draw your own conclusion. In the next verse, we find that the Lord claims this army as "his." This is not implying that this is a Godly people, only that God is using them to work his will. He's using them; they are his. When he's done with them, he will be *done* with them indeed, as we will see. As I mentioned, Joel 2:11 does give us a hint at the number of soldiers in this army; they are beyond number! So this army may be more than two hundred million! We don't know, and frankly, I don't think it matters. It will be the mightiest army ever fielded in the past or future! Now we are told that the "Day of the Lord" is great, and it is here! God, at this point, is going to intervene in world events directly. This is a fearful thing! God tells the Israelites to turn to him with their whole heart, to repent from the soul, not just with words, but in truth. We will see that this is the time that they repent as a nation, their Yom Kippur, their Day of Atonement. They have just gathered as a nation to examine themselves and prepare to repent with their Rosh Hashanah. This is the purpose of Rosh Hashanah: self-examination, looking for sin; and they recognize that they need to trust Christ. They will then repent as a nation. It will be their Day of Atonement for the sin of rejecting their God, Jesus Christ. They will finally know their God and will embrace him! We are told then that God will be jealous for them and will take pity on his people. He promises to supply them with their needs to survive. He says that he will *never* make them an object of scorn again. Never! If this weren't their Day of Atonement, this statement wouldn't be true. They are now truly his people. (We will cover this in more detail in the next chapter.) Then he says that he will drive the *northern* army far from them. This gives us the information as to whom this is referring. It can only be the Magog and its cohorts of Ezekie1.38–39, the army of the "far north." He will drive them into a "barren land." This army will be large enough that one end of it will be at one sea and the other will be at another sea! If there is any question as to the disposition of this army, God tells us that its "stench will go up; its smell will rise." I assure you, this has nothing to do with their bathing habits! They will be killed.

Then God assures the wild animals that the earth will produce food for them; they need not fear. He then assures the people of

Zion (Jerusalem) that he will provide for them too. In Joel 2:25, we have an interesting statement. He will repay Israel for what the different kinds of "locusts" have eaten. I have an interesting statement in my Bible notes that sheds some light on this verse. The meaning of the four Hebrew words translated *locusts* is unclear! This army has been likened to locusts because of the way they wipe out everything in their path, but God tells us exactly what he is talking about here. It's his mighty army that he sent among them! This was to bring them to repentance, and it works! We are told once more that *never again* will his people be shamed! Then he repeats their repentance.

Joel is an excellent book to aid in the understanding of end-times prophecies. It aids in tying scriptures together.

Now we'll look at Isaiah 17:12–18:7. This portion picks up with the events that follow the battle of Damascus. As you'll remember, the first part of Isaiah 17 was the prime portion dealing with the battle of Damascus. Here it goes on into the Battle of Magog. In the previous verses, we see that Israel is living in a time of relative peace, although not entirely successful in their endeavors, due to the fact that they still haven't repented. Then we'll see that the atmosphere has changed. It becomes violent again. In Isaiah 17, specific nations are not mentioned, but in Isaiah 18 they are, and we will see that they are nations that accompany Magog in its attempted conquest. We will also see in Isaiah 17:14 that a crucial piece of information is given that helps to pinpoint the timing of this portion with other scripture.

Let's read, starting with Isaiah 17:12.

> Oh, the raging of many nations—they rage like the raging sea! Oh, the uproar of the peoples—they roar like the roaring of great waters! Although the peoples roar like the roar of surging waters, when he rebukes them they flee far away, driven before the wind like chaff on the hills, like tumbleweed before a gale. In the evening, sudden terror! *Before the morning,*

they are gone! This is the portion of *those who loot us, the lot of those who plunder us.*

Isaiah 18:1–7:

Woe to the land of whirring wings along the rivers of *Cush*, which sends envoys by sea in papyrus boats by water. Go, swift messengers, *to a people tall and smooth-skinned*, to a people feared far and wide, an aggressive nation of strange speech, *whose land is divided by rivers.* All you people of the world, you who live on the earth, when a banner is raised on the mountains, you will see it, *and when the trumpet sounds, you will hear it.* This is what the Lord says to me: "I will remain quiet and will look on from my dwelling place, like shimmering heat in the sunshine, like a cloud of dew in the heat of *harvest.*" For, before the *harvest*, when the blossom is gone and the flower becomes a ripening grape, he will cut off the shoots with pruning knives, and cut down and take away the spreading branches. *They will be left to the mountain birds of prey and to the wild animals; the birds will feed on them all winter.* At that time gifts will be brought to the Lord Almighty from a people tall and smooth-skinned, an aggressive nation of strange speech, whose land is divided by rivers- the gifts will be brought to mount Zion, the place of the Name of the Lord Almighty.

This portion starts out clearly moving into the next battle after the battle of Damascus. This is, as we have seen, the Battle of Magog. It speaks of the "roaring of many nations." This refers to the coalition of nations accompanying Magog (Russia). It then tells us that when God rebukes them, they will be like chaff before the wind or tumbleweed before a gale. This shows that no matter how powerful a nation may be in man's sight, it is nothing before God. Then notice that, "Before the morning, they are gone!" This tells us the swiftness of God's judgment on this army. Talk about overnight delivery! God delivers judgment on Magog and delivers safety to Israel overnight! Then we have the key phrase of this portion. "This is the portion of those who loot us, the lot of those who plunder us." Please remember Ezekiel 39:10. This portion tells us, "…And they will *plunder those who plundered them and loot those who looted them…*" This is referring to the outcome of the battle after Israel has repented, and it ties the Isaiah 17 portion to the Battle of Magog in Ezekiel 39.

Then we enter Isaiah 18. This is still on the subject of the Battle of Magog, because one of the participants in this battle is "Cush." This today covers the modern day countries of Ethiopia and Sudan. They are named in Ezekiel 38 as cohorts of Magog (Russia). Today, we find that they are indeed friendly with Russia and get their arms from them. We find that this is a message of woe to Cush. They are dealing with a nation that is cryptically mentioned as a feared, smooth-skinned people, aggressive, with strange speech, whose land is divided by waters. They aren't named specifically, but we can conjecture, provided we understand that it is just conjecture. It is possible that smooth-skinned refers to an inability to grow body hair well (e.g. facial hair) due to Genesis 27:11 where Jacob is contrasted with Esau, because "Esau is a hairy man, and I'm a man with smooth skin." *Slender of build* is the general meaning of "tall," not so much that they are of greater stature than other peoples, but their height to their body mass is "tall," thus slender. They are a feared and aggressive nation, and they have "strange speech." Well, I suppose that any nation that doesn't speak your language is "strange" in their speech. And their land is divided by rivers. The KJV interprets this in an interesting manner. It says, "…whose land the rivers have spoiled." Most countries have rivers dividing their land, but most countries aren't spoiled by their rivers. If you put these facts together, some interesting conclusions may be considered. A people who don't grow facial hair easily and are generally thin could be descriptive of an Asian race. Their language is strange to foreigners who don't understand it (when an English-speaking person hears

French or German or even Spanish, he can find similarities and see that the words have some common origin), but this language doesn't have many similarities. Also, we find that it is a feared and aggressive nation. Now, over recent history, several Asian nations would come to mind that could be considered "aggressive." In the middle of the last century, Japan would fit the bill quite nicely, but now they are not feared or aggressive. Then, with the Cold War, China would leap to mind, and they still would be a prime candidate. In Revelation, we find that a nation or nations from the east will make war with an overwhelming army of two hundred million soldiers. But another country to consider is North Korea. They are exporting weapons for money because there is a famine over there presently, caused by heavy rains that flooded their rivers, carrying away their fertile top soil, so they haven't been able to feed their people. Their rivers have spoiled their land! Am I saying that this is any of these countries? No, I'm saying that presently, it would appear likely that if conditions do not change, North Korea is a possibility. This could change, though, at the drop of a hat! This is just something to consider.

Again, I believe that Isaiah 18:3 may be signaling the fulfillment of Rosh Hashanah; the trumpet sounds! Then we have the Lord saying that he will remain quiet, looking on from his dwelling place. I believe that this is referred to in Hosea 5:14–15:

> For I will be like a lion to Ephraim, like a great lion to Judah. *I will tear them to pieces and go away; I will carry them off, with no one to rescue them. Then I will go back to my place until they admit their guilt. And they seek my face; in their misery they will earnestly seek me.*

We see in Isaiah 18:5 that he likens the events that are mentioned here to pruning—pruning before the harvest, cutting down the spreading branches. I am always trying to garden and raise fruit trees and the like, but I'm not very good at it. I've been told that I need to prune my trees and thin my vegetables. I'm always afraid that I will hurt them, and I don't get a very good crop, ever! Here we find that God is likening this event to pruning, but this pruning is after God unleashes his wrath on Israel. After he leads his army against Israel, he is found quietly sitting in his dwelling place, waiting for their repentance (Isaiah 18:4 and Hosea 5:15). And here, he is saying that the animals will feed on the carcasses all winter. We find that the animals feed on the bodies of Magog and his accomplices in this battle (Ezekiel 39:17–20 confirms this nicely). Admittedly, in just this portion, it isn't very clear, but with other portions, it becomes clear. Then we find that these people (the tall, smooth-skinned people) bring gifts to the Lord in Mount Zion. If this is immediately after the Battle of Magog, it has to be before the middle of the tribulation period, because from that time onward, all nations will turn against God and attack Israel. The antichrist's power hasn't at this time been fully felt on the earth but will be very soon, as we will see in Chapter 4 of this book and Chapter 1 of volume 2. Or it could simply be skipping on ahead to the time during the millennial reign of Christ, which is certainly more likely.

So in the portion that we have just studied, we found that Isaiah has given us a logical progression from the battle of Damascus through the Battle of Magog, detailing the events and conditions even between these battles.

Next, we will find another interesting passage that introduces Israel's call to repentance, their Rosh Hashanah. In this portion, God is telling Israel and the surrounding nations of judgments being poured on the region due to their sin. In this chapter, Zephaniah speaks of general conditions that are prevalent at the time that this prophecy is fulfilled.

> Gather together, gather together, *O shameful nation,* before the appointed time arrives and that day sweeps on like chaff, before the fierce anger of the Lord comes upon you, before

the day of the Lord's wrath comes upon you. Seek the Lord, all you humble of the land, you who do what he commands. Seek righteousness, seek humility; perhaps you will be sheltered on the day of the Lord's anger.

Zephaniah 2:1–3

After this, we are given a rendition of events that have already happened by the time of their call to seek forgiveness. All of the countries that are mentioned in this portion are involved in the battle of Damascus, with the possible exception of Cush. Cush is mentioned in the Battle of Magog as one of Russia's confederates and will be destroyed there. We find in Zephaniah 2:5 that God will destroy all the inhabitants of the "land by the sea," where the "Kerethites" live; there will be no survivors! We aren't sure from the ancient Hebrew what the word *Kerethites* means, but it is a people by the sea. This could be Lebanon or Gaza. It does mention that it is where the Philistines dwell. Today, the Palestinians still live in the same area, even though they don't have their own homeland. Anyway, there is definite reference to the Damascus battle when Israel is mostly destroyed. This is because Zephaniah 2:9 mentions that the "survivors of my nation" will inherit these attacking nations. The land that the Philistines inhabit, Gaza, Palestine, also Moab, is mentioned as being taken over by Israel's "survivors." This is the annexation of the previous chapter in this book. In Zephaniah 2:11, there is a break in the rendition of judgment, and it is then resumed in verse 12 with the judgment on Cush. It is possible that the break is exactly that, a break in the action; but if it is, why does it go back to a definite Damascus battle participant with Assyria (Iraq)? It mentions that Israel will govern Iraq with a sword after the Damascus battle (Micah 5:5–6). Indeed, we find in Jeremiah 50 that Iraq is involved in the Battle of Magog in a big way! We will study this in greater detail shortly.

So in the Zephaniah portion, we have a rendition of conditions that will set the stage for Israel's call to repentance, their Rosh Hashanah. They will have had a mighty battle, which will nearly have destroyed them, and they will annex their attackers' lands, and then Russia is beginning to attack them. Now they need to repent and turn to Christ! And as we will see, they do! Indeed, after Zephaniah 2:11, it is speaking of Magog.

Next we will study Jeremiah 50. In this portion, we find that God's judgment is poured out on Babylon (Assyria, modern-day Iraq). In this portion, we find the reason why (at least God's reason!) and the outcome of this battle. We find the significance of this battle in prophecy and its timing! This is a wealth of information to us, giving us another viewpoint on the Battle of Magog. This portion is often misunderstood as a portion that is already fulfilled because of Jeremiah 51. Most of Jeremiah 51 is fulfilled with the overthrow of Babylon by the Medes and the Persians, which is named in the context, and this is what Jeremiah 51 centers on. But that time didn't see the utter destruction of *the land of Babylon*. It only centered on the destruction of the city of Babylon, which to this day lies in ruins. The destruction of Babylon as mentioned in Jeremiah 50 is over the whole land, for the most part (even chapter 50 discusses the destruction of the city some), and it is fulfilled by an unnamed nation "from the north," as we will see. Also, never before has the land of Israel entered into an everlasting covenant with God where their sin is erased! This definitely marks the time of Jeremiah 50 as future! Let's study Jeremiah 50:

> This is the word the Lord spoke through Jeremiah the prophet concerning Babylon and the *land of the Babylonians*: "Announce and proclaim among the nations, *lift up a banner* and proclaim it; keep nothing back, but say, 'Babylon will be captured; Bel will be put to shame, Marduk filled with terror. Her images will be put to shame and her idols filled with terror.' *A nation from the north will attack her and lay waste her*

*land. No one will live in it; both men and animals will flee away.
'In those days, at that time,' declares the Lord, 'the people of Israel
and the people of Judah together will go in tears to seek the Lord
their God. They will ask the way to Zion and turn their faces
toward it. They will come and bind themselves to the Lord in an
everlasting covenant that will not be forgotten. My people have
been lost sheep; their shepherds have led them astray and caused
them to roam on the mountains. They wandered over mountain
and hill and forgot their own resting place.'* Whoever found
them devoured them; their enemies said, *'We are not guilty,
for they sinned against the Lord, their true pasture, the Lord, the
hope of their fathers.'* 'Flee out of Babylon; leave the land of
the Babylonians, and be like the goats that lead the flock. For
I will stir up and bring against Babylon an alliance of great
nations *from the land of the north.* They will take up positions
against her, and *from the north she will be captured.* Their
arrows will be like skilled warriors who do not return empty
handed. So Babylonia will be plundered; all who plunder her
will have their fill,' declares the Lord. 'Because you rejoice
and are glad, you who pillage my inheritance, because you
frolic like a heifer threshing grain and neigh like stallions,
your mother will be greatly ashamed; she who gave you
birth will be disgraced. She will be the least of the nations-a
wilderness, a dry land, a desert.' Because of the Lord's anger
she will not be inhabited but will be completely desolate. All
who pass Babylon will be horrified and scoff because of her
wounds. 'Take up your positions around Babylon, all you
who draw the bow. Shoot at her! Spare no arrows, for she
has sinned against the Lord. Shout against her on every side!
She surrenders, her towers fall, her walls are torn down. Since
this is the vengeance of the Lord, take vengeance on her; do
to her as she has done to others. Cut off from Babylon the
sower, and the reaper with his sickle at harvest. Because of
the sword of the oppressor let everyone return to his own
people, let everyone flee to his own land. Israel is a scattered
flock that the lions have chased away. The first to devour
him was the king of Assyria; the last to crush his bones was

Nebuchadnezzar king of Babylon.' Therefore this is what the
Lord Almighty, the God of Israel, says: 'I will punish the king
of Babylon and his land as I punished the king of Assyria. But
I will bring Israel back to his own pasture and he will graze on
Carmel and Bashan; his appetite will be satisfied on the hills
of Ephraim and Gilead. *In those days, at that time,'* declares
the Lord, *'search will be made for Israel's guilt, but there will
be none, and the sins of Judah, but none will be found, for I will
forgive the remnant I spare.* Attack the land of Merathaim and
those who live in Pekod. Pursue, kill and completely destroy
them,' declares the Lord. 'Do everything I have commanded
you. The noise of battle is in the land, the noise of great
destruction! How broken and shattered is the hammer of the
whole earth! How desolate is Babylon among the nations! I
set a trap for you, O Babylon, and you were caught before you
knew it; you were found and captured because you opposed
the Lord. The Lord has opened his arsenal and brought out
the weapons of his wrath, for the Sovereign Lord Almighty
has work to do in the land of the Babylonians. Come against
her from afar. Break open her granaries; pile her up like heaps
of grain. Completely destroy her and leave her no remnant.
Kill all her young bulls; let them go down to the slaughter!
Woe to them! For their day has come, the time for them to be
punished. Listen to the fugitives and refugees from Babylon
declaring in Zion how the Lord our God has taken vengeance,
vengeance for his temple. Summon archers against Babylon, all
those who draw the bow. Encamp all around her; let no one
escape. Repay her for her deeds; do to her as she has done. For
she has defied the Lord, The Holy One of Israel. Therefore,
her young men will fall in the streets; all her soldiers will
be silenced in that day,' declares the Lord. 'See, I am against
you, O arrogant one,' declares the Lord, The Lord Almighty,
'for your day has come, the time for you to be punished. The
arrogant one will stumble and fall and no one will help her
up; I will kindle a fire in her towns that will consume all who
are around her.' This is what the Lord Almighty says: 'The
people of Israel are oppressed, and the people of Judah as well.

All their captors hold them fast, refusing to let them go. Yet their redeemer is strong; the Lord Almighty is his name. He will vigorously defend their cause so that he may bring rest to their land, but unrest to those who live in Babylon. A sword against the Babylonians!' declares the Lord—'against those who live in Babylon and against her officials and wise men! A sword against her false prophets! They will become fools. A sword against her warriors! They will be filled with terror. A sword against her horses and chariots and all the foreigners in her ranks! They will become women. A sword against her treasures! They will be plundered. A drought on her waters! They will dry up. For it is a land of idols, idols that will go mad with terror. So desert creatures and hyenas will live there, and there the owl will dwell. *It will never again be inhabited or lived in from generation to generation.* As God overthrew Sodom and Gomorrah along with their neighboring towns.' Declares the Lord, *'So no one will live there; no man will dwell in it.* Look! *An army is coming from the north; a great nation and many kings are being stirred up from the ends of the earth.* They are armed with bows and spears; they are cruel and without mercy. They sound like the roaring sea as they ride on their horses; they come like men in battle formation to attack you, O daughter of Babylon. The king of Babylon has heard reports about them, and his hands hang limp. Anguish has gripped him, pain like that of a woman in labor. Like a lion coming up from Jordan's thickets to a rich pastureland, I will chase Babylon from its land in an instant. *Who is the chosen one I will appoint for this?* Who is like me and who can challenge me? And *what shepherd can stand against me?'* Therefore, hear what the Lord has planned against Babylon, what he has purposed against the Babylonians: 'The young of the flock will be dragged away; he will completely destroy their pasture because of them. At the sound of Babylon's capture *the earth will tremble;* its cry will resound among the nations.'"

Wow! What a powerful piece of scripture! This passage makes clear so many other prophecies and ties up so many loose ends! First we find that this is covering the land of the Babylonians. This is often referred to in the Bible as Assyria because they cover the same land. Today, it is known as Iraq, as I have mentioned earlier.

In Jeremiah 51, we find the prophecy of the destruction of Babylon, the city, by the Medes. This was fulfilled. But most of chapter 50 is future and will be fulfilled in the Battle of Magog. We find that Israel is to lift up a banner to announce to the nations that Babylon will be captured. In Jeremiah 50:10–16, the reference is to the city of Babylon, and in verse 13, the city will be destroyed! This is not speaking of the land of Babylon, just the city. Also, Jeremiah 50:33–40 is already fulfilled. This is speaking about the city of Babylon, not the country. We find in Chapter 51 more about the destruction of the city, but most of this chapter is speaking of the land. We can know that this is future because of Jeremiah 50:20. This is speaking of Israel's "Day of Atonement," and it hasn't happened yet. It says, "In those days, at that time," which is repeated from Jeremiah 50:4. This is definitely in the future. It tells us in Jeremiah 50:4 also that the people of Israel and Judah together will go in tears to seek the Lord. This is their Rosh Hashanah! They assemble together before the Lord to seek his forgiveness. We will find many portions referring to this event. The outcome of this gathering, this Rosh Hashanah, will be their Yom Kippur, the Day of Atonement, as we find in Jeremiah 50:5 and 20. This fixes the timing of these events for us nicely. We find that the covenant that they enter into with the Lord is an everlasting one that will not be forgotten! This is very important, not only to Israel's future history, but the world's future history as well!

We are told that Israel has been lost sheep, they have been led astray and even forgot their resting place (Israel). Throughout Jewish history, from the time of their scattering after Jerusalem was destroyed in 70 AD, there has been a series of campaigns waged against the Jews. The nations attacking them have said in nearly every case, "We haven't done anything wrong; they have sinned! They put Christ the Messiah to death!" We find here that this is the excuse used in this portion for attacking them by their attackers. The latest organized effort to exterminate the Jews was carried out by Adolph Hitler in the middle of the last century. This was his excuse as well.

We find that "a nation from the north … *will attack her and lay waste her land*" (Babylon, modern day Iraq), in Jeremiah 50:3. We find that in the last days, the northern-nation alliance headed up by Russia will be attacking Israel in the Battle of Magog. As I studied this, I wondered why Russia would attack Iraq. Then I remembered that Iraq will be governed by Israel with a drawn sword (Micah 5:6). Essentially, Iraq will be part of Israel! And, perhaps as significant, Israel will control the rich Iraqi oil fields! We find that Magog is coming to plunder. I wonder if they want to take the oil fields for themselves. We don't have any scripture that clearly says that oil will be the motivating factor, but this shouldn't be a surprise. In the list of plunder, it says *goods and plunder* (Ezekiel 38:12–13). These could certainly include oil or oil fields. I wouldn't expect to find that information in scripture. The Bible merely tells us that they are coming for a great plunder. This would certainly be a possibility. Now notice that in this attack, it isn't the Medes that are attacking Babylon, but an "alliance of great nations from the land of the north." In Jeremiah 51, we are clearly told that it is the Medes that attack the city of Babylon (Jeremiah 51:11). When the Medes overthrew Babylon, it was just the Medes that accomplished this, not an "alliance of great nations." God is allowing this because Babylon (Iraq) has always persecuted Israel (my inheritance), and they continue to do so to this day. They will be plundered (verse 10) and completely destroyed (Jeremiah 50:26, 29). Jeremiah 50:17 is stated from the viewpoint of Jeremiah; here he is explaining Babylon's guilt. As already stated, Jeremiah 50:20 seals this as a future event; Israel cannot claim that today they have no guilt. They are still in rebellion against their God, Jesus Christ, or as they refer to Him, "Yeshua."

We are told in Jeremiah 50:28 that God is taking "vengeance for his temple." This is an interesting phrase. It could have several different applications to prophecy. First, it could be referring to the pillaging of the temple by Nebuchadnezzar in Daniel's time, and I feel that this is part of it, but I believe that it could also be referring to the fact that Islam is preventing Israel from erecting the temple to this day. When the Battle of Magog is over, the way will be clear for the construction of the temple where it is supposed to stand as prescribed in Ezekiel 45:1–5 and Ezekiel 48:8–20, but we will cover this in greater detail in Chapter 2 of volume 2.

Notice Jeremiah 50:32b: "I will kindle a fire in her towns that will consume all who are around her." Again, remember that this is being carried out by a human army that God is using for His means. This appears to be nuclear, because it says *the fire will consume all who are around her*. Radiation poisoning would accomplish this; the fire in the towns would consume those surrounding the areas, especially if the weapons are neutron bombs. Again, this is speculation, but it is quite likely. Notice again in Jeremiah 50:41 that it is a great nation from the north with many kings from the ends of the earth attacking here. This is the description of the Magog attack as found in Ezekiel 38, Joel 2, and others.

Jeremiah 50:10–16 and 33–40 are fulfilled in the days of the Medes in the destruction of the city of Babylon. The mix of fulfilled and future prophecy makes this portion difficult to understand, but in the light of other scripture, it becomes easier. We will find in Isaiah 19:23–25 that Assyria (Iraq) will be restored, so the never-to-be-inhabited part cannot be referring to the land, just the city, and to this day, the city of Babylon is a wasteland. Saddam Hussein wanted to rebuild the city of Babylon, but God wouldn't allow this, and the US overthrew him. Whether you agree with the war or not, God will not allow the city to be rebuilt. We will study more in Chapter 6 of volume 2 about Iraq's restoration. There are many verses dealing with their future repentance.

It appears that God is referring to the antichrist in Jeremiah 50:44b: "What shepherd can stand against me?" A shepherd will try to stand against God in this time, but he will be defeated.

Now, last of all in this portion, please notice Jeremiah 50:46: "At the sound of Babylon's capture *the earth will tremble;* its cry will resound among the nations." This goes well with Ezekiel 38:17–23. God will intervene on Israel's behalf when they repent, (Joel 2:12–20, Hosea 5:14–6:3). When He intervenes, it won't be with nuclear weapons. It will be with a worldwide earthquake! This earthquake will be accompanied by burning sulfur, rain, and hailstones. The scriptures don't refer to volcanoes specifically but refers to them as "earthquakes" with burning sulfur (or brimstone) etcetera! As I have said, I believe that it is likely a "super volcano" explosion that we have been hearing about so much lately, similar to Yellowstone. At this time, there will be many events that would seem to indicate something of this nature: billows of smoke, the sun will be darkened, the moon turned to blood (the *appearance* of blood is likely from the original Hebrew), and the stars will fall from the sky. This could likely be a meteor shower. The meteor showers may be from outer space, or they may be rocks expelled into space from exploding volcanoes and re-entering the atmosphere at great speed. This can happen! This is found in Joel 2:30–32 and Revelation 6:12–17. I believe that these scriptures are speaking of the same event, because they both come *before* the "great and dreadful day of the Lord." Revelation 6:17 places these events as already just occurred, and the people are begging the mountains to fall on them because "the great day of their" (Him who sits on the throne and the Lamb) "wrath has come." We will find that there are other events that seem to mimic this time but are distinctly different, such as Matthew 24:29, which comes *"after the distress of those days,"* and Revelation 8:12, where only *one third* of the sun, moon, and stars are affected. It will be three separate events, all of which *appear* to be super volcano explosions! It will be one of these events that will occur when Magog attempts to attack Israel proper. At that time, Israel will repent; they will enter an everlasting covenant with God and will be forgiven for their sins. Then God will intervene on their behalf with weapons that only God can control: earthquakes, volcanoes, and weather! These will defeat the most powerful armies on earth. The battle will be God's! It appears from this portion that when Russia attacks Iraq, Jews rush to Israel "in tears," seeking God's forgiveness and intervention. They gather and repent, turning the nation to Christ; this is their Day of Atonement. I gather from the reading of these portions that there will be very little time between the Rosh Hashanah and the Yom Kippur, the Day of Atonement. As these holy days are celebrated in Judaism today, there are ten days between the holidays. These days are called "the ten days of awe." Indeed, when these events come to pass, it will be days of awe, and it could very well be just ten days! Maybe less!

One of the best portions dealing with the Jews regathering at Rosh Hashanah is found in Ezekiel 36–37; this culminates in the famous dry-bones passage. Ezekiel 36 gives an excellent description of the Damascus battle and its aftermath. It gives the reason for the surrounding nations' attack on Israel and God's reason for his response to them. Please read this portion for yourself. (I am mentioning it here instead of the previous chapter because it is primarily dealing with Rosh Hashanah.) Because it is rather lengthy, I will only copy highlights here. This is a prophecy to the "Mountains of Israel." Ezekiel 36: " ...This is what the Sovereign Lord says: 'The enemy said of you, "Aha! The ancient heights have become our possession.""" Here we find that the surrounding nations consider that they can take Israel. (Sounds like tomorrow's newspaper, doesn't it?) We find in other verses in this portion that the surrounding nations ravaged and hounded Israel and made Israel the object of malicious talk and slander (Ezekiel 36:3). They suffered scorn (Ezekiel 36:7). Ezekiel 36 verses 8–11 are important here:

> But you, O mountains of Israel, will produce branches and fruit for my people Israel, *for they will soon come home.* I am concerned for you and will look on you with favor; you will be plowed and sown, and *I will multiply the number of people upon you, even the whole house of Israel. The towns will be inhabited and the ruins rebuilt.* I will increase the number of men and animals upon you, and they will become fruitful and numerous. I will settle people on you as in the past and will make you prosper more than before. *Then you will know that I am the Lord.*

Here we find that the nations that surround Israel attack and ravage it. They insult Israel. But God promised to intervene on their behalf and bring them "home" to the mountains of Israel. We find in Ezekiel 36:8 that God has the land preparing for them to come home. "For they will *soon* come home!" Their Rosh Hashanah hasn't happened yet, but God is preparing for it! How Exciting! In fact, what is referred to in Ezekiel 36:8–10 is exactly what is referred to in Ezekiel 38:8: "… a land that has recovered from war, whose people were gathered from many nations to the mountains of Israel." This reinforces the point that the war in Damascus is the war that Ezekiel is referring to in verse 38:8, because the events of the war in Ezekiel 36 match the events of the battle of Damascus. We see that *after* they come home to Israel, they will "know that I am the Lord." This is a very important detail. We will find, in this and the next chapter of this book, specifically how they come to know that He is their Lord.

In Ezekiel 36:16–20, we find that God details His reasons for His judgment on Israel. They essentially turned their back on him. They, who should have recognized Him and presented Him to the world, crucified Him! And please, dear gentile reader, don't condemn the Jews because of this. Christ died because of our sins as well as the Jews' sins. We are all equally guilty! 1 John 2:2, "He is the atoning *sacrifice for our sins*, and not only ours but also *for the sins of the whole world.* Then we find this pivotal passage:

> I had concern for my holy name, which the house of Israel profaned among the nations where they had gone. Therefore say to the house of Israel, "This is what the Sovereign Lord says: *'It is not for your sake, O house of Israel, that I am going to do these things, but for the sake of my holy name, which you have profaned among the nations where you have gone.'*"
> Ezekiel 36:21–22

God is not going to restore Israel to her land for their sake, but for His sake, so that His name will stop being profaned throughout the world. At this time, Israel still doesn't know their God (Christ!). The rest of Ezekiel 36 will be covered in better detail in Chapter 3 of this book.

Ezekiel 37 then proceeds to detail, metaphorically, (yes, he gives the metaphoric vision and then the interpretation) the regathering of Israel just before the Battle of Magog. This portion just restates what was revealed in the previous chapter. This is a rendering of what will happen when God calls Israel home for the fulfillment of Rosh Hashanah.

Jeremiah 30–31 covers the time immediately before the Battle of Magog, through the time immediately after it, and into the tribulation period. It covers such a broad span of events but such a relatively short period of time! Probably very close to seven years are covered here. The chief problem with this portion is that it mixes the events, because they are so dependant on each other. I will quote all of Jeremiah 30 and 31:1–30. The rest of Jeremiah 30:31 is Israel's Day of Atonement and following. I will cover it in great detail in the next chapter of this book. There will be mention of their "Day of Atonement" in the portion that I will be covering now, only because it is so intimately associated with the events that are occurring. To filter this event out of this portion would damage the understanding of the scripture, and I will not do that.

This is the word that came to Jeremiah from the Lord: "This is what the Lord, the God of Israel, says: 'Write in a book all the words I have spoken to you. The days are coming,' declares the Lord, 'when I will bring my people Israel and Judah back from captivity and restore them to the land I gave their forefathers to possess,' says the Lord. These are the words the Lord spoke concerning Israel and Judah: 'This is what the Lord says: *Cries of fear are heard—terror, not peace. Ask and see: Can a man bear children? Then why do I see every strong man with his hands on his stomach like a woman in labor,* every face turned deathly pale? How awful that day will be! None will be like it. *It will be a time of trouble for Jacob, but he will be saved out of it.* In that day,' declares the Lord Almighty, 'I will break the yoke off their necks and will tear off their bonds; no longer will foreigners enslave them. Instead, *they will serve the Lord their God and David their king,* whom I will raise up for them. So do not fear, O Jacob my servant; do not be dismayed, O Israel,' declares the Lord. 'I will surely save you out of a distant place, your descendents from the land of their exile. Jacob will again have peace and security, and no one will make him afraid. I am with you and will save you,' declares the Lord. *'Though I completely destroy all the nations among which I scatter you, I will not completely destroy you. I will discipline you but only with justice. I will not let you go entirely unpunished.'* This is what the Lord says: 'Your wound is incurable, your injury beyond healing. There is no one to plead your cause, no remedy for your sore, no healing for you. *All your allies have forgotten you; they care nothing for you. I have struck you as an enemy would and punished you as would the cruel, because your guilt is so great and your sins so many.* Why do you cry over your wound, your pain that has no cure? Because of your guilt and many sins I *have done* these things to you. *But all who devour you will be devoured; all your enemies will go into exile. Those who plunder you will be plundered;* all who make spoil of you I will despoil. But I will restore you to health and heal your wounds,' declares the Lord, 'because you are called an outcast, Zion for whom no one cares.' This is what the Lord says: 'I will restore the fortunes of Jacob's tents and have compassion on his dwellings; *the city will be rebuilt on her ruins, and the palace will stand in its proper place.* From them will come songs of thanksgiving and the sound of rejoicing. I will add to their numbers, and they will not be decreased; I will bring them honor, and they will not be disdained. Their children will be as in days of old, and their community will be established before me; *I will punish all who oppress them. Their leader will be one of their own; their ruler will arise among them.* I will bring him near and he will come close to me, for who is he who will devote himself to be close to me?' declares the Lord. '*So you will be my people, and I will be your God.*' See, *the storm of the Lord will burst out in wrath, a driving wind swirling down on the heads of the wicked. The fierce anger of the Lord will not turn back until he fully accomplishes the purposes of his heart.* In days to come you will understand this.

Jeremiah 30:1–24

"At that time," declares the Lord, *"I will be the God of all the clans of Israel, and they will be my people."* This is what the Lord says: *"The people who survive the sword will find favor in the desert;* I will come to give rest to Israel." The Lord appeared to us in the past, saying: "I have loved you with an everlasting love; I have drawn you with ever-lasting kindness. I will build you up again and you will be rebuilt, O virgin Israel. Again you will take up your tambourines and go out to dance with the joyful. Again you will plant vineyards on the hills of Samaria; the farmers will plant them and enjoy their fruit. There will be a day when watchmen cry out on the hills of Ephraim, 'Come, let us go up to Zion, to the Lord our God.'" This is what the Lord says: "Sing with joy for Jacob; shout for the

foremost of the nations. Make your praises heard, and say, *'O Lord, save your people, the remnant of Israel. See, I will bring them from the land of the north and gather them from the ends of the earth. Among them will be the blind and the lame, expectant mothers and women in labor; a great throng will return. They will come with weeping; they will pray as I bring them back.* I will lead them beside streams of water on a level path where they will not stumble, because I am Israel's father, and Ephraim is my firstborn son. "Hear the word of the Lord, O nations; proclaim it in distant coastlands: 'He who scattered Israel will gather them and will watch over his flock like a shepherd.' For the Lord will ransom Jacob and redeem them from the hand of those stronger than they. They will come and shout for joy on the heights of Zion; they will rejoice in the bounty of the Lord-the grain, the new wine and the oil, the young flocks and herds. They will be a well-watered garden, and they will sorrow no more. Then maidens will dance and be glad, young men and old as well. I will turn mourning into gladness; I will give them comfort and joy instead of sorrow. I will satisfy priests with abundance, and my people will be filled with my bounty," declares the Lord. This is what the Lord says: "A voice is heard in Ramah, mourning and great weeping, Rachel weeping for her children and refusing to be comforted, because her children are no more." This is what the Lord says: *"restrain your voice from weeping and your eyes from tears, for your work will be rewarded,"* declares the Lord. *"They will return from the land of the enemy.* So there is hope for your future," declares the Lord. *"Your children will return to their own land.* "I have surely heard Ephraim's moaning: *'You disciplined me like an unruly calf, and I have been disciplined. Restore me, and I will return, because you are the Lord my God. After I strayed, I repented; after I came to understand, I beat my breast. I was ashamed and humiliated because I bore the disgrace of my youth.'* Is not Ephraim my dear son, the child in whom I delight? Though I often speak against him, I still remember him. *Therefore my heart yearns for him; I have great compassion for him,"* declares the Lord. *"Set up road signs; put up guideposts.*

Take note of the highway, the road you take. Return, O virgin Israel, return to your towns. How long will you wander, O unfaithful daughter? The Lord will create a new thing on earth-a woman will surround a man." This is what the Lord Almighty, The God of Israel, says: "*When I bring them back from captivity, the people in the land of Judah and in its towns will once again use these words: 'The Lord bless you, O righteous dwelling, O sacred mountain.'* People will live together in Judah and all its towns-farmers and those who move about with their flocks. I will refresh the weary and satisfy the faint." At this I awoke and looked around. My sleep had been pleasant to me. "The days are coming," declares the Lord, "when I will plant the house of Judah with offspring of men and of animals. *Just as I watched over them to uproot and tear down, and to overthrow, destroy and bring disaster, so I will watch over them to build and to plant,*" declares the Lord. "In those days people will no longer say, 'The fathers have eaten sour grapes, and their children's teeth are set on edge.' Instead, everyone will die for his own sin; whoever eats sour grapes-his own teeth will be set on edge."

Jeremiah 31:1–30

This is another powerful portion of prophetic scripture. This shows us a time in the future that is of great importance to Israel and to the world at large. Most people would identify this as a purely tribulation passage. They are close, but we will see that it is really a Battle of Magog portion, leading into the Day of Atonement and then the tribulation.

Jeremiah 30:3 tells us that God will bring Israel and Judah back "from captivity" and restore them to their land. This introduces the theme of this portion. They come "home" in every sense of the word. They come home to the land of Israel, and they come home to God.

First we find in Jeremiah 30:4 that this prophecy is concerning Israel and Judah. We are told in Jeremiah 30:5 that there are cries of fear and terror. Then in Jeremiah 30:6, a question is posed. Can a man bear children? The obvious answer is no. That being the case, it asks why every strong man appears to be in labor. I don't feel it is a stretch to say that we can identify this portion with Christ's words in Matthew 24:8, calling this time the beginning of birth pains. We are told in Jeremiah 30:7 that this will be an awful day, and none will be like it. Then we find that "It will be a time of trouble for Jacob." This isn't directed anywhere else; this is Jacob's (Israel's) trouble. Then we find these reassuring words: "but he will be saved out of it." This is always identified as a tribulation verse. I don't think it is strictly a "tribulation" verse, though. Let's read the events that follow this. First, "I (God) will break the yoke off their necks and tear off their bonds, foreigners will no longer enslave them." They will no longer be forced to work for foreigners. Second, "they will serve the Lord their God and David their king." Wow! What a tremendous statement! They (Israel) will serve the Lord their God. Today, we don't find that Israel is a very godly nation, and they certainly don't, as a nation, trust in Christ (Yeshua). Then we find that they will also serve David their king! This is a direct reference to Christ, of the kingly line of David. He will be their king. It is not claimed here that He is on the earth, just that they serve him and that God will raise Him up, as indeed He will! Christ rose from the dead, and He will return from heaven to reign over them (and all believers) at His second coming! God tells Israel that He will save their descendents from the land of their exile. Jews today are exiled throughout all the earth. He promises that they will have peace and have no fear.

Now, even though God is specifically speaking to Israel here, this next portion refers to the rest of the nations of the world. We are told that He will save Israel, but ... *all other nations where they have been scattered are doomed!* Yes, that certainly applies to us in the USA, Russia, Great Britain, Germany, and everywhere else that they have lived! Please notice here that they (Israel) will be saved out of this time of trouble for Jacob, and then God will destroy the nations of the earth! This is the beginning of the tribulation! This is where God pours His righteous judgment out on the nations of the earth! We find also that God will not let them (Jews) go entirely unpunished though. In fact, in verse 30 of this portion, we find that they no longer die for the sins of their fathers, but they will die for their own sins. Even this does not mean that they are unsaved. On the contrary, we are clearly told that they *are* saved; they are just disobedient children in this case. This is just like today; there are believers who are in sin and are judged by God for their sin up to death (1 Corinthians 5 gives an example). But He promises to punish them with justice. He promises to be fair. We find in Matthew 24:9 that many will die for the name of Christ. This doesn't mean that they are unsaved! Many will die simply because they love Christ so much that they will willingly give up their life for Him. What this means in relation to tribulation believers is that those who do not survive till the end will not be physically saved to enter the kingdom. They will enter the kingdom, but they will not be able to raise families. There will be families raised during that time, as we will see. Those who endure to the end, those who trust in Christ and survive, will not face death immediately but will enter the kingdom, be able to raise families, and reign with Christ as God intended for the descendants of Adam and Eve before the flood. We are told that they will live to be very old, just as they were before the flood. Someone who dies at 100 years will be considered just a child. Those believers who die due to their own sin will have to be resurrected and will enter the kingdom in their glorified bodies. Their sin will be purged, but their judgment will be early death and the fact that they will not be able to raise families in the paradise God intended for them. They are punished and must perish from this life. These certainly are not unsaved! We find in Revelation 13:7 that the antichrist will make war with the saints and will overcome them. To be sure, many will die here. But they are *saints!*

Many who die will not be dying for their sin; they will die for the love of Christ. The gospel of the kingdom mentioned in Matthew 24:13–14 is simply that those who survive to the end, trusting in Christ, will enter the kingdom to live many years and raise families. The ones who are left alive in Matthew 24:40–41 are examples of these people. They are "saved" to enter the kingdom. We will cover the time of the tribulation in greater detail in Chapters 1 through 4 of volume 2.

Now in Jeremiah 30:12–13, we find that God is taking us back to the Battle of Magog. Their wound is incurable, beyond healing! It doesn't sound good. They are in very serious trouble (Jacob's trouble!). We find in Jeremiah 30:14 that all Israel's allies abandon them. That's us! We turn our back on Israel. And we find that God has struck them. This is proof that this is speaking of the Battle of Magog here. Once Israel repents, God will not strike them (Ezekiel 39:25, Joel 2:18–20, Hosea 5:14–6:3, etc). God strikes them as someone who is cruel because their sin is so great. They rejected their Messiah, their king. We are truly *all* guilty of the *death* of Christ, because He died for the sins of the world. He died because of me! He died because of you! Then we find, in Jeremiah 30:16, that when they repent, they will devour those who would devour them and plunder those who would plunder them! This is also stated in Ezekiel 39:10 (Magog!). Then, in Jeremiah 30:17–18, we find that God will restore them and heal their wounds! He will restore the fortunes of Jacob's tents. Then in the same sentence, as a continuing act of God, we find that "the city will be rebuilt on her ruins, and the *palace* will stand in its proper place." This is so interesting! We find in Ezekiel 38:8, 12 that Magog will come against a land recovered from war and also that they are attacking a people who have resettled their ruins. This is the rebuilding of the ruins after the Damascus battle. The *palace* isn't rebuilt at that time; it couldn't be. Islam, while deeply wounded, is still alive, and Israel still hasn't turned to Christ. Yes, we find that the believing Israel will worship in the temple! Ezekiel 40–47 gives an outline for temple worship. This is not a mistake! This is how God wishes Israel and all believers to worship during the millennium. But I will cover more about the temple and the millennium in volume 2. Now back to the point of this passage. We find that when God intervenes on the behalf of Israel at their repentance, He will send an "earthquake" that will level every wall, at least in Jerusalem, (personally, I believe it will be *every wall on earth*, due to Revelation 6:12–17, which we will cover in detail later in this chapter). This would level the temple if it were rebuilt after the battle of Damascus, and we find that they worship in it after the tribulation and that the antichrist defiles it in the middle of the tribulation. This is *not* figurative speech here. There is no indication that it is figurative. This is God's promise to Israel! Also, the battle of Damascus ruined everything by the hand of man, not God with His earthquake! So now we find that the ruins of Israel will be rebuilt (from the earthquake), and the palace (temple) will be rebuilt in its proper place. All of this recovery will be by the restoration of *God!* This is important! The rebuilding of Israel and the temple is considered to be an act of God. I will explain in more detail why this is so important in Chapter 2 of volume 2. This does place this battle at Magog though, because of the different details involved in the two battles.

Now notice Jeremiah 30:19–21. This will be the condition during the tribulation and millennium. We'll have more about this in Chapters 1 through 4 of volume 2. We will find that it bounces back and forth in these next verses from the Battle of Magog to the time of the tribulation. Jeremiah 30:22 is clearly setting the stage for the protection of God because of their repentance, the Day of Atonement. Then in Jeremiah 30:23–24, we find God's intervention in the Battle of Magog and into the tribulation.

Jeremiah 31:1–6 covers the Day of Atonement into the tribulation in good detail, and so will I in volume 2.

In Jeremiah 31:7–11, we find a rendition of Rosh Hashanah. Here, God is telling us how He calls them out of the nations to which they have been scattered. This portion is actually a song about God saving them out of the nations (Rosh Hashanah) that is sung after the Day of Atonement. It tells us that they will come weeping. Women in labor will even make the journey at that time (Wow)! The lame and the blind—no one will be left behind of the house of Israel! This song tells us that even though the countries where they come from are stronger than they are, God is stronger yet and will protect His people and gather them to Himself.

Notice Zechariah 8:6–8:

> This is what the Lord Almighty says: "It may seem marvelous to the remnant of this people at that time, but will it seem marvelous to me?" declares the Lord Almighty. This is what the Lord Almighty says: "I will save my people from the countries of the east and the west. I will bring them back to live in Jerusalem; they will be my people, and I will be faithful and righteous to them as their God."

Even more remarkable is the passage in Isaiah 66:7–9:

> "Before she goes into labor, she gives birth; before the pains come upon her, she delivers a son. Who has ever heard of such a thing? Who has ever seen such things? Can a country be born in a day or a nation be brought forth in a moment? Yet no sooner is Zion in labor than she gives birth to her children. Do I bring to the moment of birth and not give delivery?" says the Lord. "Do I close the womb when I bring to delivery?" says your God.

Here we find Israel being born in a day. This is their going from Rosh Hashanah to their Yom Kippur. Their repentance is sudden and quick.

Jeremiah 31:12–14 is telling us of God's provision for them after their repentance. Jeremiah 31:15–17 goes back to Rosh Hashanah and God's delivering them from the land of their enemies.

Jeremiah 31:18 is speaking about the Battle of Magog. We are told that it was God's discipline and that they return because of it.

Jeremiah 31:19 details Israel's repentance (Yom Kippur, the Day of Atonement). They finally understand that they strayed, and they bear their humility (Zechariah 12:10–14). We will study this in the next chapter.

Then we find in Jeremiah 31:20 God's reason for His gathering them back; He loves them! Ephraim is His son! His heart yearns for them, and He has compassion on them!

In Jeremiah 31:21–23, we find another mention of Rosh Hashanah. He cautions them to be careful on their return to not get lost. Get a map, essentially. He refers to them as "virgin Israel"! This is how deeply He will cleanse them! We are told that it is God who brings them back!

Jeremiah 31:24–27 deals with God's blessing them after they repent.

Jeremiah 31:28 gives us the time covered here in a nutshell. God tore them down, and He will raise them up!

Jeremiah 31:29–30 covers the time after their repentance. Israel will no longer be punished for the sins of their fathers. They will only answer for their own sins.

This portion is so involved with the time of Magog and events immediately after resulting from the Magog battle that they are inseparable. It is a beautiful portion showing God's compassion and care for His people, Israel.

This next portion covers the Battle of Magog and the involvement of the antichrist. In fact, it covers his involvement better than any other portion of Scripture. He appears to be very much in power and well established at the time of this battle. The description in this portion is unmistakable as the Battle of Magog because the

armies and countries involved are the same as the ones in Ezekiel
38–39. This portion is Daniel 11:40–45, as it pertains to the Magog
battle. Jeremiah 31:36–39 introduces him to the reader as a leader
and some of his politics. We will concentrate on the battle here and
the man in Chapter 4 of this book.

> At the time of the end the king of the South will engage him
> in battle, and the king of the North will storm out against
> him with chariots and cavalry and a great fleet of ships. He
> will invade many countries and sweep through them like a
> flood. He will also invade the beautiful land. Many countries
> will fall, but Edom, Moab and the leaders of Ammon will be
> delivered from his hand. He will extend his power over many
> countries; Egypt will not escape. He will gain control of the
> treasures of gold and silver and all the riches of Egypt, with
> the Libyans and Nubians in submission. But reports from the
> east and the north will alarm him, and he will set out in a
> great rage to destroy and annihilate many. He will pitch his
> royal tents between the seas at the beautiful holy mountain.
> Yet he will come to his end, and no one will help him.
>
> Daniel 11:40–45

This tells us details that would be lost if not described here. This
much detail is not found anywhere else. The antichrist appears to
be in power over several countries; in fact, there are hints that the
antichrist is not Jewish. In Jeremiah 30:21, we are told that when
the Jews turn to Christ, "Their leader will be one of their own; their
leader will arise among them." This seems to indicate a change. We
are told in many scriptures that until they repent, they are subject
to foreigners (Jeremiah 30:8 is an excellent example). I have conjectured that perhaps he is in a similar role, as the leader of the United
Nations. He would represent many nations, and they would all be
subject to him. We are told that the "king of the South will engage
him in battle." This would be Ethiopia and Sudan, along with
Libya. Libya is named later in this portion, as well as the Nubians.

Nubian is another term for the Ethiopians and Sudanese. It seems that the southern force will engage him in battle, exposing his flank so that the king of the North (Magog) will be able to deliver the knockout punch. But this doesn't work. God intervenes in support of His people (certainly not for the antichrist), and Magog and his allies are defeated. The antichrist uses this to establish his power over the entire earth, with the exception of Israel, who rejects him at this point (we will discuss this in more detail in Chapters 3 and 4 of this book). You will notice here that Edom, Moab, and "the leaders of Ammon will be delivered from his hand." This is important for events during the seven years of tribulation that is coming up very soon after this battle. These areas will be a safe haven for Jewish refugees during that time. Also, we find that Israel has annexed these territories for themselves at the battle of Damascus. It is important to note that they will be part of Israel at the time of the Magog battle, and the *antichrist will not get possession of them!* Even though they are owned by Israel, and he is a shepherd over Israel, he doesn't possess the Jordan area at the time of the Battle of Magog. This shows that Israel isn't giving in to him from the time of the Battle of Magog. This also weakens the argument of those who claim that Israel goes into the tribulation in subjection to him.

The antichrist will be very interested in treasure and will gain all the treasure of Egypt. He will have power over the countries that attacked him from the south. We are told that he will "invade the beautiful land." Other translations simply say he will "enter" the beautiful land. If he is a shepherd over Israel, as we are told in Zechariah 11:15–17, it wouldn't be an invasion. When the Jews fulfill their Day of Atonement and truly repent, they will reject his leadership over them, and then he will desecrate the temple, as told in Matthew 24:15–20, Mark 13:14–17, and Luke 21:20–24. The Luke 21:20–24 portion tells us of Jerusalem being surrounded by armies. The antichrist will take the temple by force. This event was shown to the Jews at the destruction of Jerusalem by Titus, but will be fulfilled again by the antichrist in the end times. We will study more about this in chapter 4 of this book. We are told in Daniel 11:44 that reports from the east and the north will alarm him. This is in the direction of Iraq, and at the time leading up to this Magog battle, Israel will own Iraq. There is a lot of wealth to be had in the oil fields, and anyone attacking "his" (he will believe they are his) oil fields would alarm him. (The oil field connection is just speculation, of course, but it is very likely, because we find that he is only in it for personal gain and wealth anyway, Daniel 11:39.) Daniel closes with the comforting words (to God's people, at least) that he will come to his end, and no one will help him.

One of the problems that the book of Daniel has faced throughout history is that it is too detailed, so it is claimed that it must have been written after the event (like God doesn't know and can't tell us the future). This is an argument used by skeptics for years, and I am curious what they will say when these things are fulfilled that are still future. God blessed Daniel with very detailed information during the time of Babylonian and Persian empires and not later. Sorry skeptics! God is a mighty God, and He will reveal what He wishes when He wishes and to whom He wishes!

It should be no surprise that Zechariah has a mention of this event as well. I would be amazed if he didn't, and he does. Zechariah is a powerful prophetic piece, with many important details to add to God's Word. He gives added light to this event, and we can learn more details from him. The portion is Zechariah 11:15–12:14.

> "Then the Lord said to me, '*Take again the equipment of a foolish shepherd.* For I am going to raise up a shepherd over the land who will not care for the lost, or seek the young, or heal the injured, or feed the healthy, but *will eat the meat of the choice sheep*, tearing off their hoofs. Woe to the worthless shepherd, who deserts the flock! *May the sword strike his arm and his right eye! May his arm be completely withered, his right eye totally blinded!*"
>
> Zechariah 11:15–17

This is the word of the Lord concerning Israel. The Lord, who stretches out the heavens, who lays the foundation of the earth, and who forms the spirit of man within him, declares: *"I am going to make Jerusalem a cup that sends all the surrounding peoples reeling. Judah will be besieged as well as Jerusalem.* On that day, when all the nations of the earth are gathered against her, I will make Jerusalem an immovable rock for all the nations. All who try to move it will injure themselves. On that day I will strike every horse with panic and its rider with madness," declares the Lord. "I will keep a watchful eye over the house of Judah, but I will blind all the horses of the nations. Then the leaders of Judah will say in their hearts, *'The people of Jerusalem are strong, because the Lord Almighty is their God.' On that day I will make the leaders of Judah like a firepot in a woodpile, like a flaming torch among sheaves. They will consume right and left all the surrounding peoples, but Jerusalem will remain intact in her place."* The Lord will save the dwellings of Judah first, so that the honor of the house of David and of Jerusalem's inhabitants may not be greater than that of Judah. On that day the Lord will shield those who live in Jerusalem, so that the feeblest among them will be like David, and the house of David will be like God, like the Angel of the Lord going before them. *"On that day I will set out to destroy all the nations that attack Jerusalem. And I will pour out on the house of David and the inhabitants of Jerusalem a spirit of grace and supplication. They will look on me, the one they have pierced,* and they will mourn for him as one mourns for an only child, and grieve bitterly for him as one grieves for a firstborn son. On that day the weeping in Jerusalem will be great, like the weeping of Hadad Rimmon in the plain of Megiddo. The land will mourn, each clan by itself, with their wives by themselves: the clan of the house of David and their wives, the clan of the house of Nathan and their wives, the clan of the house of Levi and their wives, the clan of Shimei and their wives, and all the rest of the clans and their wives."

Zechariah 12:1–14

This portion is one of the most profound and important scriptures in the Old Testament dealing with the deity of Christ. We will find that it is also one of the most misunderstood portions dealing with prophecy. This is a shame too, because when properly understood, it is very important to a true understanding of end-times prophecy. This portion takes us from the uprising of the antichrist through the Battle of Magog and into the Day of Atonement. This shows us again the importance of Magog and its role in bringing about the repentance of the nation of Israel, as many other portions have shown, but this one is clear about the reason for God's judgment on Israel. It's because they have rejected the Christ, the Messiah.

It starts out with a pronouncement against Israel. First, we find that this is the word of the Lord. In the Hebrew, this is the word *Yahweh*, which we today transliterate as *Jehovah*, a name for God. He tells us that He is going to set up a "foolish shepherd" over the land (Israel). This shepherd will not care for the ones who need caring for, but he will use Israel and it's needs for his own personal gain. This is before the Battle of Magog, and I believe that it is started around the time of the battle of Damascus. We are told of his selfishness in Daniel 11:43, where he takes the treasures of Egypt. Daniel 11:39 tells us that he distributes the land at a price. This could be referring to him taking the land that Israel has gained in the battle of Damascus and selling it for profit, or it could also be translated *"land for a reward."* This is because in the Hebrew language, it could be properly translated either way. Seeing that it follows him honoring those who acknowledge (worship, Revelation 13) him, it is probably likely that it is a reward. Either way, he owns the land (in his eyes) and uses it for his own personal gain, either monetarily or for political and religious power. Then we find that he will be struck a violent blow in judgment of his blasphemous sin. He doesn't repent though, as we will find in Revelation 13. We will study this in greater depth in Chapter 4 of this book.

So here we find that the antichrist is in power over Israel, and he is using them for his own personal gain in his grab for worship, power, and wealth. This is the situation before the Battle of Magog.

Again in Zechariah 12:1, we find a reminder of just who is speaking here. This is the word of the Lord; it concerns Israel. This is the Lord, who stretches out the heavens, who lays the foundation of the earth, and who forms the spirit of man. Wow! This is God the almighty! Maker of heaven, earth, you, and me! He tells us that he is going to make Israel (Jerusalem represents Israel as its capital, just as Damascus represents Syria as its capital and Judah is the location of Jerusalem in Israel) a great difficulty to the nations surrounding it. I have conjectured, and I emphasize that is just conjecture, that this could be because Israel owns Iraq's oil fields at this time as a result of the Damascus battle. They will own Iraq, which is not conjecture, as I have already pointed out. No matter what, though, Israel will be a great burden to the nations around Israel, and the whole world will be either against them or at least will not support them (Jeremiah 30:11, 14). This will continue to be the situation through the entire tribulation. We are told that God will strike every horse and rider with panic and madness. I guess so! We found in Ezekiel 38–39 that he is going to send an earthquake, probably with at least one great volcano. All volcanic activity is referred to as "earthquake" in the Bible, because the word *volcano* is from the Roman god Vulcan, the pagan god of fire. This event will be felt around the world *on that day*. God uses the phrase "on that day" frequently through this passage. This is to inform us that it is a special time, also known as the "Day of the Lord." Notice Zechariah 12:5. The leaders of Jerusalem (this is important, because it again shows that Israel is not in submission to the antichrist by then!) say, "The people of Jerusalem are strong, because the Lord Almighty is their God." If the Lord Almighty is their God, they have repented, and if the leaders are saying it, the antichrist isn't their leader! We find that all the countries around will be destroyed, but Jerusalem and Judah will be safe. We find that the feeble of Israel will fight with might, and the "house of David will be like God because He is with them." All the nations that attack Israel will be destroyed. Then we find that great verse, Zechariah 12:10. Please remember who is speaking here; it's Yahweh, Jehovah God! He will pour out on Israel (as a nation!) a "spirit of grace and supplication." This will be the Holy Spirit, as mentioned in Joel 2 and Acts 2. "They will look on me, (Yahweh, Jehovah God!) *the one they have pierced*!" The deity of Christ couldn't be proven any more plainly anywhere in the Old Testament than it is here! This is Christ, crucified on the cross *for the sins of the whole world.* He is truly God! The whole world is guilty of the death of Christ, and at the time of the end, the whole world will reject Him, with the exception of Israel. How sad for the world! How happy for Israel!

Now for the misinterpretation: the word *on* in this verse (upon, King James) is not correct. I have a note in my Scofield study Bible; it could be translated *to*. This is correct. The word in the original Hebrew can mean *to look at*, but it also can mean *to regard* or *respect*! This is the proper meaning of this word. Israel is not looking at Him with their eyes! They are looking at Him with their hearts! They believe! They repent! We will study more about this in the next chapter of this book.

In Chapter 1 of this book, we studied the battle of Damascus. In that chapter, we examined Zechariah 9:1–7. There we found Zechariah's account of the battle of Damascus. Zechariah 9:8 tells us something very interesting: "But I will defend my house against marauding forces. *Never again* will an oppressor overrun my people, for now I am keeping watch."

Here we find that never again will an oppressor overrun His people! Israel will feel completely threatened and helpless when Russia begins their attack against Iraq. They will come together in fear as a people and meet before God as the fulfillment of their Rosh Hashanah. They will make a solemn covenant with Jesus

Christ, Yeshua, and accept Him as their Messiah and God. They will repent! This is their Yom Kippur! God will forever protect them from this point. They will not be overrun in the Magog battle, because they repent—only because they repent.

In the next portion, we will discuss this time as it is found in the book of Revelation. John discusses this time in the sixth chapter: the seven seals. I used to think that everything in the book of Revelation chapters 5 through 19 was tribulation. I have had to rethink this. The reason I had to rethink this is because Ezekiel 38:8 and 11 speak of Israel having recovered from war and living safely in peace. This doesn't describe any part of the tribulation. Also, almost every report on this battle found in Scripture tells us that it is followed by the "day of the Lord." It isn't during the "day of the Lord." Back to our subject here. Revelation 6 is the time of birth pains, as described in Matthew 24. We will go over Revelation 6:7–17 in this chapter. We studied Revelation 6:1–8 in Chapter 1 of this book, dealing with the time around the Damascus battle. Now we will deal with things surrounding the Battle of Magog.

> When the Lamb opened the fourth seal, I heard the voice of the fourth living creature say, "Come!" I looked, and there before me was a pale horse! Its rider was named Death, and Hades was following close behind him. *They were given power over a fourth of the earth to kill by sword, famine, and plague, and by the wild beasts of the earth.* When he opened the fifth seal, I saw under the altar the souls of those who had been slain because of the word of God and the testimony they had maintained. They called out in a loud voice, "How long, Sovereign Lord, holy and true, until you judge the inhabitants of the earth and avenge our blood?" Then each of them was given a white robe, and they were told to wait a little longer, until the number of their fellow servants and brothers who were to be killed as they had been was completed. *I watched as he opened the sixth seal. There was a great earthquake. The sun turned black like sackcloth made of goat hair, the whole moon*

turned blood red, and the stars in the sky fell to earth, as late figs drop from a fig tree when shaken by a strong wind. The sky receded like a scroll, rolling up, and every mountain and island was removed from its place. Then the kings of the earth, the princes, the generals, the rich, the mighty, and every slave and every free man hid in caves and among the rocks of the mountains. They called to the mountains and the rocks, *"Fall on us and hide us from the face of him who sits on the throne and from the wrath of the Lamb! For the great day of their wrath has come, and who can stand?"*

Rev 6:7–17

This portion puts the whole prophecy of Magog and the time of birth pains in perspective when we properly understand the sequence of events from prophecy. We can only learn this from an in-depth study of all Scripture, not just a portion. You can't understand the book of Revelation just by studying Revelation. You need all the prophetic books that deal with end-times prophecy. You need to compile all the details and compare scripture with scripture. Only then can you begin to understand what God has in store for us in the end times.

We find that the fourth horse carries Death as a rider, and Hades followed close behind him. Here we find that one quarter of the earth's population is killed at this time! How can this not be the tribulation? Well, it introduces the tribulation time. It sort of kicks it off. This may be speaking only of the Magog battle; of course it could include the Damascus battle. It may be speaking of all killed during the time of birth pains—only time will tell. Certainly, the great majority of the number killed will die at the time of the Magog battle, we can be sure. The Magog battle will cover a much greater number of people and nations. By the way, later we will find that another event will kill one third of the remainder of the earth's population. That adds up to half of the world's population just in two events! Let us compare this with other scripture:

I will send fire on Magog and on those who live in safety in the coastlands, and they will know that I am the Lord.

Ezekiel 39:6

On that day I will give Gog a burial place in Israel, in the valley of those who travel east toward the Sea. It will block the way of travelers, because Gog and all his hordes will be buried there. So it will be called the Valley of Hamon Gog. For seven months the house of Israel will be burying them in order to cleanse the land.

Ezekiel 39:11–12

Son of man, this is what the Sovereign Lord says: Call out to every kind of bird and all the wild animals: "Assemble and come together from all around to the sacrifice I am preparing for you, the great sacrifice on the mountains of Israel. There you will eat flesh and drink blood. You will eat the flesh of mighty men and drink the blood of the princes of the earth as if they were rams and lambs, goats and bulls—all of them fattened animals from Bashan. At the sacrifice I am preparing for you, you will eat fat till you are glutted and drink blood till you are drunk. At my table you will eat your fill of horses and riders, mighty men and soldiers of every kind," declares the Sovereign Lord.

Ezekiel 39:17–20

Here we find that tremendous devastation will be poured out on the earth by the hand of God and man. Israel alone will be months burying the dead, and we are told that devastation will be spread over the entire earth (distant coastlands).

Joel 2:20 says, "I will drive the northern army far from you, pushing it into a parched and barren land, with its front columns going into the eastern sea and those in the rear into the western sea. And its stench will go up; its smell will rise." Surely he has done great things.

Here we find that this great attacking army is all killed.

After the mention of one fourth of the earth's population being killed, we find the fifth seal: the martyred souls under the altar in heaven asking for God's vengeance on their killers. At first, I used this as a proof that this was a tribulation passage. We find that during the tribulation, there will be many people put to death for their testimony of Christ. This activity will rank high on the antichrist's to-do list. Then I remembered that he will be in power for some time *before* the tribulation begins. We are told in Daniel 11:39 that the antichrist "will greatly honor those who acknowledge him." He will give honor to those who worship him! How about those who won't? One thing to remember about the antichrist is that he will try to fulfill the role of Christ, the Messiah! As such, as we will learn when we study Chapter 4 of volume 2, when Christ returns, He will destroy all unbelievers (Revelation 19:17–21, Matthew 24:37–41; no, this is *absolutely not* a rapture portion). If someone doesn't put their trust in the antichrist, he will have him or her destroyed and claim that he is doing the right thing! What John is telling us here is that the antichrist will actively be killing Christians, even before the tribulation begins. And yes, he will be waging an even greater war against them during the tribulation, especially during the second half, but it will have begun even earlier. This is important to our understanding of what goes on with Israel during the time of "birth pains." We found that there was a worldwide revival after the battle of Damascus (Isaiah 17:7–8 and other portions we have covered), but then they turn away from Him (Isaiah 17:10 again and other portions we have studied). I speculated that the reason they turn from Him is the activity of the antichrist. I believe that this portion of Revelation bears up this theory. He is beginning a campaign of genocide against Christians! Apparently, this is somewhat successful, in that he destroys any organized Christian movement until Israel's Day of Atonement, Yom Kippur, but more about this in Chapter 4 of this book. People will die for Christ's testimony before the tribulation even begins, and that has been happening throughout history; when he comes on the scene, it will just be stepped up a notch. Also, in Revelation 6:11, we find that these martyrs are given a white robe and an admonition to "wait a little longer *until the number of their fellow servants and brothers who were to be killed as they had been was completed.*" This tells us that there are more to be killed during this period.

Then we come to Revelation 6:12–17, the sixth seal. Notice the effects of the sun, moon, and stars. This is a familiar theme in the end-times events. We read about this in Matthew 24 and in Revelation 8. We will find that these are similar events, but not the same, as we will see. We see the sun turned black, the moon turned to (the appearance of) blood, and the stars fell to the earth. I have always found this very interesting and still do. Perhaps one reason for this is that, for most of my life, I have been fascinated by astronomy. So I try to imagine how God will accomplish these amazing feats. I believe that His word gives us some strong clues. Notice also in this portion that every mountain and island was removed from its place. This accompanies the events seen in the sky.

Let's look at Ezekiel 38:19–20. God is speaking here and says:

> "In my zeal and fiery wrath I declare that at that time there shall be a great earthquake in the land of Israel. The fish of the sea, the birds of the air, the beasts of the field, every creature that moves along the ground, *and all the people on the face of the earth* will tremble at my presence. *The mountains will be overturned, the cliffs will crumble and every wall will fall to the ground.*"

Wow, this doesn't sound good! It appears to be a worldwide event. Every creature and every human on earth will tremble at the presence of God! Ezekiel 39:21 says, "I will display my glory among the *nations, and all the nations will see the punishment I inflict and the hand I lay upon them.*" This is continuing commentary on the

Battle of Magog by Ezekiel. This is a worldwide event. This event in Revelation 6 is also a worldwide event.

Now let's look at Joel's account of the end of the Battle of Magog. Joel 2:30–31. "I will show wonders in the heavens and on the earth, blood and *fire and billows of smoke*. The sun will be turned to darkness and the moon to blood *before* the coming of the great and dreadful day of the Lord."

You will notice that this reads very much like the Revelation 6 portion. In fact, the moon turning to blood (the ancient languages allow this to mean that it gives the appearance of blood) only occurs in these two places. In Joel 2, we find that there will be wonders in the heavens and *on the earth*. Joel concentrates on the events in the heavens, mainly the sun and moon phenomenon, which come before the Great and Terrible Day of the Lord. But he alludes to fire and billows of smoke, which would be an earthly event. If we look at Ezekiel 38:19–22, we find that there will be an earthquake that is felt around the world. There is "burning sulfur." Burning sulfur is very much associated with volcanoes. In Ezekiel 39:6, we find that God will send "fire on Magog and on those who live in safety in the coastlands." This is clearly not a local event. So this supports the comment in Joel that there will be "fire and billows of smoke." This also goes well with John's rendition in Revelation 6:12–17. Every mountain is moved (many are exploding!), and islands are moved out of their places.

Then notice in Joel 2:31, these things will occur "before the coming of the *great and dreadful day of the Lord*." Now look in Revelation 6:16–17: "They called to the mountains and the rocks, 'Fall on us and hide us from the face of him who sits on the throne and from the wrath of the Lamb! For *the great day of their wrath* has come, and who can stand?'"

There is much discussion as to the exact meaning of the phrase, "Day of the Lord," and similar phrases. I believe it is clear that God's Word points to the time when He intervenes in the affairs of man in the end time with wrath as the "Day of the Lord." It begins at the end of the Battle of Magog and ends at the second coming of Christ. Again, I need to caution the reader—God isn't trying to fool us; don't make it more complicated than it already is.

To restate Joel 2:31, this event happens before the day of the Lord. And in Revelation 6:16–17, the people of the earth want to die because they are at the starting of the day of the Lord, and they're terrified! So the events of Ezekiel 38–39, Joel 2, and Revelation 6:12–17 all mark the same occurrence, the transition from "birth pains" to "tribulation." I find it sadly interesting that the people in Revelation beg to die instead of just repenting and turning to God. They know it is God (in fact, they know it is Christ!) pouring out wrath, and they still refuse to trust Him! I don't get it! Although it is an interesting fact that the newly popular religion known as the New Age religion worships rocks, crystals, and the earth as part of their idolatry, so it is actually likely that these deluded people are asking the rocks and mountains to protect them! This agrees with Daniel 11:38, which states that he honors, *"a god unknown to his fathers."* We find in Ezekiel 39:21 that God displays His glory among the nations. Ezekiel 39:23 tells us that the nations will know that God poured His wrath on Israel because they were unfaithful to Him. They know who He is, yet they won't acknowledge Him. Ezekiel 38:23 tells us that many nations will know that He is the Lord, but they won't repent. How sad!

So, I will recap what we have found in this chapter. First, we found in Ezekiel a great army from the north, of a country referred to as Magog, is coming against Israel. This army is stressed in many portions as from the north or from the far north. Some even say *the uttermost parts of the north.* There is no place north of Israel more "uttermost" than Russia. That is the simple answer and, in my opinion, the correct one. All other northern nations (north of Israel) are mentioned as coming with Magog or having been destroyed at the Damascus battle. The accompanying nations are specifically mentioned and named (as they were known in Ezekiel's day). We found that they were made by God to attack Israel, but they weren't aware that they were fulfilling God's will. They want plunder. At this time, we found that Israel controls Iraq's oil fields, and this may be the motivating factor, but this is, of course, speculation, but a likely scenario. The nations accompanying Magog are the Islamic countries of Turkey (today Turkey is mostly Islamic), Iran, Ukraine, from the area near Russia, and Ethiopia, Sudan, and Libya. Interestingly, these nations are all allies of Russia today and anti Israel.

We found the leader of this coalition is referred to here as *Gog*. He is referred to in Revelation 20:7–9, but we found that here it is another thousand years past the time of the Battle of Magog. So I believe it is safe to say that this Gog is Satan empowering the human leader. While Gog is evil, he is not the antichrist. The antichrist may very well claim that he is, but Gog is not the antichrist.

We found that Russia is attacking Israel after they have recovered from war. Also, we found that all the countries that attacked Israel in the Damascus battle are absent in this one (at least as self-governing entities). This is important for the timing of the Damascus battle as well as the Magog battle. We do find one country mentioned in a different portion of scripture that is associated with the Damascus battle, and that is Babylon, modern-day Iraq. It is mentioned that Israel will possess Iraq and rule it with a "drawn sword." We found in Jeremiah 50 that the army from the north will attack the land of Babylon (Iraq). This will be the opening phase of the Battle of Magog. Being Israel owns Iraq at that point, this will be the beginning of the attack on Israel. Israel is rebuilt by Jews coming from all over the world. We also found that Israel owns the modern-day country of Jordan. This will be important when tribulation is being poured out on earth.

We found that Israel is at peace and unsuspecting when they will be suddenly attacked in this battle. We found that it comes as a shock.

It is evident that the antichrist will be a "shepherd" to Israel at the time of the Magog battle, but not a good one. He will be greedy for money, power, and worship. It is only when Magog attacks that Israel rejects him.

We found that Israel's Rosh Hashanah, their Feast of Trumpets, is fulfilled. They will call a solemn assembly before God with the purpose of repenting as a nation for their sin of rejecting their Messiah, Christ. Scripture tells us that every Jew from all over the world that is still alive at this time will go back to Israel. Not one will be left behind!

We found that the word translated *horse* in these scriptures can also be translated *swallow* or *crane*, because they skip or fly. So horses as we know them needn't be involved in this battle. Likewise, *horsemen* need not have anything to do with horses. They merely need to be drivers (or pilots). In fact, in Joel 2:5, we find that these "horses" leap over mountaintops! Wow! Quite a horse!

It is also obvious that the United States of America is mentioned in scripture at this time! Not specifically, but we are told that all the allies of Israel abandon her, and that every nation where God has scattered the Jews will be destroyed! That does include the United States of America.

This battle, as well as the battle of Damascus, are both during the time Christ mentioned as the beginning of birth pains, or the beginning of sorrows. The battle of Damascus is near the beginning of that time, and the Battle of Magog is at the very end.

Another thing that we learned is that Israel will use the weapons of their enemies as fuel for seven years after this battle. We found that Russia is using a new substance known as lignostone as armor in their weapons. It is derived from wood; it is stronger than steel, lightweight, and relatively inexpensive. It also has the property of burning at a very high temperature!

The reason they are using the armor as a fuel is because God intervenes on behalf of Israel and destroys their attackers. In fact, in this battle, we find in Revelation 6 that one quarter of the earth's population will be killed at this time, either by the attackers or God's intervention! This time also is the beginning of the seven years of tribulation.

We find that at the time of the Battle of Magog, the entire earth is involved, either actively as combatants or passively, because when God intervenes, He does so through an earthquake that is felt around the world. It is so powerful that Ezekiel tells us that every wall will fall to the ground. This is also a great time marker, in that we are told that the antichrist will desecrate the temple in the middle of the tribulation time. If the temple were built before this, it would be destroyed, so the temple seems to be built at the beginning of the tribulation time, during the recovery of the Battle of Magog. Notice Jeremiah 30 tells us that "the city will be rebuilt on her ruins and the palace will stand in its proper place." This is speaking of the Magog battle and its aftermath. Here, we are told that when they rebuild the city, the "palace" will stand in its proper place, on the temple mount! Also, the Islamic Dome of the Rock will be destroyed, clearing the way for the temple's construction, and Islam will be, at least for the most part, destroyed in this battle. This will make the construction of the temple to be just a building project (albeit a precious one!) instead of an international incident. Although at this time, every country on earth will turn against Israel because Israel turns against the antichrist, whom the world worships. So an international incident will not matter at this point anyway. With the construction of the temple at the beginning of the tribulation, the way will be clear for the antichrist to desecrate it three and one half years into the tribulation. So this battle has to happen at or before the beginning of the tribulation. As mentioned, Israel repents because of this battle, and they turn to Christ. (We will study this more in the next chapter of this book.)

Interestingly, we find that the antichrist will not gain possession of the area of Jordan after the Battle of Magog. This will be important when the middle of the tribulation comes, as we will see in Chapter 3 of volume 2. But we also find that he will get possession of Egypt and its treasures. So Egypt, after all its problems during the time of birth pains of withering on the vine, will suffer the sacking of its ancient treasures that it so jealously guards. There will be no sparing Egypt as a nation. The antichrist will greedily snatch up all he can.

I find it interesting that so many Bible scholars don't know what to do with the Battle of Magog or simply ignore it as just another incident in the parade of events that will happen in the tribulation. This event is pivotal to Israel and all believers in the world at the time that this will be fulfilled! This is when Israel comes to Christ once and for all! God uses the instrument of this battle to bring Israel to Himself, and it is through Israel that the entire world will be able to come to Christ in that day, further fulfilling God's promise to Abraham: "through you all the world be will blessed." (The most important fulfillment was at the incarnation of Christ, of course.)

In the next chapter of this book, we will look at the rebirth of Israel as God's own.

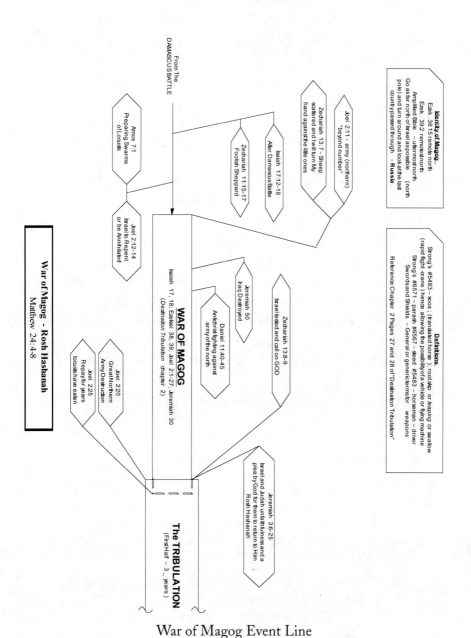

War of Magog Event Line

138

CHAPTER 3

Israel Believes - Yom Kippur,
the Day of Atonement
Matthew 24:9

Then you will be handed over to be persecuted and put to
death, and you will be hated by all nations because of me.

Here we have an interesting statement by our Lord that is often
overlooked for its importance to prophecy. "You will be handed over
to be persecuted and put to death ..." Here Christ is speaking to a
group of interested Jews (specifically His disciples) about the end
times. He is telling them that they will be undergoing great persecution. In light of history, this isn't surprising; Jews have undergone
persecution for thousands of years, from the time of Abraham even
to this day. I don't believe that there is much question that Jews are
the single-most persecuted people on the face of the earth. The very
interesting part is the reason for their persecution in this case: "you
will be hated by all nations *because of me.*" This persecution is because
of Christ! Not because of their *lack* of faith in Him, but because of
their *faith in Christ!* Also of note is the fact that, at least in this
verse, they are hated by nations—all nations. This is significant in
that it clearly agrees with other prophecies found throughout the

Old Testament. Please bear this in mind as we review Israel's Day of Atonement throughout the Old Testament. We will begin with verses that fix the timing of this great event.

We have just covered the Battle of Magog in the previous chapter. In Ezekiel 39:22, we find an interesting statement about the end of that battle. Ezekiel 39:22: "From that day forward the house of Israel will know that I am the Lord their God."

From the end of the Battle of Magog, Israel will know that "I am the Lord their God." This is a profound statement, because it gives the timing of the Jewish Day of Atonement. It comes at the end of the Battle of Magog. In fact, we will see that it is a direct result of the Battle of Magog, as we will see in other scriptures. It is also profound because it gives more weight to Christ's statement that the nations will hate Israel "because of me." Here, Christ is giving claim to deity. Yes, Christ is indeed Jehovah God!

Please remember the previous chapter as we discussed Zechariah 13:8–9. This is where Israel repents because Magog is destroying them, and two thirds die.

> "In the whole land," declares the Lord, "two-thirds will be struck down and perish; yet one-third will be left in it. This third will I bring into the fire; I will refine them like silver and test them like gold. *They will call on my name and I will answer them; I will say, 'They are my people,' and they will say, 'The Lord is our God.'*"

Here we have the battle raging. Many die, and they call on the name of the Lord. This is their Rosh Hashanah. They repent as a nation, and then they say, "The Lord is our God." This is their Yom Kippur, their Day of Atonement.

You will remember that Ezekiel gives a rendition of the Battle of Magog as this great army from the uttermost parts of the north with its allies coming to attack Israel. Israel suspects nothing; they are living at peace, having conquered their surrounding Islamic enemies in the battle of Damascus. They are being shepherded by the antichrist, and he has fooled them, along with the rest of the nations. Yes, there are believers at this time, but they are hunted down and destroyed as troublemakers during the time of birth pains. But then Russia sees the great wealth that Israel commands and decides to take it from them, and they attack in the Battle of Magog. I conjecture that a great part of the wealth that is tempting to Russia is the rich oil fields that Israel owns because they own Iraq. Russia is fielding the greatest army ever assembled, and modern armies need oil. I'm sure we all know the oil reserves of the world are limited and that it will only become more and more valuable and essential. This will become a great need for Russia.

You will notice that I keep harking back to history for pictures of prophecy. I believe that God gives us events that foreshadow future events, and I find it interesting that the reason Japan attacked the United States was so that they could cripple our fleet and be able to take the rich oil fields of the Dutch East Indies. We (the US) had promised to defend Java and Sumatra from aggressors, and Japan needed their oil for their war machine. Japan had no natural oil of its own and had to take it or quit the war. They plundered the Dutch East Indies for their oil so they could continue their conquest of expansion, thus catapulting the United States into World War II.

I don't feel it is unlikely that this could be a great reason for Russia's attack. We are told that they come to plunder. Oil isn't mentioned, but petroleum wasn't known at the time the Bible was written. If you look at the wealth and possessions of Saudi Arabia because of their oil sales, they have great riches. This could very well be the condition of Israel when Russia attacks; they will probably be a very wealthy nation due to their oil sales. So, indeed, it could be that the great wealth of goods that are mentioned as Russia's plunder in the Ezekiel portion will include oil as well, and the wealth could be because of oil.

Anyway, Russia attacks Israel with an overwhelming army, far greater than Japan fielded in World War II. Also, Israel is caught sleeping; they are unsuspecting. Russia considers that it should be a cakewalk, nothing to it; and indeed, by all reasonable considerations, it should be. Russia doesn't consider God's involvement in this issue though, and God does indeed get involved. God made promises to Abraham, David, and many others about His defending them forever. God doesn't go back on His word, *ever!* Russia makes a big mistake here in not considering God in this, because they are messing with His people. No, "the Church" doesn't supplant Israel in God's plan. It merely fills in while Israel is set aside due to their unbelief. God is going to pick them up again.

Ezekiel 39:23–25 tells us:

> And the nations will know that the people of Israel went into exile for their sin, because they were unfaithful to me. So I hid my face from them and handed them over to their enemies, and they all fell by the sword. I dealt with them according to their uncleanness and their offences, and I hid my face from them. Therefore this is what the sovereign Lord says: "I will now *bring Jacob back from captivity and will have compassion on all the people of Israel,* and will be zealous *for my holy name."*

The last almost 2000 years has seen God turning His face from Israel, but He will have compassion on them, and it will be soon.

Isaiah 43:25 repeats this theme: "I, even I, am He who blots out your transgressions, *for my own sake,* and remembers your sins no more." Here we find that Isaiah mentions that God will forgive Israel's sins, but not for their sake; it is for God's own sake. *It is for God's own sake that He forgives Israel!* On this basis, we can be sure that He will again deal with Israel in love and compassion. Never think that God will not again deal with Israel. He gave His word, and He never lies. It is because of His word that He will restore Israel. In Isaiah 48:11, it says, "For my own sake, for my own sake, I do this. *How can I let myself be defamed?* I will not yield my glory to another." Here God explains His motives in restoring Israel. If He doesn't, He will be defamed. His enemies will be able to say, "See, their God isn't real, He didn't come through for them." God will not allow that.

So in these first portions, we have found that Israel, as a nation, discovers that Christ is their God and Messiah. This is in direct response to the Battle of Magog. They realize that without divine intervention, they will be destroyed, and they find that Christ fulfilled all the requirements for their Messiah according to the Old Testament prophets. They also realize that they are better off offending the whole world than God. (At this point, the whole world is very impressed by the antichrist and gives their devotion and even worship to him.)

In this next portion, we will find the condition Israel is in at the time prior to their Day of Atonement and their subsequent repentance.

> These are the words the Lord spoke concerning Israel and Judah: "This is what the Lord says: 'Cries of fear are heard— terror, not peace. Ask and see: *Can a man bear children? Then why do I see every strong man with his hands on his stomach like a woman in labor*, every face turned deathly pale? How awful that day will be! None will be like it. It will be *a time of trouble for Jacob, but he will be saved out of it. In that day,' declares the Lord Almighty, 'I will break the yoke off their necks and will tear off their bonds; no longer will foreigners enslave them. Instead, they will serve the Lord their God and David their king*, whom I will raise up for them.'"
>
> Jeremiah 30:4–9

And we find in Jeremiah 30:22–24:

> "*So you will be my people, and I will be your God.*" See, *The storm of the Lord will burst out in wrath*, a driving wind swirling

down on the heads of the wicked. *The fierce anger of the Lord will not turn back until he fully accomplishes the purposes of his heart.* In days to come you will fully understand this.

This sets the time for this event in relation to Ezekiel 39:22, which we have already addressed, as at the end of the Battle of Magog. Here we find that the famous "time of Jacob's trouble" is prior to their Day of Atonement, not after, and it is also prior to the time of tribulation! This is contrary to everything that I've ever been taught, but it has to be, as we will find.

We will find that there is a lot of overlap in this book from the previous chapter to this one. This is necessary because of the dependency of each on the other. While we will mention the Battle of Magog here, the emphasis will be on Israel's repentance, their Day of Atonement, as opposed to the battle.

First we find the reaction similar to a woman in labor, but it is men that are exhibiting the symptoms. This tells me that it is starting out by what Christ mentions as the time of birth pains. It mentions that it will be an "awful" day, a time of "terror and not peace." Now, if that were the only reason for saying that the time of Jacob's trouble (as it is stated in the KJV and is commonly known) is not the tribulation as we know it, I would reject this notion. But it goes on. The second half of Jeremiah 30:7 says, "...but he will be saved out of it. In that day...I will break the yoke off their necks...no longer will foreigners enslave them." So in that day, God will intervene, and they will no longer serve a foreigner (the antichrist); instead, they will serve Christ. Christ is from the line of David, and God not only did raise Him from the dead, He will raise Him up to be king on the earth as soon as the tribulation is over. You will notice that the portion only says that they will serve Him as king, not that He would be bodily present on the earth at that time. As we will find, when He returns, it will be at the end of this time, and when He does return, it will be with judgment on those who have witnessed His wrath and glory. Ezekiel 38:21: His glory here *is* the tribulation. He is showing us that with Israel's repentance, the Battle of Magog is ending, but the tribulation is just beginning! Matthew also refers to this in chapter 24:38–41 (we will cover this in more detail in Chapter 4 of volume 2).

This same chapter of Jeremiah 30:11 alludes to the actual time of tribulation. "'I am with you and will save you,' declares the Lord. '... *Though I completely destroy all the nations among which I scatter you, I will not completely destroy you. I will discipline you but only with justice; I will not let you go entirely unpunished.*'"

The reason that it isn't given as much attention here is because Israel is being protected at this point. Notice that even though they are being protected, they will still be disciplined. This is at the time He is completely destroying all the nations where He has scattered them. He promises not to *completely* destroy them, but that He will discipline them with justice. This is the time of the tribulation! He is now saving them from annihilation but *not* from discipline. If God didn't intervene, they *all* would die!

So this fixes the "time of Jacob's trouble" as prior to the tribulation. The tribulation will follow, and the nations where Israel was scattered will all be destroyed! That includes just about anywhere that we have permanent habitation! During this time of tribulation, Jews will still have much persecution, even death, but not annihilation. This is mentioned in Matthew 24:9, with which we started this chapter.

The time of birth pains, culminating with the time of trouble for Jacob, will be ended with God's intervention and salvation. "So you will be my people, and I will be your God" (Jeremiah 30:22). Their salvation, in every sense of the term, will hinge on their repentance, their turning to Christ on the fulfillment of Yom Kippur!

So here we find that this event will precede the time of tribulation and will insure Israel God's divine protection during that time. We will find more about this as we study God's Word in this chapter of this book.

In the next portion, we will find a continuation of the thought begun in Jeremiah 30. It will cover their conversion and their restored relationship with God.

Jeremiah 31:1–40:

> *"At that time,"* declares the Lord, *"I will be the God of all the clans of Israel, and they will be my people."* This is what the Lord says: "The people who survive the sword will find favor in the desert; I will come to give rest to Israel." The Lord appeared to us in the past, saying: "I have loved you with an everlasting love; I have drawn you with loving-kindness. *I will build you up again and you will be rebuilt, O Virgin Israel.* Again you will take up your tambourines and go out to dance with the joyful. Again you will plant vineyards on the hills of Samaria; the farmers will plant them and enjoy their fruit. There will be a day when watchmen cry out on the hills of Ephraim, 'Come, let us go up to Zion, to the Lord our God.'" This is what the Lord says: *"Sing with joy for Jacob; shout for the foremost of the nations. Make your praises heard, and say, 'O Lord, save your people, the remnant of Israel.'"* See, I will bring them from the land of the north and gather them from the ends of the earth. Among them will be the blind and the lame, expectant mothers and women in labor; a great throng will return. They will come with weeping; they will pray as I bring them back. I will lead them beside streams of water on a level path where they will not stumble, because I am Israel's father, and Ephraim is my firstborn son. "Hear the word of the Lord, O nations; proclaim it in distant coastlands: 'He who scattered Israel will gather them and will watch over his flock like a shepherd.' For the Lord will ransom Jacob and redeem them from the hand of those stronger than they. They will come and shout for joy on the heights of Zion; they will rejoice in the bounty of the Lord—the grain, the new wine and the oil, the young of the flocks and herds. They will be like a well-

watered garden, and they will sorrow no more. Then maidens will dance and be glad, young men and old as well. I will turn their mourning into gladness; I will give them comfort and joy instead of sorrow. I will satisfy the priests with abundance, and my people will be filled with my bounty," declares the Lord. This is what the Lord says: "A voice is heard in Ramah, mourning and great weeping, Rachel weeping for her children and refusing to be comforted, because her children are no more." This is what the Lord says: "Restrain your voice from weeping and your eyes from tears, for your work will be rewarded," declares the Lord. "They will return from the land of the enemy. So there is hope for your future," declares the Lord. "Your children will return to their own land. "I have surely heard Ephraim's moaning: *'You disciplined me like an unruly calf, and I have been disciplined. Restore me, and I will return, because you are the Lord my God. After I strayed, I repented; after I came to understand, I beat my breast. I was ashamed and humiliated because I bore the disgrace of my youth.'* Is not Ephraim my dear son, the child in whom I delight? Though I often speak against him, I still remember him. Therefore my heart yearns for him; I have great compassion for him," declares the Lord. "Set up road signs; put up guideposts. Take note of the highway, the road that you take. Return, O Virgin Israel, return to your towns. How long will you wander, O unfaithful daughter? *The Lord will create a new thing on earth- a woman will surround a man.*" This is what the Lord Almighty, the God of Israel, says: "When I bring them back from captivity, the people in the land of Judah and in its towns will once again use these words: 'The Lord bless you, O righteous dwelling, O sacred mountain.' People will live together in Judah and all its towns—farmers and those who move about with their flocks. I will refresh the weary and satisfy the faint." At this I awoke and looked around. My sleep had been pleasant to me. "The days are coming," declares the Lord, "when I will plant the house of Israel and the house of Judah with the offspring of men and of animals. *Just as I watched over them to uproot and tear down, and to overthrow, destroy and bring disaster, so I will watch over them to build and to plant," declares the Lord. "In those days people will no longer say, 'The fathers have eaten sour grapes, and the children's teeth are set on edge.' Instead, everyone will die for his own sin; whoever eats sour grapes—his own teeth will be set on edge. "The time is coming," declares the Lord, "when I will make a new covenant with the house of Israel and with the house of Judah. It will not be like the covenant I made with their forefathers when I took them by the hand to lead them out of Egypt, because they broke my covenant, though I was a husband to them," declares the Lord. "This is the covenant I will make with the house of Israel after that time," declares the Lord. "I will put my law in their minds and write it on their hearts. I will be their God, and they will be my people. No longer will a man teach his neighbor, or a man his brother, saying, 'Know the Lord,' because they will all know me, from the least of them to the greatest," declares the Lord. "For I will forgive their wickedness and will remember their sins no more."* This is what the Lord says, he who appoints the sun to shine by day, who decrees the moon and stars to shine by night, who stirs up the sea so that its waves roar—the Lord Almighty is his name: *"Only if these decrees vanish from my sight," declares the Lord, "will the descendants of Israel ever cease to be a nation before me." This is what the Lord says: "Only if the heavens above can be measured and the foundations of the earth below be searched out will I reject all the descendants of Israel because of all they have done," declares the Lord.* "The days are coming," declares the Lord, "when this city will be rebuilt for me from the Tower of Hananel to the Corner Gate. The measuring line will stretch from there straight to the hill of Gareb and then turn to Goah. The whole valley where dead bodies and ashes are thrown, and all the terraces out to the Kidron Valley on the east as far as the corner of the Horse Gate, will be holy to the Lord. The city will never again be uprooted or demolished."

Here we find the repentance of Israel and its results. We find many interesting things in this passage.

First, in Jeremiah 31:1, we have a restatement from the previous chapter, Jeremiah 30:22. "I will be the God of all the clans of Israel, and they will be my people." What a wonderful statement! How reassuring! This shows God's unfailing kindness and forgiveness, even though Israel rejected their Messiah. Due to our own sin, we are all guilty of His death. His death was the only way we could be cleansed from our sin and given life! Even though they had the prophets to tell them of what to expect, and they killed them also, He forgives them. He will not go back on His promises! His forgiveness is that great! Notice Jeremiah 3:2: those "who survive the sword will find favor in the desert." This relates to Revelation 12:13–17. God will protect them in the wilderness during the tribulation.

There are those who will tell us that Israel is forever rejected and that the promises made to Israel have been transferred to the "church." There are many problems with this premise. First, God promised to Israel specifically, in fact, tribe by tribe, how He would bless them in the end times. I will agree that the promises of grace and forgiveness are passed on to us as Gentiles today and that Jews who believe will be saved the same as Gentiles today, but this does in no way negate the promises God made unconditionally to Israel. Notice Jeremiah 31:3: "I have loved you with an everlasting love" this is *unconditional!* We are merely temporary caretakers of His wonderful promises! The day is coming, and soon, when the Gentiles will reject Him even more fully than Israel did.

Romans 11:13–24 tells us what will happen when Gentiles finally reject Christ and God turns back to His people, Israel.

> "I am talking to you Gentiles. Inasmuch as I am the apostle to the Gentiles, I make much of my ministry in the hope that I may somehow arouse my own people to envy and save some of them. For if their rejection is the reconciliation of the world, *what will their acceptance be but life from the dead?* If the part of the dough offered as first fruits is holy, then the whole batch

is holy; if the root is holy, so are the branches. If some of the branches have been broken off, and you, though a wild olive shoot, have been grafted in among the others and now share in the nourishing sap from the olive root, *do not boast over those branches. If you do, consider this: You do not support the root, but the root supports you. You will say then, 'Branches were broken off so that I could be grafted in.' Granted. But they were broken off because of unbelief, and you stand by faith. Do not be arrogant, but be afraid. For if God did not spare the natural branches, he will not spare you either.* Consider therefore the kindness and sternness of God: sternness to those who fell, but kindness to you, provided that you continue in his kindness. Otherwise, *you also will be cut off. And if they do not persist in unbelief, they will be grafted in, for God is able to graft them in again.* After all, if you were cut out of an olive tree that is wild by nature, and contrary to nature were grafted into a cultivated olive tree, how much more readily will these, the natural branches, be grafted into their own olive tree!"

(*Emphasis* of course is mine.)

Here we find that Paul is giving us as Gentiles a solemn warning. God is very able to graft Israel back into the "tree." Notice Romans 11:15: *What will their acceptance be but life from the dead?* This will happen. It is promised throughout Scripture. When Israel believes, they will be grafted back into the "tree." It will happen. And Gentiles will reject Him even worse than the Jews did almost 2000 years ago! This will be at the time of the tribulation. At that time, God will pour out His wrath on the gentile world due to their unbelief.

In Jeremiah 31, we find that a specific tribe is mentioned as a recipient of God's favor. Ephraim is mentioned as loved by God and longed for. We may be the temporary caretakers of God's promises as spiritual children of Abraham, but we are not spiritual Ephraim! When God mentions the twelve tribes in Revelation, He is not speaking to Gentiles! This is to Jews! Notice also in

Jeremiah 31:4 that God refers to Israel as "Virgin Israel"! He has cleansed Israel so completely that He refers to Israel as "Virgin"! Only God can do this. In Jeremiah 50:20, it is speaking about the same time as Jeremiah chapters 30 and 31, specifically Israel's Day of Atonement. It tells us, "'In those days, at that time,' declares the Lord, 'search will be made for Israel's guilt, but there will be none, and for the sins of Judah, but none will be found, for I will forgive the remnant I will spare.'" This is how Israel can be called "Virgin." It is an act of God! Just as you and I can be justified (made just) in God's sight, Israel will be pure by God's forgiveness! What a picture of God's kindness and love! In Jeremiah 31:7, we find that they are to "sing with joy." I find this interesting, when you follow the events that are coming. Many will be killed (Jeremiah 30:11, 31:30)! But this is not important, because they finally realize that there is something more important than this physical life! There is life eternal with Christ, and that is more important than life on this earth. This eternal life was what they were lacking, and now they have it! Indeed, they will sing with joy. Also notice that God refers to the "remnant of Israel." Certainly many Jews will die leading up to this joyous time, but the remnant will be delivered! The nation will be virtually wiped out in the battle of Damascus. In the Battle of Magog, many more may die before repentance is made. After all, the battle begins in Iraq, and Israel governs Iraq at that time. We are told that many will die during the time of birth pains because they accept Christ. The genocide of Christian believers, Jew and gentile, will begin before the tribulation officially starts (Revelation 6:9–11). This will effectively squash the revival that we find mentioned in Isaiah 17:7–8. We will find that this genocide coincides with the rise of the antichrist, as covered in Chapter 4 of this book.

Jeremiah 31:8–17 refers to the time of Rosh Hashanah. God will gather Jews from the ends of the earth. The blind, lame, pregnant, and even those women in labor will be gathered to Israel! We find in Ezekiel 39:28 that God will not leave any behind! Not one! In fact, this event will be so great that we are told in Jeremiah 23:7–8, in reference to this event:

> "So then, the days are coming," declares the Lord, "when people will no longer say, 'As surely as the Lord lives, who brought the Israelites up out of Egypt,' but they will say, 'As surely as the Lord lives, who brought the descendants of Israel up out of the land of the north and out of all the countries where he had banished them.'"

Then they will live in their own land. The exodus will not be considered a great event in light of the fulfillment of Rosh Hashanah. The reason being this is not just a physical re-gathering, but a spiritual one as well. They will be gathered to God as a result of this; it is their Yom Kippur!

Jeremiah 31:18 refers to the Battle of Magog. This is the discipline that will bring them to Christ. Discipline is not ever intended to utterly destroy those it is being administered to (contrary to my opinion as a child!), but to correct them. Such is the case here. God is correcting Israel. He is telling them that they need to trust Christ, God in the flesh. He will not destroy them, but He will bless them.

The result of this discipline is mentioned in Jeremiah 31:19. Israel is repentant. They understand. They are ashamed of their unbelief. They are humiliated! If you are humiliated, it means that you are humbled. Humiliation is not a bad thing! All it hurts is our pride, and pride is just a stumbling block. Pride can lead a person to hell! God loves a humble person. Here we find that Israel discovers humility. They bear disgrace and beat their breasts. Now they can have a relationship with God. Now they have the right attitude.

We find in Jeremiah 31:20 that even though Ephraim strayed, God still loves him. He is still His son. God speaks against Ephraim (Israel) because he strayed, and God is righteous. God is honest; He won't lie and say, "He's a good child!" That would be a lie. But God still loves him and will accept him when he repents, as any father will accept a repentant child.

Jeremiah 31:21 and 22 have interesting comments. In verse 21, we find that the children of Israel are on their way to the land of Israel in repentance, and God calls them "virgin." As they gather, repentant, in obedience to Him, He calls them "virgin"! But in verse 22, while they are still wandering aimlessly, they are referred to as "unfaithful daughter." How interesting! The moment they obey Him, they are restored, whether they realize it or not!

There is some controversy concerning the next part of this verse. "The Lord will create a new thing on earth—a woman will surround a man." The word *surround* means to *woo and win over* and *to protect*, according to Strong's Exhaustive Concordance and Lexicon. It is suggested that this is Israel seeking forgiveness from God. I believe that the context bears this up. But the interesting thing is that it is God who orchestrates it! He leads Israel to woo Him! He is sovereign! I have been told that in the early church, some believed that this was referring to the virgin birth. While Christ was, indeed, born to a virgin, I don't believe that this is referring to that. There is nothing in the context to support that conclusion.

In Jeremiah 31:28, we find that just as God was in control in the destruction that Israel suffered, He will be in control as they rebuild.

In Jeremiah 31:29 and 30, we find that at this time, the children of Israel will no longer be paying for their fathers' sin! They will only suffer the consequences of their own sin.

In Jeremiah 31:31 through 34, we find a great promise to Israel. He will make a new covenant with them that will not be broken. He will put His law in their minds and write it on their hearts. He (Christ) will be their God, and they will be His people! People will not need to teach Jews to know the Lord, because they will all know Him. And God will forgive them and remember their sins no more! Wow! What forgiveness! In the next verse, we are reminded

Thomas Farr

of just who is making this promise here. It is the Almighty God! In Jeremiah 31:36 and 37, we are informed essentially that it is impossible for God to go back on this promise. Then in the last verses of this chapter, just to reaffirm that God is speaking here to physical Israel, He gives the physical boundaries of the city (Jerusalem) for its rebuilding. Remember, it is destroyed in the Battle of Magog. Every wall will fall in the earthquake!

This portion, along with Jeremiah 30, has given us a very detailed account of the events surrounding Israel's repentance and conversion to Christ and where it fits into the end-times plan. I am amazed at the rich information that God has given us! This is truly the fulfillment of Yom Kippur! We have found in Jeremiah 30 that there is a time of "Jacob's trouble." We learned in the previous chapter of this book and in this chapter that the time of Jacob's trouble is the Battle of Magog. We are told that Israel will be saved out of it and that God will provide for them, and they will live in relative peace. In fact, they will have peace for a while, because they will be able to rebuild Israel, the city of Jerusalem, and the temple. While this is going on, God tells us that He will destroy all the nations where He has scattered them! This is the tribulation that we all have heard about! Now, why doesn't it get more attention in this portion? Because during this time (the first three and one half years of the tribulation), Israel is living in safety, protected by God. Until the temple is desecrated by the antichrist, Israel will have freedom to go about their business and worship as they will. During this time, Israel will thrive. The destructions that are poured out on the rest of the world will not affect Israel, and this book is written to Israel. The entire Old Testament is written to Israel specifically, and as such, it will always be Israel centric.

We are told in Romans 15:4, "For everything that was written in the past was written to teach us, so that through endurance and the encouragement of the Scriptures we might have hope." Here we find that the Old Testament was given to us so we can learn.

154

Now, most of this book series is covering material found in the Old Testament, because most of prophecy has to do with Israel specifically. However, we can see things that have to do with us as Gentiles and even, to a very limited extent, with American citizens in the Old Testament. One of the things mentioned in passing here is that *every nation where God has scattered them will be destroyed!* This is the seven years of tribulation! It will be a far greater tribulation for the rest of the world than it will be for Israel! God will be protecting them at that point, as He has shown us in these two chapters of the Bible and others. This will become even more apparent in the next portion that we will cover.

Let's turn now to Joel 2:12–29, where we will find Israel's fear (they are in *trouble* here, Jacob's *trouble!*) and their repentance and then God's forgiveness and provision.

> "Even now," declares the Lord, "return to me with all your heart, with fasting and weeping and mourning." *Rend your heart and not your garments. Return to the Lord your God, for he is gracious and compassionate, slow to anger and abounding in love, and he relents from sending calamity.* Who knows? He may turn and have pity and leave behind a blessing—grain offerings and drink offerings for the Lord your God. *Blow the trumpet in Zion, declare a holy fast, call a sacred assembly. Gather the people, consecrate the assembly; bring together the elders, gather the children,* those nursing at the breast. Let the bridegroom leave his room and the bride her chamber. *Let the priests, who minister before the Lord, weep between the temple porch and the altar. Let them say, "Spare your people, O Lord. Do not make your inheritance an object of scorn, a byword among the nations. Why should they say among the peoples, 'Where is their God?'"* Then the Lord will be jealous for his land and take pity on his people. The Lord will reply to them: "I am sending you grain, new wine and oil, enough to satisfy you fully; never again will I make you an object of scorn to the nations. *"I will drive the northern army far from you, pushing it into a parched and barren land,*

with its front columns going into the eastern sea and those in the rear into the western sea. And its stench will go up; its smell will rise." Surely he has done great things. Be not afraid, O land; be glad and rejoice. Surely the Lord has done great things. Be not afraid, O wild animals, for the open pastures are becoming green. The trees are bearing their fruit; the fig tree and the vine yield their riches. Be glad, O people of Zion, rejoice in the Lord your God, for he has given you the autumn rains in righteousness. He sends you abundant showers, both autumn and spring rains, as before. *The threshing floors will be filled with grain; the vats will overflow with new wine and oil.* "*I will repay you for the years the locusts have eaten—the great locust and the young locust, the other locusts and the locust swarm—my great army that I sent among you. You will have plenty to eat, until you are full, and you will praise the name of the Lord your God, who has worked wonders for you; never again will my people be shamed. Then you will know that I am in Israel, that I am the Lord your God, and that there is no other; never again will my people be shamed.* "*And afterward, I will pour out my Spirit on all people. Your sons and daughters will prophesy, your old men will dream dreams, your young men will see visions.* Even on my servants, both men and women, I will pour out my Spirit in those days."

As we learned in the last chapter of this book, this is a portion dealing with Russia's attack on Israel, known as the Battle of Magog. God uses this battle to drive Israel to Him, and they do come to Him and repent. Here we have their repentance detailed from their Rosh Hashanah through God's Spirit being poured out on them after their Day of Atonement. We have in this portion even more detail that helps us fill in the gaps in our understanding.

The first thing we find in this portion is that they are to return to Him with their "heart," with fasting and weeping. Then it goes on to say that they are to rend their heart, not their garments. This means that it is a true repentance, not just an outward showing and not a ceremonial thing. God doesn't want and isn't impressed with actors. He wants a real response from the heart. Then we find that they are encouraged to return to Him because He is gracious and compassionate. I get the impression here that they may think they have gone too far, committed too great a sin, because it is emphasized that they need to return to Him because He can forgive them. It isn't a lost cause! I have heard some say that the Jews have committed too great a sin and so God has forsaken them. God is greater than that! He will forgive! We are told that He is slow to anger and "relents from sending calamity." Then it goes on with "Who knows? He may turn and have pity … and leave a blessing … " This reinforces the feeling that I have that they may feel too far gone. "Who knows?" This also reinforces the impression that it is from the heart. They recognize the depth of their sin. This is good. This is the first step in anyone's repentance, recognition of the condition, humiliation, a humbling. God does look for that in a human. This will be a national attitude at this time.

Joel 2:15 brings us a notification of Rosh Hashanah. Their hearts have been prepared by the attack of Russia. They recognize that they are in sin and in need of forgiveness. They recognize that they need to act as a corporate body. As a corporate body, they gather in a sacred assembly to seek God's forgiveness. They are called together with a "trumpet sound." Whether it's a literal or figurative trumpet sound is irrelevant. It doesn't matter. I feel that it may very well be literal. They will do what they must to gather all. It may be like the sounding of a siren, but all Jews will be notified and alerted. They will come back to Israel, even if they are in labor. Ouch! Think about that one, ladies! When the people call on God, notice that they don't say, "Have mercy on us because we are about to be squished!" They say, essentially, "Defend your Holy name! Don't let the world say, 'their God isn't real!'" They know this from Isaiah 43:25: "I, even I, am he who blots out your transgressions, *for my own sake,* and remembers your sins no more," Isaiah 48:11:

"*For my own sake, for my own sake,* I do this. *How can I let myself be defamed?* I will not yield my glory to another," and Ezekiel 36:22: "Therefore say to the house of Israel, 'this is what the Sovereign Lord says: It is not for your sake, O house of Israel, that I am going to do these things, but for the sake of my holy name, which you have profaned among the nations where you have gone.'" Israel is humbled enough now to recognize that if they are to survive, it will be because God will defend His holy name and not because they deserve it.

Do you *deserve* forgiveness? If you say yes, then rethink your relationship with God! No one deserves God's forgiveness! Not you, not me, no one! We are all sinners! We all deserve eternal punishment! We have all failed God and are guilty of the death of Christ (God in the flesh)! Don't be so high and mighty that you elevate yourself above anyone. In God's eyes, we are all guilty and deserve punishment. But He loves us and will extend forgiveness to *anyone* who asks for it, *freely.* This includes Israel.

Now notice that they ask for forgiveness and admit their guilt. They truly repent *as a nation.* Only then will God remove the northern army from them. The Magog battle is over at that point. God intervenes and destroys the northern army (Russia and her cohorts), and He blesses them with their physical needs as well. God even tells Israel that He will repay them for what the "locusts" have eaten. We have found that *locusts* is the term God gave the northern army earlier in Joel 2. God reinforces the fact that the "locusts" are the human army when He refers to them as "my great army." He tells them that he will provide all their needs. They will have plenty to eat until they are full. He will work wonders for them. Then we have an interesting verse: Joel 2:27. I didn't make much of it at first, but as I studied it, it brought to light other scriptures. Jeremiah 30:8–9 speaks of Israel serving "David, their king," after they are no longer serving "foreigners." This is during the tribulation, because during this time, God is destroying "all the nations where I have scattered you" (Jeremiah 30:11). When they have plenty, when they see the wonders that He is doing for them after they repent, when they are praising the name of the Lord, then they "will know that I am in Israel." It is not when they *see* Him. It is when they see the evidence of His presence. He is not there physically. He is there spiritually.

After they repent, after they know that He is in Israel, God will pour out His spirit on them. Their children will prophesy, old men will dream dreams, and the young men will see visions. This is the portion spoken of in Acts 2:16–17. Luke quotes this portion and tells us that the pouring out of the Holy Spirit on Pentecost was the fulfillment of Joel 2:28–29. If Israel had indeed accepted Christ as their Messiah and king, He would have reigned as king. They have Pentecost now as a picture of future prophecy. It will finally be completely fulfilled in the future. It will happen again. The events of Pentecost will be fulfilled again, and this time Israel will repent.

These are the events immediately following the Battle of Magog. Israel (the people), in terror, gathers to Israel (the country) which is their Rosh Hashanah, conducts a solemn assembly before the Lord, and repents. They turn to Christ (Yom Kippur), and then, realizing that their repentance has given them favor with God, they know that the antichrist is a deceiver and reject him, turning the world against them.

In the next portion, we find a narration from God discussing His viewpoint of the events surrounding Israel's Day of Atonement. He explains His actions and His motives. Then it moves to a narrative from Israel's point of view in response to God's actions toward them. I feel that it is unfortunate that the people who divided the Bible into chapters and verses divided it right here. The thought is a continuing one, and it seems to break the natural flow of the thought.

"For I will be like a lion to Ephraim, like a great lion to Judah. I will tear them to pieces and go away; I will carry them off, with no one to rescue them. Then I will go back to my place until they admit their guilt. And they will seek my face; in their misery they will earnestly seek me."

[6:1] "Come, let us return to the Lord. He has torn us to pieces but he will heal us; he has injured us but he will bind up our wounds. After two days he will revive us; on the third day he will restore us, that we may live in his presence. Let us acknowledge the Lord; let us press on to acknowledge him. As surely as the sun rises, he will appear; he will come to us like the winter rains, like the spring rains that water the earth."

Hosea 5:14–6:3

This is very to the point. God tells us that He is pouring His wrath on Israel for the purpose of bringing them to repentance. He will put them into a hopeless situation and then let them sweat it out until they admit their guilt. What is their guilt? The fact that Israel as a nation rejected their Messiah. This will involve a humiliation, a humbling; this is what God desires in a person and in a nation. God desires humility. They will be miserable. The result will be that they will finally, corporately, earnestly seek Him. And yes, at that point, it will be out of desperation.

I remember my own salvation experience. When I gave my life to Christ, it wasn't because I loved Him. I was told that I should accept Him in love, but I couldn't. I didn't *know* Him. I accepted Him in fear! I knew one thing; I was going to hell! This prompted me to give my life to Him and commit my future to His care. Since then, I have learned to love Him. We are told, "The fear of the Lord is the beginning of wisdom…" (Psalm 111:10a), but then we are also told, "There is no fear in love. But perfect love drives out fear, because fear has to do with punishment. The one who fears is not made perfect in love. We love because he first loved us" (1John

4:18–19). When I first accepted Him, I feared eternal punishment! That was the *beginning* of wisdom for me. I knew that I needed to keep from going to hell. This life may average a little over seventy years, but heaven and hell are seventy years times *infinity!* The only way was to trust Him. Then over the years, as I learned more about Him, I learned to love Him. I am no longer *afraid* of Him. I do regret when I fail Him, but not because I fear eternal punishment any more than a child in a "normal" home would fear being disowned by his earthly father for an infraction. "You lousy kid! You told a lie! So you are no longer my child!" Would this be a good father? *No!* Will God be a worse father than any earthly father? Again *no!* He is better, not worse! Does an earthly father understand grace better than God? *No!* So many well meaning people paint a picture of a God who is impossible to please, to the detriment of people's souls! How tragic! He wants a *relationship* with us, and He makes it simple. Just *trust* Him! There may be a penalty, but any father will reprimand his child out of love to *help* the child be a better-adjusted individual. This is God's desire for us, that we grow in Him to be better prepared for what life has in store for us in this life and in the next. We are told in 1 Corinthians that we will have eternal reward for what we do right, and God doesn't want us to lose eternal reward. That is the eternal consequence for our actions on this earth as Christians. (We will talk more about our eternal reward in Chapter 5 in this book and Chapter 8 of volume 2.)

Then we find that Israel will *trust* Him to help them out of their problems. They trust that He will let them live in His presence. They agree to acknowledge Christ as Messiah and Lord and trust Him to bless them. We find that this trust is not misplaced. God's aims are accomplished!

In Isaiah 66:1–12, we have another portion dealing with God bringing Israel to final repentance:

This is what the Lord says: "Heaven is my throne, and the earth is my footstool. Where is the house you will build for me? Where will my resting place be? Has not my hand made all these things, and so they came into being?" declares the Lord. *"This is the one I esteem: he who is humble and contrite in spirit, and trembles at my word.* But whoever sacrifices a bull is like one who kills a man, and whoever offers a lamb, like one who breaks a dog's neck; whoever makes a grain offering is like one who presents pig's blood, and whoever burns memorial incense, like one who worships an idol. *They have chosen their own ways, and their souls delight in their abominations; so I also will choose harsh treatment for them and will bring upon them what they dread.* For when I called, no one answered, when I spoke, no one listened. They did evil in my sight and chose what displeases me." Hear the word of the Lord, you who tremble at his word: *"Your brothers who hate you, and exclude you because of my name, have said, 'Let the Lord be glorified, that we may see your joy!' Yet they will be put to shame.* Hear that uproar from the city, *hear that noise from the temple! It is the sound of the Lord repaying his enemies all they deserve. "Before she goes into labor, she gives birth; before the pains come upon her, she delivers a son. Who has ever heard of such a thing? Who has ever seen such things? Can a country be born in a day or a nation be brought forth in a moment? Yet no sooner is Zion in labor than she gives birth to her children. Do I bring to the moment of birth and not give delivery?" says the Lord. "Do I close up the womb when I bring to delivery?" says your God. "Rejoice with Jerusalem and be glad for her, all you who love her; rejoice greatly with her, all you who mourn over her. For you will nurse and be satisfied at her comforting breasts; you will drink deeply and delight in her overflowing abundance." For this is what the Lord says: "I will extend peace to her like a river, and the wealth of nations like a flooding stream; you will nurse and be carried on her arm and dandled on her knees."*

Here we have a portion that at first can be difficult, but when studied carefully, it yields new insights. This is covering the time of Israel's repentance. In the beginning of the portion, it is dealing with people who believe they are serving God but are not. When I read the part about sacrifices, I was confused for a moment. Animal sacrifice was practiced and instituted in the Law of Moses by God, yet here it was being condemned. At first, I thought it was speaking about unbelieving Jews, those who still reject Christ, but there are some things wrong with this theory. First, let's look at Isaiah 66:4. God will give them "Harsh treatment." This still goes along with Israel, because at the time of Magog, Israel will be treated harshly. We are told this over and over. But I noticed that it doesn't say "Israel" anywhere in the first few verses. In fact, it refers to "they" and "them." Then I looked at Isaiah 66:5. "Your brothers," it says. This still seems to reinforce the idea of it being Israel, but I also remember that God tells us in other portions that He will bring every Jew to Him at the fulfillment of Rosh Hashanah, even the blind, lame, and those women in labor! It even says that He will not leave *any* behind! Here we have a problem then, if this is talking about unbelieving Jews! So I read on. Then I read Isaiah 66:6 mentioning the "noise from the temple." At the time of the Magog battle, the temple will not be standing. So this has either already come to pass or it is during the tribulation. Then we find the noise is the Lord repaying Israel's enemies all they deserve. This is in complete agreement of events that occur during the tribulation. If you will recall, Ishmael was a brother to Isaac. Isaac was the father to Jacob (Israel); Ishmael is the father of the Arabic peoples of the world. In fact, much of the Islamic world is a distant cousin of Jews. Then I read it in the King James Version. "Your brethren that hated you, that cast you out for my name's sake, said, 'Let the Lord be glorified.' But he shall appear to your joy, and they shall be ashamed." I believe that the brothers are today's Islamic world. They claim to be worshipping the God of Abraham (they of course don't know the God of Abraham). This is why God tells us in this portion that he looks on their worship as idolatry! And if we look at the countries who align themselves against Israel, most of them are of this religion and lineage. And we find that Islam will be virtually wiped out at the time of the Battle of Magog. This is at the same time that Israel repents and the tribulation begins. This hasn't been fulfilled historically, to my knowledge, but it will be fulfilled at the time of the tribulation. So it is referring to Israel and their relationship to the Arab world. Israel is in repentance, just in repentance, because this is exactly at the time of their repentance, at the height of the Magog battle. Now God intervenes on Israel's behalf and punishes the Islamic Arab world for their opposition to Israel. The Islamic world believes they are serving God, but they are not. They have chosen what offends God. Israel is going to build the temple for God, but the Islamic world is arrayed against them right at the time of Magog. We find that the Islamic world is rendered impotent at that time. This is speaking of the time, the moment, of Israel's repentance.

Now what brings us to this point in this chapter is the next thought of this passage. A nation is born quickly, in a day! God doesn't recognize Israel as a nation prior to this point. Before this, they aren't reconciled to Him. He treats them as an enemy (Jeremiah 30:14). But when they turn to Christ, they are indeed His people, dearly beloved! They are born in a day; in fact, they are born *again* in a day! We are told in this portion that the delivery of this nation is swift. They are born before the mother goes into labor! (My wife would have liked that!) This also indicates that this is the ending of the time of labor pains mentioned by Christ. God recognizes her when she (Israel) gathers to him at the fulfillment of Rosh Hashanah. They repent in a day! This tells me that they repent in a day, and God accepts them. This portion is definitely speaking of the moment of Israel's repentance. Hosea 6:2 tells us that the recovery begins in two to three days! Indeed, that is quick!

Isaiah 66:8 says, "Can a country be born in a day or a nation be brought forth in a moment? Yet no sooner is Zion in labor than she gives birth to her children." Many suggest that this is speaking of Israel's becoming of a nation in 1948. First, it didn't happen over night. Second, God hasn't begun repaying all Her enemies. Third, Israel hasn't repented yet; God will still treat them as an enemy. As I've already said, the existing nation of Israel is just a place for Jews to go to when God calls them home in the future.

Micah 5:3–5a tells us an encapsulation of events covering this time:

> Therefore Israel will be abandoned until the time when she who is in labor gives birth and the rest of his brothers return to join the Israelites. He will stand and shepherd his flock in the strength of the Lord, in the majesty of the name of the Lord his God. And they will live securely, for then his greatness will reach to the ends of the earth. And he will be their peace.

This covers the birth of Godly Israel (the Day of Atonement) through the reign of Christ in the millennium.

Isaiah 66:10 following says that those who love Jerusalem will be blessed by her. I don't get from the context that this is only speaking to Jews! I believe that all who love Israel in that day will be blessed by her. This is the part of the beginning of the fulfillment of Scripture, which says that through Israel all nations will be blessed (Geneses 22:18). (The first part was when Christ came to die for our sins!)

So here we found that Israel believes and is born in a moment. Then God repays all the nations who are Israel's enemies and blesses Israel and all who love her.

This next portion gives us a detailed overview of the time from the gathering of Rosh Hashanah through the Day of Atonement's repentance of the nation of Israel. It gives the overview and then gives us the details of how God will bring it about in Ezekiel 38–39 in the Battle of Magog.

"I had concern for my holy name, which the house of Israel profaned among the nations where they had gone. Therefore say to the house of Israel, 'This is what the Sovereign Lord says: *It is not for your sake, O house of Israel, that I am going to do these things, but for the sake of my holy name,* which you have profaned among the nations where you have gone. I will show the holiness of my great name, which has been profaned among the nations, the name you have profaned among them. *Then the nations will know that I am the Lord, declares the Sovereign Lord, when I show myself holy through you before their eyes. 'For I will take you out of the nations; I will gather you from all the countries and bring you back into your own land. I will sprinkle clean water on you, and you will be clean; I will cleanse you from all your impurities and from all your idols. I will give you a new heart and put a new spirit in you; I will remove from you your heart of stone and give you a heart of flesh. And I will put my Spirit in you and move you to follow my decrees and be careful to keep my laws. You will live in the land I gave your forefathers; you will be my people, and I will be your God. I will save you from all your uncleanness. I will call for the grain and make it plentiful and will not bring famine upon you.* I will increase the fruit of the trees and the crops of the field, so that you will no longer suffer disgrace among the nations because of famine. *Then you will remember your evil ways and wicked deeds, and you will loathe yourselves for your sins and detestable practices. I want you to know that I am not doing this for your sake, declares the Sovereign Lord. Be ashamed and disgraced for your conduct, O house of Israel!' 'This is what the Sovereign Lord says: On the day I cleanse you from all your sins, I will resettle your towns, and the ruins will be rebuilt.* The desolate land will be cultivated instead of lying desolate in the sight of all who pass through it. They will say, "This land that was laid waste has become like the garden of Eden; the cities that were lying in ruins,

desolate and destroyed, are now fortified and inhabited."
Then the nations around you that remain will know that I
the Lord have rebuilt what was destroyed and have replanted
what was desolate. I the Lord have spoken, and I will do it.'
This is what the Sovereign Lord says: 'Once again I will yield
to the plea of the house of Israel and do this for them: I will
make their people as numerous as sheep, as numerous as the
flocks for offerings at Jerusalem during her appointed feasts.
So will the ruined cities be filled with flocks of people. Then
they will know that I am the Lord.'

Ezekiel 36:21–37

The hand of the Lord was upon me, and he brought me
out by the Spirit of the Lord and set me in the middle of a
valley; it was full of bones. He led me back and forth among
them, and I saw a great many bones on the floor of the valley,
bones that were very dry. He asked me, "Son of man, can
these bones live?" I said, "O Sovereign Lord, you alone know."
Then he said to me, "Prophesy to these bones and say to
them, 'Dry bones, hear the word of the Lord! This is what
the Sovereign Lord says to these bones: I will make breath
enter you, and you will come to life. I will attach tendons
to you and make flesh come upon you and cover you with
skin; I will put breath in you, and you will come to life. Then
you will know that I am the Lord." So I prophesied as I was
commanded. And as I was prophesying, there was a noise, a
rattling sound, and the bones came together, bone to bone.
I looked, and tendons and flesh appeared on them and skin
covered them, but there was no breath in them. Then he said
to me, "Prophesy to the breath; prophesy, son of man, and say
to it, 'This is what the Sovereign Lord says: Come from the
four winds, O breath, and breathe into these slain, that they
may live.'" So I prophesied as he commanded me, and breath
entered them; they came to life and stood up on their feet—a
vast army. Then he said to me: "*Son of man, these bones are the
whole house of Israel. They say, 'Our bones are dried up and our
hope is gone; we are cut off.'* Therefore prophesy and say to them:

167

'This is what the Sovereign Lord says: O my people, I am going to open your graves and bring you up from them; I will bring you back to the land of Israel. Then you, my people, will know that I am the Lord, when I open your graves and bring you up from them. *I will put my Spirit in you and you will live, and I will settle you in your own land. Then you will know that I the Lord have spoken, and I have done it, declares the Lord.*" The word of the Lord came to me: "Son of man, take a stick of wood and write on it, 'Belonging to Judah and the Israelites associated with him.' Then take another stick of wood, and write on it, 'Ephraim's stick, belonging to Joseph and all the house of Israel associated with him.' Join them together into one stick so that they will become one in your hand. "When your countrymen ask you, 'Won't you tell us what you mean by this?' say to them, 'This is what the Sovereign Lord says: I am going to take the stick of Joseph—which is in Ephraim's hand—and of the Israelite tribes associated with him, and join it to Judah's stick, making them a single stick of wood, and they will become one in my hand.' Hold before their eyes the sticks you have written on and say to them, 'This is what the Sovereign Lord says: I will take the Israelites out of the nations where they have gone. I will gather them from all around and bring them back into their own land. There *I will make them one nation in the land, on the mountains of Israel. There will be one king over all of them and they will never again be two nations or be divided into two kingdoms.* They will no longer defile themselves with their idols and vile images or with any of their offenses, for I will save them from all their sinful backsliding, *and I will cleanse them. They will be my people, and I will be their God.* "*My servant David will be king over them,* and they will all have one shepherd. They will follow my laws and be careful to keep my decrees. They will live in the land I gave to my servant Jacob, the land where your fathers lived. They and their children and their children's children will live there forever, and David my servant will be their prince forever. *I will make a covenant of peace with them; it will be an everlasting covenant.* I will establish them and increase their numbers, and I will put my sanctuary among them forever. *My dwelling place will be with them; I will be their God, and they will be my people. Then the nations will know that I the Lord make Israel holy, when my sanctuary is among them forever."*

Ezekiel 37:1–28

This is a very detailed overview. It includes many focal points that help us identify the order of events.

First, God repeats over and over that He isn't doing this for Israel's sake, but His own! He explains that Israel profaned His name throughout the earth. How did Israel "profane" God's name throughout the nations? When Israel was scattered throughout the world at the time that Jerusalem was sacked by Titus (not the recipient of the epistle from Paul), they carried with them the teaching that Jesus wasn't the Messiah. This profaned the name of God, because Jesus was God in the flesh! Despite the fact that Israel profaned His name in the nations, He will show Himself to the nations through Israel.

Ezekiel 36:24 details the fact that God will gather Israel out of the nations and bring them to Israel. This is the Rosh Hashanah. Please notice that He doesn't cleanse them until after they are gathered to Israel. This gathering is the solemn assembly before the Lord where Israel prepares to repent as a nation. Then we find that God will cleanse them. Ezekiel 36:26 tells us that God will give them a new heart and a new spirit. This is the same prophecy that we find in Joel 2:28–29. God pours out His Spirit on Israel! God will move them to obedience. It will be a function of God, not of man. Then we find in Ezekiel 36:28 that He will give them the land of their forefathers, and "you will be my people, and I will be your God." This is the pivotal phrase that gives us the timing of these events. It is repeated in Ezekiel 39:22 and Jeremiah 30:22. In Ezekiel 39:22, it gives us the timing as exactly when the Battle of Magog is brought to a close by the intervention of God.

Then we find that God blesses them, and He gives us a detailed description of the blessings He will pour on them. As He blesses them, they will remember their sins and will hate themselves for it. They will be truly humbled. God tells us that He will raise their towns from the ruins (Ezekiel 38:20: "every wall will fall"). Notice that it says, the "towns around you that remain." This speaks of the destruction that will be poured on the earth at the time of this battle. It tells us that the towns will know that the Lord intervened on the behalf of Israel, but we also find that they will still not believe. Remember the Revelation 6:16–17 passage that tells us that the world will call on the mountains to fall on them because they know that this is the "wrath of the Lamb" (Christ). The world will know, but they will not repent. The gentile world will at this time reject Christ even more soundly than the Jews did 2000 years ago. How sad!

Then we have the famous "dry bones" passage of Ezekiel 37. The dry bones are a metaphor. God gives the interpretation of this metaphor in the same chapter. God tells us that these bones are the "whole house of Israel." It doesn't say, "house of Israel"; it says, "whole house of Israel." This is to emphasize that He will not leave any behind (Ezekiel 39:28: "He didn't leave *any* behind"). God is telling us here that Israel was dead. But He gave it new life and regenerated it. We are told later in this chapter that the two nations (Judah and Israel) will no longer be two but will be one. No one today divides Israel into two nations. But in Ezekiel's day, that was a miraculous idea.

God refers to "my servant David." This is none other than Christ. He will set up His reign on earth after the tribulation is over. But we find that He will be reigning in the hearts of Israel before that, and they will know that He is restoring Israel after the Battle of Magog (Joel 2:23–27 speaks of Israel's blessing and the fact that they know Christ is in Israel by virtue of the miraculous restoration *after* they repent and commit to Him). They will give the credit and the glory to Him! His reign starts when they acknowledge Him as their Messiah, just as He reigns in us when we accept His salvation.

We find also that He will make an everlasting covenant with Israel at the time of their repentance. At that point, He tells us that He will dwell with man forever. Ezekiel 37:21–28 is a brief overview of end-time events, and then Ezekiel gets more detailed again in chapters 38–39, dealing with the Battle of Magog and Israel's repentance.

The next portion is another prophetic Psalm dealing with this topic. Psalm 102 is giving us another view of Magog and Israel's resulting repentance.

Psalm 102:1–27:

> Hear my prayer, O Lord; let my cry for help come to you. Do not hide your face from me when I am in *distress.* Turn your ear to me; when I call, *answer me quickly. For my days vanish like smoke; my bones burn like glowing embers.* My heart is blighted and withered like grass; I forget to eat my food. Because of my loud groaning I am reduced to skin and bones. I am like a desert owl, like an owl among the *ruins.* I lie awake; I have become like a bird alone on a roof. All day long my enemies taunt me; those who rail against me use my name as a curse. For I eat *ashes* as my food and mingle my drink with tears *because of your great wrath, for you have taken me up and thrown me aside.* My days are like the evening shadow; I wither away like grass. But you, O Lord, sit enthroned; your renown endures through all generations. *You will arise and have compassion on Zion, for it is time to show favor to her; the appointed time has come.* For her stones are dear to your servants; her very dust moves them to pity. The nations will fear the name of the Lord, all the kings of the earth will revere your glory. *For the Lord will rebuild Zion and appear in his glory. He will respond to the prayer of the destitute; he will not despise their plea. Let this be written for a future generation, that a people not yet created may praise the Lord:* "The Lord looked

down from his sanctuary on high, from heaven he viewed the earth, to hear the groans of the prisoners and release those condemned to death." *So the name of the Lord will be declared in Zion and his praise in Jerusalem when the peoples and the kingdoms assemble to worship the Lord.* In the course of my life he broke my strength; he cut short my days. So I said: "Do not take me away, O my God, in the midst of my days; your years go on through all generations. In the beginning you laid the foundations of the earth, and the heavens are the work of your hands. They will perish, but you remain; they will all wear out like a garment. Like clothing you will change them and they will be discarded. But you remain the same, and your years will never end. The children of your servants will live in your presence; their descendents will be established before you."

As I study this topic, I am amazed at the amount of prophetic material there is in the Bible! God keeps revealing more and more as I study. This portion is clearly prophetic, as is made clear in Psalm 102:18. And we will see that it deals with Israel's reclamation by God on the fulfillment of their Yom Kippur.

First we find that they are in distress, and that in and of itself is not unusual. Many prophets were distressed throughout the Bible; in fact, I can't think of any that weren't distressed at some time in their life, often by their own countrymen. But let's read on. They request that the Lord answer their prayer quickly. We are told throughout the prophecies that God will respond quickly to them at this time, because it is truly a life-and-death situation for the nation of Israel. Psalm 102:3 is interesting in the choice of wording: "My days vanish like *smoke*; and my *bones burn* like *glowing embers*." The descriptions we have of the Battle of Magog all seem to be nuclear on the part of man (Joel 2:3, Ezekiel 39:14–16, etc.). Again, I will say nuclear war is only speculation, but the descriptions are all likely. Psalm 102:6 describes the person relating this as

Destination

an "owl among the ruins." We find that during the Battle of Magog, Israel will be ruined. God will ruin what isn't ruined by Russia with the earthquake. (But, of course, God will restore Israel.) Also, we find that their food will be ashes. Again, this could be describing a nuclear confrontation. Also notice that the wrath poured out by Israel's enemies is actually God's wrath (Psalm 102:10)!

Psalm 102:13 brings us to an interesting point. It says that "You" (God) "will arise" and have compassion on Zion. In Jeremiah 30:9, it says, speaking of this very time, "Instead, *they will serve the Lord their God and David their king, whom I will raise up for them.*" God will arise and have compassion. I should mention this about the Hebrew language: often, a person is referred to by their father's name or by the name of an important ancestor. This is the case here. They will serve God and David their king. These are the same person. Christ is God, He is the descendant of David their king, and He will reign over them (Revelation 20:6). The reason He will have compassion on them is it is the *appointed time.* It tells us here in Psalm 102:15, "The nations will fear the name of the Lord." This is reiterated in Revelation 6:16–17, where the people ask the mountains to fall on them to hide them from the wrath of the Lamb. They will fear the Lord, but, as I have said over and over, they will not repent!

Psalm 102:16 moves to the restoration of Israel, telling us that God will rebuild Zion. We are told that Israel will know that God is with them when they see Israel rebuilt, not when they *see* Him (Joel 2:26–27). He will rebuild Zion, and then "He will appear in His glory." The order given in this verse is correct! Whether Zion is rebuilt solely by God's hand or if people build it with God's help may be unimportant. We find that the Messiah is given credit for building the temple, but we are told that the regathered Jews build it Zechariah 6:15.

Now notice this very important verse, Psalm 102:18. We are being told here that this is prophecy! There is no ambiguity about it

173

here! This is prophecy! "Let this be written for a future generation, that a people not yet created may praise the Lord." This is written to inspire Israel to repentance when they are faced with destruction in the Battle of Magog. Wow!

Then we find Psalm 102:21–22 referring back to the fulfillment of Rosh Hashanah. We are told that the Lord will be praised in Jerusalem when the *peoples and the kingdoms* assemble to worship the Lord. We know already that the Jews will all assemble to repent. Their repentance is true worship. I was, at first, confused about the term *the kingdoms* until I remembered that Israel will be coming out of all the kingdoms of the earth. Probably every kingdom of the earth will be represented! It is possible too that it may be leaping ahead to the time of the kingdom. Either would work here, as we find that the following portion is dealing with Israel and all believing people in the time of the kingdom.

The rest of the chapter is telling us that the children of God's people will live with Him forever. This is a promise that God will accept Israel's repentance in the end time. And it is a promise that we, all who trust Him, will be with Him forever.

In the next portion, we find God's viewpoint of Israel's reconciliation to Him. We find God banishing Israel from the land, such as occurred in 70 AD, and His eventual restoration of them spiritually and physically to the land. He also promises to bless them forever. Jeremiah 32:37–44:

> "*I will surely gather them from all the lands where I banish them in my furious anger and great wrath; I will bring them back to this place and let them live in safety. They will be my people, and I will be their God. I will give them singleness of heart and action, so that they will always fear me for their own good and the good of their children after them. I will make an everlasting covenant with them: I will never stop doing good to them, and I will inspire them to fear me, so that they will never turn away from me. I will rejoice in doing them good and will assuredly plant them in*

this land with all my heart and soul. This is what the Lord says: *As I have brought all this great calamity on this people, so I will give them all the prosperity I have promised them.* Once more fields will be bought in this land of which you say, 'It is a desolate waste, without men or animals, for it has been handed over to the Babylonians.' Fields will be bought for silver, and deeds will be signed, sealed and witnessed in the territory of Benjamin, in the villages around Jerusalem, in the towns of Judah and in the towns of the hill country, of the western foothills and of the Negev, because I will restore their fortunes," declares the Lord.

As we look at this portion, we find the common theme of God gathering them to the land of Israel after having scattered them in anger for their rejection of Christ. Then we have the very important phrase, "They will be my people, and I will be their God." Again, this pinpoints the timing of this event at the time of Israel's repentance. Notice that God doesn't say, "they will have singleness of heart and action," but He says, "I will give them singleness of heart and action." This again stresses that it is an act of God and not man. It will be for their good and the good of their children. God tells us He will make an *everlasting* covenant with them. The fear of God comes from God; He inspires it, and they will *never* turn from Him. God tells us that He will bring calamity on Israel, and He will bring prosperity on them as well.

The substitution theologians seem to me to not understand the nature of God. God doesn't make mistakes, and He knows the end from the beginning. He knows the future as though it has already been accomplished (Isaiah 46:9–10). When He created this earth, He already knew that He would have to die to pay for the sins of the world, and He knew that Israel would reject Him. When they did that, it was no surprise to Him! This is why God gave so many verses to tell the world that they would do just that. If He would forever reject them, He wouldn't have chosen them in the first place. It would be illogical. God chose them to show His great compassion and forgiveness, just as He did when He paid for my sins and yours. He forgives!

In Jeremiah 50:20, we are shown how great the forgiveness of God is in dealing with Israel at their true Day of Atonement. "In those days, at that time," declares the Lord, "search will be made for Israel's guilt, but there will be none, and for the sins of Judah, but none will be found, for I will forgive the remnant I spare." This shows the extent of God's forgiveness in dealing with the people He has chosen.

In the next portion that we are covering, we find some details of events at the time of Israel's repentance. When the nation seeks Christ, we find God ready to help them in a big way!

> *On that day the Lord will shield those who live in Jerusalem, so that the feeblest among them will be like David, and the house of David will be like God, like the Angel of the Lord going before them. On that day I will set out to destroy all the nations that attack Jerusalem. And I will pour out on the house of David and the inhabitants of Jerusalem a spirit of grace and supplication. They will look on me, the one they have pierced, and they will mourn for him as one mourns for an only child, and grieve bitterly for him as one grieves for a firstborn son.* On that day the weeping in Jerusalem will be great, like the weeping of Hadad Rimmon in the plain of Megiddo. The land will mourn, each clan by itself, with their wives by themselves: the clan of the house of David and their wives, the clan of the house of Nathan and their wives, the clan of the house of Levi and their wives, the clan of Shimei and their wives, and all the rest of the clans and their wives.
>
> *[13:1] On that day a fountain will be opened to the house of David and the inhabitants of Jerusalem, to cleanse them from sin and impurity. On that day, I will banish the names of the idols from the land, and they will be remembered no more, declares the Lord Almighty. I will remove both the prophets and the spirit of*

impurity from the land. And if anyone still prophesies, his father and mother, to whom he was born, will say to him, "You must die, because you have told lies in the Lord's name." When he prophesies, his own parents will stab him. On that day every prophet will be ashamed of his prophetic vision. He will not put on a prophet's garment of hair in order to deceive. He will say, "I am not a prophet. I am a farmer; the land has been my livelihood since my youth." If someone asks him, "What are these wounds on your body?" he will answer, "The wounds I was given at the house of my friends."

Zechariah 12:8–13:6

This is a very rich portion of scripture. It starts with "On that day the Lord will shield those who live in Jerusalem." We find the phrase, "on that day," specifying that it is a certain day that the Lord is referring to here. He will refer to this particular day throughout this portion. God will shield those who live in Jerusalem. We find that He will protect them, just as was promised in Jeremiah 30:8–11, which we covered earlier in this chapter and the previous one. Specifically, we find God saving Israel while He destroys the nations where He has scattered them in the Jeremiah portion, and this is what He refers to here. The nations that attack Israel will be all of them! Every nation on earth will turn against Israel "on that day"! Jeremiah 30:14 tells us, "all your allies have forgotten you." Here we find that they indeed attack Israel. My friend, that includes the US, Great Britain, and all others! Why? Because "on that day," God will "break the yoke off their necks..." and "...no longer will foreigners enslave them" (Jeremiah 30:8). This is talking about Israel no longer serving the antichrist, whom the *rest of the world worships!* Suddenly, Israel is every nation's enemy. The only one on Israel's side is God, and that is good for Israel and bad for the world! God will strengthen Israel and protect it. And "on that day," God will set out to destroy all the nations that attack Israel. God will pour out His Spirit on "the House of David" and the "inhabitants of Jerusalem" on the day that they "look on" (the word here is *to look unto* or *respect*, not necessarily to see with the eyes, but to see with the heart, and so Israel will respect and look unto Christ) "me" (God is speaking here), "whom they have pierced, and they will mourn for him…" Here we have an interesting sentence structure. Remember, God is speaking here, and he tells us that Israel will look unto and regard God (Christ), whom they pierced on the cross, which is the Christ, and they will mourn for Him. Here we have an interesting change to the third person in the middle of the sentence. This is because God exists in the trinity. He can refer to Himself in the third person and be entirely proper, and so He does!

After this, He refers to a historic event that Israel can relate to: when a righteous king, Josiah, was killed. There was great mourning over this event. There will be great mourning when Israel realizes that they killed their Messiah.

Then we find in Zechariah 13:1 that Israel will be cleansed from their impurities. They will be clean *before God*! Then we find that God will banish all idols from Israel, and they will be remembered no more. This is very different from the portion in Isaiah 17 when they no longer regard the idols. In Isaiah 17 (at the battle of Damascus), they just turn from their idolatry, but they turn back. Here it is gone! Never will it be remembered again! Those who were false prophets will be ashamed. They will in truth say that they were never prophets. They were just liars, but now they know the truth. This has apparently led them to not lie in the strictest sense, but it does look like they are being evasive in their answers. They are ashamed and embarrassed.

There are many who believe that Zechariah 12:10 of this portion is speaking of Christ's return to earth after the tribulation. I was one of them just a couple of years ago! Then, as I studied it more deeply, I was shown that it isn't possible. This time is obviously referring to the same time as Joel 2:12–32 (especially verse 27, where they know that God is in Israel, not because they see Him, but because they see the things He is doing), Ezekiel 39:21–29 (verse 21 is referring to the tribulation beginning after God intervenes on Israel's behalf when Israel repents), and Jeremiah 30:7–24 (verses 23–24 are speaking of the tribulation time *following Israel's conversion!*).

Here we have found a portion detailing the conversion of Israel. We find a true change of heart among the people of the whole nation as they turn to Christ (whom they have pierced). They will *never turn away from Him again!* What a wonderful promise to Israel and through them to the world! They will finally be the blessing of the world as was prophesied to Abraham (Genesis 12:3).

In the next portion, we find another case of multiple fulfillments. Luke 21 covers the same subject as Matthew 24 and Mark 13. This is Christ's Olivet discourse. This is where Christ details the end times. In Luke, we find that Christ is giving them some details that were soon to be fulfilled that the Apostles could recognize when it came (Luke 21:12–19). This was a personal message to the apostles. Indeed, there will be people in the end times that will very much relive these events. Then we move into Luke 21:20–24. Luke 21:24 is definitely only an end-times event. But the sacking of Jerusalem in 70 AD fulfilled verse 20. "When you see Jerusalem being surrounded by armies, you will know that its desolation is near." But it was *not* completely fulfilled in that time. Christ was careful to say in Luke 21:22, "For this is the time of punishment in fulfillment of *all* that has been written." The sacking of Jerusalem does not fulfill all that has been written. The Matthew 24 and Mark 13 passages make it clear that this is also referring to a future event by tying this in with the desecration of the temple by the antichrist in the middle of the tribulation. This didn't happen when Jerusalem was destroyed. The temple was simply robbed and razed. So in the tribulation, we find that Jerusalem will be surrounded by armies, and the antichrist will take the temple, desecrating it with the abomination of desolation, as mentioned in Daniel 9:27, Matthew 24:15, Mark 13:14, 2 Thessalonians 2:4, and Revelation 13:14–15 (we will cover this in greater detail in Chapter 3 of volume 2). The Jews never welcome him into the temple; he simply takes it! This is illustrated by the example Christ makes of the first abomination of desolation as committed by Antiochus Epiphanes. Daniel prophesied this event, and it happened to the letter. Christ referred to Daniel's prophecy to let His listeners know that it will happen again. The point to this is the Jews never welcomed Antiochus Epiphanes into the temple the first time, and they won't again in the future. The reason that they will *not* welcome him is because they have already come to Christ! Israel as a nation has *already rejected the antichrist* at the end of the Battle of Magog and the beginning of the tribulation!

In the next portion, we find Paul explaining a "mystery." A mystery, we will find, is something that has been hidden, something not prophesied. Now we know that Israel's repentance is prophesied throughout Scripture. The mystery part is that Israel was set aside so Gentiles could be saved. When the "full number of the Gentiles" has come in, the program will be given back to the Jews. This is found in Romans 11:25–27:

> I do not want you to be ignorant of this mystery, brothers, so that you may not be conceited: Israel has experienced a hardening in part until the full number of the Gentiles has come in. And so *all Israel will be saved*, as it is written: "The deliverer will come from Zion; he will turn godlessness away from Jacob. And this is my covenant with them when I take away their sins."

So when the full number of Gentiles has come in, Israel will be saved. This is at the time of the beginning of the tribulation, immediately following the Battle of Magog.

In the next portion, we will take another approach to prove that Israel cannot wait to accept Christ until His second coming to earth. This approach is doctrinal. (Don't worry; this will be quick and painless!)

Second Corinthians 5:7: "We live by faith, not by sight."

This is a portion that I'm sure most of us are familiar with. But let's examine the implications of this verse. *Sight is not faith!* If Israel waited to see Christ coming to earth, it wouldn't be faith! Let's look at another portion, Hebrews 11:1: "Now faith is being sure of what we hope for and certain of what we *do not see.*" Again, faith is not of sight! Now what does this mean? Let's look at Hebrews 11:6: "And *without faith it is impossible to please God,* because anyone who comes to him must believe that he exists and that he rewards those who earnestly seek him." If they don't have faith, it is impossible to please God!

So if Israel followed the antichrist through the tribulation and then only repented when they saw Him coming back to the earth, they would be condemned with the earth! Their repentance would not be of faith, but sight, and without faith, it is impossible to please God! This only verifies that the Zechariah 12:10 portion means that they *regard* Christ, not *see* him.

In the next portion, we will find something that simply surprised me when I seriously studied it. This is the portion that many use to identify one of the two witnesses of Revelation 11. Because of the wording of this verse, I no longer believe that this identifies either of the two witnesses. I will explain why that is in Chapter 3 of volume 2. Now I will explain what this person is doing at the Day of Atonement for Israel. The portion is Malachi 4:5–6.

Malachi 4:5–6: "See, I will send you the prophet Elijah *before the great and dreadful day of the Lord* comes. He will turn the hearts of the fathers to their children, and the hearts of the children to their fathers; *or else I will come and strike the land with a curse.*"

Here we find some interesting facts. We find the mission of Elijah, the prophet, in the end times. His mission is to reconcile

Jews and unite them. This is apparently a part of their repentance. We are told in Ezekiel 11:19–20, which speaks of this very event:

> ...*I will give them an undivided heart and put a new spirit in them*; I will remove from them their heart of stone and give them a heart of flesh. Then they will follow my decrees and be careful to keep my laws. *They will be my people, and I will be their God*...

This speaks of them uniting; they have an undivided heart. This is part of their repentance. God promises to never curse them again after they repent, so the Malachi portion is speaking of the time of their repentance when they repent or are killed! Elijah will come at the Battle of Magog to call the nation of Israel to repentance. He will unite them all with a new heart and help bring them to repentance so that God doesn't curse the land. God will not curse the land after Israel repents! In fact, we have found that that is how Israel will know that God is in Israel (Joel 2:26–27).

Now we will recap what we have found in this chapter.

In Matthew 24:9, we found that Jews will be persecuted because of their faith in Christ. This is at least before the tribulation is over. We also found in Ezekiel 39:22 that from the end of the Magog battle onward, Israel will know who their God is! This is repeated in Jeremiah 30:22 and other portions.

We found that the time of Jacob's trouble is the Battle of Magog and *not the tribulation!* We found that after the time of Jacob's trouble, God will destroy all the nations where He has scattered them; that is the tribulation!

We found that God will forgive Israel and cleanse them so completely that their sins cannot be found. He will even refer to them as "Virgin Israel"!

Another important thing that we learned is that God doesn't do this for Israel's sake but for His own, so His holy name will not be profaned any more.

Another thing is that Israel woos Christ back to them, but God orchestrates this! This shows the sovereignty of God. We find that this relationship will be eternal, unconditional, and unbreakable!

Something else that is important is that Israel looks unto Him whom they have pierced. This shows the deity of Christ. Also, when properly understood, we see that this isn't speaking of physically looking at Him, but looking unto Him with their heart, regarding and recognizing Christ as God and Messiah without *seeing* Him!

We also found that when Israel believes in Christ, He will bless them, to the amazement and destruction of the world. We found that the world will *know* who Christ is; they will *know* that they are wrong, but they will still not repent!

We learned that it is indeed Israel that God will turn to and that the "church" was just a caretaker of God's promises until He returned to them. By the way, you probably noticed that I often put quotation marks around the word *church*. This is because the word *church* is the Greek word *ekklesia,* which means, essentially, *a called out assembly.* As such, God has always had and will always have a "church" present on this earth from the time of Adam until the end of the world! The time that we are in, as I write this book series, is popularly called the "church age."

And we learned that Israel will have to accept Christ before He comes back to this earth, because if they waited, they would be lost!

And last of all, we learned that Elijah will be very instrumental in the repentance of Israel. That is Elijah's mission.

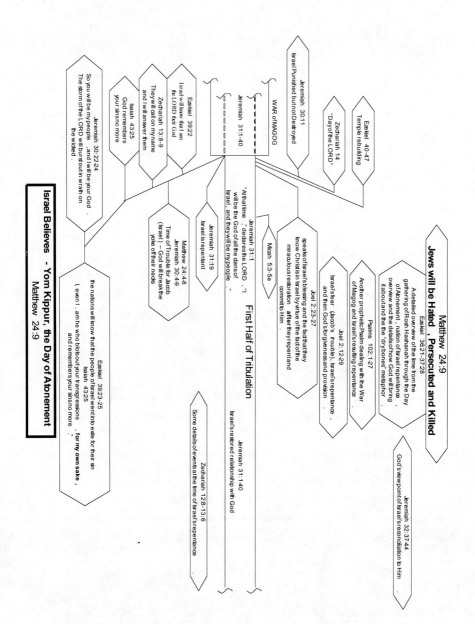

Israel Believes - Yom Kippur, the Day of Atonement Event Line

CHAPTER 4

The Antichrist
Matthew 24:4–14, 23–26

In this chapter, we will be dealing with a very dark subject. This is the antichrist. He plays a very large and destructive part in end-times prophecy. But before we start, we need to understand some things about the term *antichrist*.

First, we need to understand what *Christ* means. *Christ* is the Greek form of the word *Messiah*. The word *Messiah* is found in Daniel 9:25–26, in his prophesy of Christ. It is not translated *Messiah* in the NIV. In the NIV, it is translated *Anointed One*. The word means *delivered by God*. He is the one promised by God for the healing of the world, the forgiveness of sins and salvation. He is none other than God in the flesh, Jesus. He is known by many names in the Old Testament, including the Prince, Immanuel (which means *God with us* or, more properly, *God has become one of us*), Branch, Arm of the Lord, Counselor, Desire of All Nations, Desire of Women (in the sense of virgins desiring to give birth to Him), Everlasting Father (yes, these are names of Jesus, the Son, because it speaks of the trinity.), Jehovah, King, Mighty God, Redeemer, Seed of Woman, and Son of Righteousness, among others. We can get a picture of who Jesus is by how He is referred to in the Old Testament prophecies of Him.

Then we get the word *antichrist*. This is introduced to us by Apostle John in 1 John 2:22, 4:3, and 2 John 7. The *anti* part of the name means more than what *anti* means to us who speak English. It does have the aspect of *against*, as we know it, but it also includes the aspect of *in place of*, or *substitute*. So when we have the term *antichrist*, we have the idea of *a substitute to God in the flesh, who is opposed to Him*. This is Satan's plan to remove Christ from the minds and hearts of mankind. He found that he couldn't defeat Him by killing Him, so now he will try to substitute Him with a counterfeit.

There are many names in the Bible for the antichrist. In the Old Testament, we find him referred to as the little horn, the beast, the ruler who will come, the abomination, another king, the king who will do as he pleases, and foolish shepherd, among others. In the New Testament, he has many names also. He is known as the man of lawlessness, the man doomed to destruction, the beast, and of course, the antichrist and others. Here we have a good picture of his character and ambition, as well as his fate. He is evil, and he will ultimately fail.

Now let's begin our study of the scriptures that deal with this evil person.

Matthew 24:4–15:

> Jesus answered: "Watch out that no one deceives you. *For many will come in my name, claiming, 'I am the Christ,' and will deceive many.* You will hear of wars and rumors of wars, but see to it that you are not alarmed. Such things must happen, but the end is still to come. Nation will rise against nation, and kingdom against kingdom. There will be famines and earthquakes in various places. All these are the beginning of birth pains. *Then you will be handed over to be persecuted and put to death, and you will be hated by all nations because of me. At*

that time many will turn away from the faith and will betray and hate each other, and many false prophets will appear and deceive many people. Because of the increase of wickedness, the love of most will grow cold, but he who stands firm to the end will be saved. And this gospel of the kingdom will be preached in the whole world as a testimony to all nations, and then the end will come. *So when you see standing in the holy place 'the abomination that causes desolation,' spoken of through the prophet Daniel*—let the reader understand…"

Here we don't have the antichrist mentioned specifically, but we do have some of his actions mentioned specifically.

First, we find that there will be many who will claim to be Christ, and we are told to be careful to not be fooled by them. The antichrist will be one of them, or he may just claim that he is powerful enough to beat God, and unlike Jim Jones, David Koresh, Moon, and others, he will have power. He will have political and religious power. He will have power over the law, and he will be backed by the world's most powerful religious system of the time. We are told that when he comes to power, it will be during a time of military upheavals, as well as geological upheavals. Sound familiar? We are seeing this begin today. The difference is that then, it will be turned up a notch. The wars will be more devastating, and so will the earthquakes and volcanism. There will be famines. Again, we see this in the news frequently.

We already discussed some of the events of the time of "birth pains," as Christ called it in Chapter 1 of this book. And, as we will see, this is when he becomes active. In Matthew 24:9, we find the words, "Then you will be handed over to be persecuted and put to death." This will be a campaign of genocide that will begin shortly after the battle of Damascus and will extend through the time of tribulation. To be sure, it will be stepped up considerably during the tribulation, but it will be the same campaign. The phrase, "and you will be hated by all nations because of me," marks a shift in the program of God. Suddenly, we find that Israel is, *as a nation,* dedicated to Christ. They will be hated because of Him, and many will die *because of Him!* This marks the time discussed in Chapter 3 of this book: Israel's repentance, their Yom Kippur fulfilled! We will find that the antichrist will be putting believers to death before that from all nations, but here we find that he is concentrating on Jews specifically. He is here speaking to Jews being hated by all nations because of Christ. This happens after they reject the antichrist and accept the true Christ. This is why the world hates them. Israel will be rejecting the world's god! Still, all believers will be subject to death from the antichrist; it is just that the only *nation* that will be the recipient of his wrath, as a nation, will be Israel, because they reject him. As it is the time of the repentance of Israel, it also would mark the beginning of the tribulation period, the seven years.

In Matthew 24:10, we have the statement, "Many will turn away from the faith and will betray and hate each other." These cannot be Jews! We found in Chapter 3 of this book that *every Jew* will be brought to Jerusalem at the time of the Battle of Magog (Ezekiel 39:28). *Every Jew* will be given a new heart of flesh and have their heart of stone removed (Ezekiel 36:26). *Every Jew* will have the Law of God written on their heart so that they will not need a teacher (Jeremiah 31:33–34)! From this, I would think that Matthew 24:10 is speaking of non-Jews specifically, but we also find that God gives them all a new heart and writes His Law on their hearts "from the least of them to the greatest." Are they incapable of sin? No. We find in Jeremiah 31:29–30 that they will no longer die for the sins of their fathers but will die for their own sins. Does this mean that these redeemed of Israel will go to hell? No! It goes on after that to say in Jeremiah 31:31–34 that God will make a new, everlasting covenant with Israel that will apply to *all Jews* from the least to the greatest! He says, "I will be their God, and they will be my people"! He says this *after He says that they will die for their own sins.* Also, after He says this, He tells us in Jeremiah

31:34, "For I will forgive their wickedness and remember their sins no more." Now, I realize He is specifically speaking of the nation here, but He is also speaking of individuals, as is mentioned earlier in this same verse. In Zechariah 13:9, it tells us, "This third (the remnant after the Battle of Magog) I will bring into the fire; I will refine them like silver and test them like gold. *They will call on my name and I will answer them; I will say, 'they are my people,' and they will say, 'The Lord is our God.'"*

This entire remnant is capable of sin, according to Jeremiah, but they are still saved! Even if God has to take their life! An example of this is found in 1 Corinthians 5. In this portion, Paul is talking about a member of the Corinthian congregation that is having sexual relations with his stepmother! Paul tells them that this cannot be tolerated! Notice 1 Corinthians 5:5: (I will use the New American Standard Bible here, because it seems to capture the full intent of the verse.) "I have decided to deliver such a one to Satan *for the destruction of his flesh, so that his spirit may be saved in the day of the Lord Jesus.*" Read this carefully! Paul was going to hand him over to Satan to be *killed!* The destruction of his flesh! To what purpose? That his spirit may be saved in the day of the Lord Jesus! If this man wouldn't repent (which he did, as we find in 2 Corinthians), he would die in his sin. This is the sin unto death as spoken of by John in 1 John 5:16. Does a believer go to hell? No, but they lose rewards in heaven for all eternity. Read 1 Corinthians 3:11–15.

While they will still be capable of sin, they will not turn from the faith. Matthew 24:10 is speaking of Gentiles who have heard and decided not to believe.

Now, what is the result of a believing Jew sinning? Jeremiah 30:11 tells us that God will not leave them completely unpunished. Even though He is protecting them and will *save* them, they will still be punished, justly. Let's read Jeremiah 30:11. "'I am with you and will save you,' declares the Lord. 'Though I completely destroy all the nations among which I scatter you, I will not *completely* destroy you. I will discipline you but only with justice; I will not let you go entirely unpunished.'" This discipline is severe. Does this mean the ones who are disciplined are unsaved? No! Jeremiah 30:11 speaks of His saving them even though He punishes them. They *all* proclaim God is their God, and God claims them as His people (Ezekiel 39:22, Jeremiah 30:22, Jeremiah 31:1, Jeremiah 32:38, and others).

If you will recall, in Chapter 2 of this book, we found that two thirds of the Jews will die in the Battle of Magog. These are the ones that will not believe! God destroys them so He can bring the others through the fire and refine them. If they were perfect to start with, they wouldn't need refining! And yes, some will die during that awful time, and some of the deaths will be due to their own sin. They will be saved, "but only as one escaping through the flames" (1Corinthians 3:15b).

Remember, we are sons of God! And yes, even women are *sons*! This is important to understand. As sons, we can be heirs, whether male or female. Women, in Bible times, except in rare cases, couldn't be heirs to the family wealth. So women, when you accept Christ as your savior, you become a "son" of God, so you can inherit the family fortune! Cool, huh? As sons of God, we have a certain place in the family of God. We are His sons. No matter what, if we are indeed His sons, *we are His sons*! This is the very same as being a child of your parents. No matter what, you will always be your parents' child. This is even truer with God. He is the perfect father. He doesn't choose His words loosely. Let's read Hebrews 12:5–11:

And you have forgotten that word of encouragement that addresses you as sons? "My son, do not make light of the Lord's discipline, and do not lose heart when he rebukes you, because the Lord disciplines *those he loves*, and punishes *everyone he accepts as a son*." Endure hardship as discipline; *God is treating you as sons*. For what son is not disciplined by his father? If you are not disciplined (and everyone undergoes discipline), then you are illegitimate children and not true sons. Moreover, we have all had human fathers who disciplined us and we respected them for it. How much more should we submit to the father of our spirits *and live*! Our fathers disciplined us *for a little while as they thought best*; but God disciplines us *for our good, that we may share in his holiness.* No discipline seems pleasant at the time, but painful. Later on, however, it produces a harvest of righteousness and peace for those who have been trained by it.

First, notice that God disciplines everyone that He accepts as a son! Not those who are going to hell. He disciplines those He accepts and those He loves! (Although many that are going to hell will experience the consequences of their own actions and will die from their own foolishness.) The writer of Hebrews cautions us to check to see if we are being disciplined by God. If not, you had better examine yourself to see if you are indeed His son! This discipline brings us life (Hebrews 12:9). (It may not include physical life Jeremiah 31:30, but it will bring us life in Heaven!) Now notice Hebrews 12:10; God disciplines us for our good. If He banishes us to hell, that wouldn't be for our good, now would it? And He disciplines us that we may share in His holiness. This is sharing in His sinlessness; while we are not sinless in ourselves, we are sinless through His blood, which we are cleansed with once and for all (Romans 6:10). Does this give a license to sin? No! In fact, as Paul says in response to this very question: "God forbid!" The penalty is severe. It can cause hardship and pain, even death, but even that is for our good!

Please pardon my excursion into doctrine here. It was necessary because of the prophetic statement by Jeremiah that these who call Him God and God calls His people will still die for their own sins.

We find in Matthew 24:12–13: "Because of the increase of wickedness, the love of most will grow cold, but he who stands firm to the end will be saved." This seems to infer salvation by works, and if it were speaking of eternal salvation, it would be. But that isn't it. Does this mean that those who die during the tribulation weren't spiritually saved? No, we are told that many will be in heaven that died during the tribulation (Revelation 7:14, 12:11). These are physically saved to see the Lord Jesus Christ return to the earth after the tribulation. They will go into the millennial reign with Christ physically to raise families and worship during the thousand years. This is what the passage in Matthew 24:36–41 is talking about, physically entering the millennial reign of Christ. The ones "taken" are killed! The ones who believe are *left behind* to enter the kingdom! We will discuss this more thoroughly in Chapter 4 of volume 2 and chapter 5 of this book. Does this mean that all who are believers that die in the tribulation died because of their sin? Again, no. Revelation 12:11 tells us that many will willingly lay down their lives for the love of Christ during that time. There is no allusion to their sinning here. These will not be saved in the physical sense, but they will receive great reward for their sacrifice. They will be saved in the more important sense; their soul will be saved. What this does mean has nothing to do with their being saved by their works, and it has nothing to do with their surviving the tribulation! This portion is translated in a very confusing manner. If it were speaking of salvation by works, it would conflict with many other scriptures, and if it meant surviving the tribulation, it would also conflict with many other scriptures. The proper translation of this verse, one that would agree with other scriptures and agree with the context of this chapter, would read along the lines of, "He who trusts Christ at the end will be saved (to enter the kingdom)." There are a couple of translations that give this very meaning. One is the Young's Literal Translation, which reads, "But he who did endure to the end, he shall be saved," and the Wycliffe New Testament, which reads, "but he that shall dwell still into the end, shall be safe." Perhaps the Wycliffe translation is the most accurate in this case. It agrees with the portion later in this chapter, Matthew 24:36–41.

These verses speak of those being left behind to enter the kingdom of Christ. No! These verses are not "rapture" verses. I will say this more than once.

Now please notice Matthew 24:14. This is the "gospel of the kingdom," specifically, whoever stands firm at the end will be saved to be left behind at the final harvest by Christ and will enter the millennial reign of Christ. What is preached now *is not the gospel of the kingdom.* Today's gospel (at the time this is being written) is "the gospel"! It is the good news that Christ has paid for your sins and is yours as a gift! Free! All you need to do is accept it, but it has nothing to do with preparing yourself for Christ's physical return. It has to do with your eternal spiritual state! The gospel of the *kingdom* will be preached throughout all the earth to every person, regardless of nationality. Jew and Gentile will all be subject to this gospel, and *if* they stand firm for Christ at the end, they will survive. Salvation of the soul will be the same then as it is now. Believe on the Lord Jesus Christ; trust in Him to save you by his death on the cross, and you will not see hell! Always remember Ephesians 2:8–9: "For it is by grace you have been saved, through faith—and this not from yourselves, it is the gift of God—not by works, so that no one can boast." You are never saved because you are good enough! Not now and not then. Furthermore, at "the end," Christ will come to judge the world, as we will see in Chapter 4 of volume 2. Those who haven't trusted Christ as their Savior will not survive to go into the kingdom. I mentioned this earlier. Those who are unsaved, who haven't trusted Christ to save them, will not stand firm. They will not survive. Christ will destroy them in the final harvest of the earth prior to the millennium.

The gospel of the kingdom is essentially, "Prepare yourselves to meet Christ face to face; He is coming very soon! Within your lifetime, if you survive."

When this gospel of the kingdom has been preached to the entire earth, the end will come. Everyone must hear. Everyone will have the opportunity to believe.

Now in Matthew 24:15, we have Christ telling us to watch for the abomination of desolation that was prophesied by Daniel. This is definitely a work of the antichrist *specifically*. While he is not specifically mentioned here, there are many portions that do mention him in relation to this act, as we will see.

Matthew 24:16 through 22 dwell on what people living then should expect, what to look out for, and how to survive. We won't go into this at this time; we will cover this in Chapters 1 and 3 of volume 2.

The account of the antichrist picks up again in Matthew 24:23 through 26 of this portion. Again, he is not specifically named here, but his works are covered without question.

> At that time if anyone says to you, "Look, here is the Christ!" or, "There he is!" do not believe it. *For false Christs and false prophets will appear and perform great signs and miracles to deceive even the elect—if that were possible.* See, I have told you ahead of time. "So if anyone tells you, 'There he is, out in the desert,' do not go out; or, 'Here he is, in the inner rooms,' do not believe it."
>
> Matthew 24:23–26

In this portion, we have Christ giving a general explanation of how to recognize a false Christ. This is so they will not be deceived.

Now in Matthew 24:24, He gives some pointed advice. The antichrist will use great signs and wonders, enough to deceive the very elect. That sounds rather grave until we read the next part of the verse: "if that were possible." Praise the Lord; it isn't possible to deceive the elect! Now this has implications with the earlier portion that we studied, Matthew 24:4 through 15. Since it isn't possible to deceive the elect, the "many" that turn away from the faith weren't saved to start with! If they were, they would be elect, and Christ tells us they cannot be deceived! What words of comfort! Also, if someone doesn't stand firm for Christ to the end to the point that they are deceived and deny Christ, by this portion, we can know that they aren't elect and are unsaved in every sense of the word. We will cover the second coming of Christ in depth in Chapter 4 of volume 2.

In this next portion of this book, we will study the rise of the antichrist. We will search for information about how he comes to power.

> After that, in my vision at night I looked, and there before me was a fourth beast—terrifying and frightening and very powerful. It had large iron teeth; it crushed and devoured its victims and trampled underfoot whatever was left. It was different from all the former beasts, and it had ten horns. *While I was thinking about the horns, there before me was another horn, a little one, which came up among them; and three of the first horns were uprooted before it. This horn had eyes like the eyes of a man and a mouth that spoke boastfully.*
>
> Daniel 7:7–8

> I also wanted to know about the ten horns on its head and about the other horn that came up, before which three of them fell—the horn that looked more imposing than the others and that had eyes and a mouth that spoke boastfully. *As I watched, this horn was waging war against the saints and defeating them, until the Ancient of Days came and pronounced judgment in favor of the saints of the Most High, and the time came when they possessed the kingdom.* He gave me this explanation: "The fourth beast is a fourth kingdom that will appear on earth. It will be different from all the other kingdoms and will devour the whole earth, trampling it down and crushing it. *The ten horns are ten kings who will come from this kingdom. After them another king will arise, different from the earlier ones; he will subdue three kings. He will speak against the Most High*

and oppress his saints and try to change the set times and the laws.
The saints will be handed over to him for a time, times and half a
time. But the court will sit, and his power will be taken away and
completely destroyed forever."

Daniel 7:20–26

This covers the ascension of the antichrist to power. It came with the symbolic vision, but as is true of God, it is followed by an explanation. Daniel 7:24–26 explains the vision.

There are things we can learn from this cryptic portion of Scripture. First we find that there are ten horns. These all exist at the same time. We can know this because, when the little horn comes up, he comes up among them, and it uproots three of them. We find that the little horn had eyes like a man and spoke boastfully. At this point, it already becomes apparent that it is speaking of a man.

We find that the antichrist will persecute the believers during the tribulation, and here we find that he makes war with the saints. In fact, we find that he is defeating them (this very event is also mentioned in Revelation 13:5–7). So we can be assured that this evil "little horn" is indeed the antichrist, the beast.

The ten horns are ten kings that come from "this" kingdom. It is generally assumed that this kingdom is the ancient Roman Empire, and I have no problem with that view. The description of the fourth beast aligns well with the historical record of the Roman Empire. The problem comes from people trying to read into this more than God gives us in this portion. All it tells us is that it is ten kings that come from this old Roman Empire! We have had much speculation as to whom these kingdoms are, based on confederations of nations born from this Empire. We have had suggested to us that it is the European Union (too many, there are more than ten), United Nations (too many again, and not all were members of the ancient Roman Empire), the western Roman Empire, the eastern Roman Empire (again, too many for both of these), and other possibilities.

None perfectly fit the information given, and people try to make them fit. Let's not do that!

What does it tell us here? It tells us that there will be ten kings that will arise that will have in common the background of being from the ancient Roman Empire. Does it say that they will be all the kings that arise from this Empire? Certainly not! It just says that there will be ten kings of note (I say "of note" because the Bible takes note of them here). It *does not say* that they will be all of the kings of the Roman Empire, or for that matter, it does not say that they will be all the kings of the western or the eastern Roman Empire. It just tells us that they will come from the Roman Empire.

Then this portion tells us that *after* these kings are established (Daniel 7:24), another king will arise. He will come up *among* them (Daniel 7:8). He will be a "little one" (also Daniel 7:8). This indicates to me that he will rise from an obscure background, similar to Adolph Hitler. He started out as a corporal in the German army in World War One, who was captured and held in a British POW camp. Then, on his release he made his living as a house painter before becoming a major troublemaker. But this is speculation on my part. I just don't know what else it could mean. It doesn't mean that he isn't powerful. He subdues three of the kings as he comes to power. And we will find that he certainly isn't insignificant in the future history of the world. In fact, we will find that he has a starring role, though not a good one. To me, the only thing that his being a "little one" could mean is that he starts out as an insignificant person. We are told in this portion that he will be different from the ones who are established when he arises, although it doesn't tell us how he will be different. To be sure, he will be different! We could list many ways that he could be different from anyone else who will live on this earth. I won't try to go into that here. And as mentioned, he will subdue three kings (Daniel 7:24). These three kings will be part of the ten kings (Daniel 7:8). He will speak against God (Daniel 7:25). He will be very boastful (Daniel

7:8). He will "oppress the saints", which, contrary to some popular teachings, "saints" are not dead people. They are believers. If you have trusted in Jesus Christ as your Savior, you are a saint. Daniel 7:25: He will try to change the times and the laws (Daniel 7:25). Again, I'm not sure how he will try to change the times and the laws. My guess, and it's just a guess, would be that he will try to get the years to not be based on Christ. This is just a guess. And probably every new world leader (king) changes the laws somehow. We will find things that he will change later as we continue in this book series.

We are also told in Daniel 7:25 that the "saints will be handed over to him for a time, times, and half a time." We will find that this is specifically three and a half years (a time equals one year).

Then we find that the court will sit. This, we will find, is the court of God. The antichrist's power will be taken away and completely destroyed forever (Daniel 7:26). Then in Daniel 7:27, we find that Christ will set up His kingdom, as we will study later in this book series.

Now, is there any information in Scripture as to just who the ten kingdoms may be? There may be some information. There will not be names, of course, but the people that they represent may be available to us.

I have alluded to the fact that I feel the antichrist will make his appearance in the battle of Damascus. There are hints to this in Scripture. They are just hints though; there are no scriptures that say, "the antichrist will make his appearance at the battle of Damascus."

A careful study of the participants of the Damascus battle will show us that there apparently are ten members of this coalition. Psalm 83 gives us the most complete list of members. Contrary to popular opinion, there are only nine listed, not all ten. There are Edom, the Ishmaelites, Moab, the Hagrites, Gebal, Ammon, Amalek, Philistia, people of Tyre, and Assyria. Yes, there are ten mentioned, but one is redundant. Many say that "Ishmaelites" and "Hagrites" are redundant, but since they are in the same verse, I believe that they are two separate peoples. Ishmael descended from Hagar and as such may refer to the descendants of Ishmael's half brothers as Hagrites (the descendants of Ishmael are known today as Arabs). Both Ishmael and Isaac (the father of the Jews) were born to Abram (later Abraham) but to different mothers. Isaac was born to Sarah, and Ishmael was born to Hagar, Sarah's handmaiden. The Arabs believe that Hagar had no other children, but that is debatable. Either she had other children, or there was a group of Ishmaelites that broke off and became a separate group. Anyway, there appear to be two separate groups here. The more likely redundancy is Gebal and Edom. The Gebal that is found here is in Edom. (Again, there is another Gebal, which is in Lebanon, which is a sister city of Tyre and would be redundant also if this were the intended city.) Edom is mentioned, and the city of Gebal in Edom is also mentioned. There may be significance too. Edom will have a special place in Israel's future, as we will find in Chapter 3 of volume 2. So this leaves us with nine. That's good though, because there is one participant missing, and that is, of course, Damascus! We find many of these members mentioned in Amos 1 and 2. We also find a detailed report on the battle in Isaiah 17, but this only covers Syria and Israel. If you put all the passages together, we get ten! All of these countries and peoples were subject to the Roman Empire. I say "countries and peoples" because not all have a home-land at this time, but all have a leader (king).

This list of ten includes Edom, which is southern Jordan (and includes Gebal). The Ishmaelites are the Arabic peoples. Moab is central Jordan. The Hagrites are generally considered to be located along the eastern side of Saudi Arabia and may include parts of Saudi Arabia, Qatar, the United Arab Emirates, and perhaps part of Oman. Ammon is northern Jordan. Amalek were an ancient people possibly predating Abraham. They were nomadic but likely settled in later times in the south (1 Samuel 15:7 and Numbers 13:29). They were enemies of Israel from the earliest times. Their likely area of residence is the Sinai Peninsula of eastern Egypt. While Egypt itself is not mentioned as a participant, there will be a lot of internal strife, which may involve some splinter factions. Philistia: today there is a group of people that call themselves Palestinians. They claim to be directly descended from the Philistines. They are waiting for a homeland and are closely associated with Gaza. We find in Amos that the Philistines of Gaza will be destroyed in the battle of Damascus. They exist today throughout Gaza, Israel, Lebanon, and Jordan. Tyre is a city in Lebanon. Tyre was destroyed in ancient times and has been rebuilt to some extent. It is not nearly as important as it was many centuries ago. Interestingly, as I write this, there is a war going on in Israel with Lebanon, and Tyre is being mentioned in the newscasts. Then there is Assyria. Assyria is present-day Iraq. It is said in Psalm 83 that they will help others in their attack on Israel. This completes the list in Psalms, but there is one key player missing, which, of course, is Damascus, along with its mother country, Syria. This is mentioned in Isaiah 17 and Amos 1. Amos 1 and 2 is the portion that ties all these other passages together. It ties them together by listing many of the participants that are listed in Psalm 83. While no single passage lists all of them, when put together, there are ten. I believe that we can put them together because this battle that is mentioned in these portions has never been fulfilled as it is told in these scriptures, and the circumstances found in each of these portions is the same. We find that they are bent on Israel's destruction, all three have members found in the other portions that are common to this battle (Isaiah has Damascus, as does Amos, and Amos has the Philistines and Jordan, as does Psalms), and all three portions end up with them being destroyed. I am convinced that these passages can only be speaking of the same event. To be speaking of different events would introduce problems that become insurmountable. You would have events that are still future resulting in these cities being destroyed, some never to be inhabited again, and the people being killed with no survivors *more than once*, unless it is speaking of the same battle!

This is a list of ten countries that will form a confederation in the end times. They have never all at once done this, but it is very understandable how it could happen today. It will happen, probably soon. We are told that the antichrist will arise from a conflict involving ten "kings." It seems logical that this coalition of ten that will attack Israel could be the one of Daniel 7, from which the antichrist will arise.

In Daniel, we find that the antichrist will "uproot" three kings. What three kings will be uprooted?

We find only three that seem to be destroyed. These are Edom's house of Esau (Edom, southern Jordan: "There will be no survivors from the house of Esau" [Obadiah 18b]), Moab (central Jordan; Moab shall die, KJV, Amplified bible, and NASB. NIV says, "shall go down" [Amos 2:2]), and Palestine ("till the last of the Philistines is dead" [Amos 1:8]). No mention of the others being destroyed is found. And even at that, in reference to Moab, while Moab will die, there is reference to there being some survivors in Isaiah 16. But this reference tells us that the survivors will be very few ("a servant bound by contract would count them"). So, truly, Isaiah mentions more than just Damascus in this battle. Damascus is only mentioned in Isaiah 17, while Moab (central Jordan) is mentioned in Isaiah 16. This leads me to believe that these three are the ones "uprooted." Can I be sure? I'm sorry, but I cannot. God deliberately makes this somewhat obscure so the players will be off their guard. There is no scripture I have found that makes this absolutely clear. I will be happy to hear of any other ideas that have scriptural merit though. This seems to be the most logical scenario that I have heard, and it follows Scripture, which is an absolute prerequisite.

In the Daniel 7 portion, we are told that the antichrist ("beast," forgive me, but I will continue to call him the "antichrist" for clarity sake) will "subdue" three kings. This tells us that he will come to power or at least make his first appearance on the world stage at this point and will have an active role in this great battle. The reason that I think it will be his first appearance is this is what we are told in Daniel 7:8. We find that he comes up amid the other ten horns that are already established, destroying ("uprooting") three in the process. Exactly what his role or motives will be in this battle, we cannot say for certain, but we know from this scripture and others that he is very self serving and boastful, as we will find. On this basis, we can safely assume that the reason is for personal gain.

Another reason I believe the antichrist will arise during the Damascus battle is that he is very much in power and active in the Magog war. We will find this in Daniel 11:36–45. To make this point, we must leap ahead somewhat to a point near the middle of his evil career.

Daniel 11:36–45:

> The king will do as he pleases. *He will exalt and magnify himself above every god and will say unheard-of things against the God of gods. He will be successful until the time of wrath is completed,* for what has been determined must take place. He will show no regard for the gods of his fathers or for the one desired by women, nor will he regard any god, but will exalt himself above them all. Instead of them, he will honor a god of fortresses; a god unknown to his fathers he will honor with gold and silver, with precious stones and costly gifts. He will attack the mightiest fortresses with the help of a foreign god and *will greatly honor those who acknowledge him. He will make them rulers over many people and will distribute the land at a price. At the time of the end the king of the South will engage him in battle, and the king of the North will storm out against him with chariots and cavalry and a great fleet of ships.* He will invade many countries and sweep through them like a flood. He will also invade the Beautiful Land. *Many countries will fall, but Edom, Moab and the leaders of Ammon will be delivered*

from his hand. He will extend his power over many countries; Egypt will not escape. He will gain control of the treasures of gold and silver and all the riches of Egypt, with the Libyans and Nubians in submission. *But reports from the east and the north will alarm him, and he will set out in a great rage to destroy and annihilate many.* He will pitch his royal tents between the seas at the beautiful holy mountain. *Yet he will come to his end, and no one will help him.*

It is clear from this passage that this is speaking of the antichrist. He will magnify himself above all gods and above the God of gods (Daniel 11:36). He will have great political power, as well as military might. We are also told here that this is speaking of the time of the end (Daniel 11:40). He will honor those who acknowledge him (Daniel 11:39). The line stating that he will "distribute the land at a price" could be accurate, but it could also mean that he will "distribute the land for a reward." This isn't unlikely, because it follows the line about him honoring those who acknowledge him. This means those who worship him acknowledge him as god.

Then we find that "at the time of the end" the king of the south will attack him. Many believe that this is speaking of Egypt, but Egypt is in no position to attack anyone in a coordinated military manner. In fact, we find him plundering Egypt of its treasures. Egypt is just in the unenviable position of being in the way. The king of the south is speaking of a coalition between Sudan, and Ethiopia, with Libya. It will probably be led by Sudan, although this is just speculation on my part. They are working in cooperation with the king of the north, which is Magog, which is Russia and her cohorts, as listed in Chapter 2 of this book. These nations are all mentioned in Ezekiel 38. We are told that Russia will attack with a coordinated military operation. All its forces will work in cooperation with each other. The southern forces will work in a coordinated attack with Magog in what is often called a pincer attack, attacking an opponent from two sides, thus dividing its forces.

Thomas Farr

Then we find the narrative continuing with the antichrist's activities in this battle. It says that he will invade many countries. The NIV says that he will "invade the beautiful land." This will be Israel. At this time though, it will not be a true invasion. Until Israel repents, he is still Israel's shepherd, Israel's leader. The NIV is the only translation that reads "invade." The NASB, KJV, and the Amplified Bible say, "enter," and Young's literal says, "come in to." In this case, I am convinced that the other translations are correct. This may at first seem like a minor difference, but when the Battle of Magog is begun, he is welcome in Israel. It would be merely an entrance. But we find something interesting here. Jordan is kept out of his possession. We will find that Jordan (Edom, Moab, and the main part of Ammon), especially southern Jordan (Edom), will be a safe hiding place for Israelis during the last half of the tribulation. God keeps it out of the antichrist's hands, and it *is* in Israel's hands (Obadiah 21). This shows the change in power in Israel from the antichrist to the true Christ! The Jews reject the antichrist at this point. They deny him possession of Jordan!

By the way, Obadiah is a very important book when it comes to end-times prophecies, because it takes us from the battle of Damascus through the Day of the Lord (tribulation) and on into the millennium. It deals with these prophecies from the aspect of God's dealing with Edom (southern Jordan).

Then we find that the antichrist will plunder Egypt, and Sudan and Ethiopia will be in subjection to him. Then we are told that "reports from the east and the north will alarm him, and he will set out in great rage to destroy and annihilate many." I believe it will be at this point that God intervenes on behalf of repentant Israel. The reason I say this is because he is in control up to this point. When the earthquake hits and every wall falls to the ground, he will not be able to operate either, but it will no longer be important, because the battle will be over. It will appear that he won! It seems that Daniel 11:41 looks ahead to the eventual outcome of this battle to inform us that he doesn't gain control over Jordan. This goes with Revelation 12:13–17 and Isaiah 16:1–5. (We will cover this in Chapter 3 in volume 2.)

So, Magog is a threat to the antichrist's personal gain. They probably want his oil fields in Iraq. He defends his territory, and in the middle of the battle, Israel recognizes just who he is and rejects him, turning to Christ. God saves His people, and the antichrist, being the opportunist that he is, claims credit for it. The world buys it, worshipping the antichrist and despising Israel for rejecting their god, when he is right here and, in their minds, proves he is bigger than God with this great miracle and other miraculous signs. But Israel will be the only nation that will have it right! The true God devastates the mighty armies of Magog and her allies, and the antichrist takes an armistice to the many nations involved in this battle, claiming it was he who did it. This is the "many" mentioned in Daniel 9:27, *not Israel!* It's the same "many" that is mentioned in Daniel 11:41. This will be a peace treaty with the nations of the Magog battle, or what's left of them. There is no scripture that says that Israel signs a treaty with the antichrist at the beginning of the tribulation! This was just an assumption based on the idea that Israel still accepts the antichrist as God during the tribulation, which, as we have seen, is a false assumption.

Okay, now back to the activities of the antichrist after his rise to power in the Damascus battle.

There are references to his activities during the time of "birth pains." One that gives us some insight into his rise to power is Daniel 8:19–26:

> He said: "I am going to tell you what will happen *in the time of wrath, because the vision concerns the time of the end.* The two horned ram that you saw represents the kings of Media and Persia. The shaggy goat is the king of Greece, and the large horn between his eyes is the first king. The four horns that replaced the one that was broken off represent four kingdoms

that will emerge from his nation but will not have the same power. In the latter part of their reign, when rebels have become completely wicked, a stern faced king, a master of intrigue, will arise. He will become very strong, but *not by his own power. He will cause astounding devastation and will succeed in whatever he does. He will destroy mighty men and the holy people.* He will cause deceit to prosper, and he will consider himself superior. *When they feel secure, he will destroy many and take his stand against the prince of princes. Yet he will be destroyed, but not by human power.* The vision of evenings and mornings that has been given you is true, *but seal up the vision, for it concerns the distant future."*

This is a very difficult portion for one reason. It is detailing the reign of Antiochus Epiphanes. We can know this because the vision that Daniel had in the first place (Daniel 8:1–14) included certain elements that pertained only to the reign of this tyrant. The goat was the kingdom of Greece, from which Antiochus Epiphanes came. The way we can know this is Antiochus Epiphanes is, first of all, he fulfilled the vision entirely, even to the 2,300 days of Daniel 8:14. There is nothing in the antichrist's reign that comes specifically to 2,300 days. The tribulation lasts for 2,520 days or slightly less (Matthew 24:22) to preserve life on earth as Christ has told us. But it won't be 2,300 days, because Christ also told us, "No one knows about that day or hour" (Matthew 24:36). If it were shortened to 2,300, then we would know.

The explanation on the other hand gives strong reason to believe that it is speaking of future events. This can be very confusing, but I believe that it will become apparent to the Jews when they see these things happen during the tribulation. I have always said that Antiochus Epiphanes was a type of the antichrist, and this seems to give very strong support to this.

The first thing in the explanation that refers to the antichrist is in Daniel 8:17b, which says, "Understand that the vision *con-*

cerns the time of the end." Then in Daniel 8:19, which was quoted above, this is reiterated. "I am going to tell you what will happen later *in the time of wrath*, because the vision *concerns* the time of the end." All that was ending at the time of Antiochus Epiphanes was the preeminence of the kingdom of Greece. From the time of the Roman Empire to today, Greece has not been a world power. God makes it clear that this is the end time because He also refers to the time it *concerns* as the "time of wrath." "The time of wrath" refers to the tribulation time. But notice a great clue to understanding the duplicity of this vision: the fact that it seems to cover two prophetic (to Daniel) events, Antiochus Epiphanes and the antichrist. The wording of the explanation of the vision of Daniel 7:23 states, "The fourth beast *is* a fourth kingdom..." but we are told twice in the explanation of the vision of Daniel 8, "the vision *concerns* the time of the end." The vision *concerns*, not *is* the time of the end. I believe that God was giving Israel a snapshot of events that will transpire in the tribulation when Antiochus Epiphanes came to power, not an exact duplicate so that people would think that the fulfillment was already complete, but a strong foreshadowing. So this vision *is* of Antiochus Epiphanes, but the explanation *concerns*, or applies to, the time of the end.

The four horns definitely picture the Grecian Empire. When Alexander the Great died, he divided his kingdom into four states. These were Macedonia, Syria, Egypt, and Asia Minor. Antiochus Epiphanes came out of the Syrian state, the northern horn.

The things that seem to apply to the antichrist in the explanation are: a) Daniel 8:24 - He will become very strong, *but not by his own power.* The antichrist's power comes from Satan (Revelation 13:2). He will cause *astounding devastation.* Antiochus Epiphanes did great harm to Godly believers, and he did do harm to many cities, but other kings did greater physical damage. The antichrist will cause truly astounding devastation. b) Daniel 8:25 - "When they feel secure, he will destroy many and take his stand against the

Prince of Princes." While Antiochus Epiphanes did stand against God, he didn't knowingly stand against the Prince of Princes, Jesus Christ. The only time I have seen God referred to as the "Prince," it is speaking of Christ (Isaiah 9:6 "Prince of Peace"). God in general is usually referred to as the "King."

We do find, though, that Antiochus Epiphanes died by a sudden illness or physical collapse. I have read that he died of being eaten with worms and ulcers. I have read other reports that simply state that he died suddenly while attempting to squash the Maccabean revolt. However he died, it was not by the hand of man. He was definitely struck down by God. This will be true of the antichrist also. He will be destroyed by God at the end of the tribulation (Revelation 19:20); he will be thrown alive into the lake of fire, along with the false prophet, which is his false John the Baptist. We will study him a little later.

An interesting point to consider is the fact that while the reference to 2,300 was mentioned in the vision, it was never mentioned in the explanation. This is likely because of the mention that this "concerns" the time of the end. The 2,300 days isn't at the time of the end. The explanation of this vision "concerns the *distant* future" (Daniel 8:26). It seems that from Daniel 8:24 on, it is speaking of the antichrist more than Antiochus Epiphanes.

There are those who consider that this is telling us the country of origin of the antichrist. They believe that he will come out of Syria, because that is where Antiochus Epiphanes came from. This seems to me to be a weak argument though. There is probably better information that he will be of Roman descent, and I don't think I would say that he has to be Roman on just this basis either. He could just as well be Iraqi, according to another scripture. We will discuss this in Chapter 1 of volume 2.

Now a point that I do wish to make here is that it says in Daniel 8:25, "When they feel secure, he will destroy many and take his stand against the prince of princes." This is the NIV translation.

King James reads, " … and by peace shall destroy many." The NASB translation reads, "He will destroy many while they are at ease." And the Amplified Bible says, "In their security he will corrupt and destroy many." Young's Literal translation says, "By ease he destroyeth many." I feel that all these translations paint a picture of how he will harm believers. You may want to read about Antiochus Epiphanes. When he came to power, he didn't begin his massacres immediately, and apparently, the antichrist won't either. The parallels are amazing.

There may be more than one way to interpret this. One way is to suggest that by giving the people a sense of security, he can make them forget about God. Another way would be in the name of peace he destroys many. (To keep things peaceful, he must destroy all those religious fanatics). Or He will lull people into a false sense of security, telling them that their freedoms are protected. They are free to worship as they wish, while he builds a database on believers, and then he proclaims himself to be God. He demands worship, making Christianity illegal. Or perhaps he comes to power after a devastating war. He proclaims that we must never have another war like this again! We must do all in our power to prevent such bloodshed. "I have come to bring peace and prosperity, just trust me!" Then Christianity will be considered a destabilizing influence. "After all," he will say, "more wars have been fought in the name of Christ than any other excuse!" (Who hasn't heard that one?) "And, frankly, I am God anyway, and I will no longer tolerate this false teaching that only promotes violence." Christianity is made illegal, in the name of peace and security. Believers are removed from society and quietly killed.

Although this is just conjecture, I tend to lean toward the last view, because it seems to have the most scriptural backing. This is because there is a great revival after the Damascus battle (Isaiah 17:7–8), but we find it quickly forsaken (Isaiah 17:10). In Isaiah 17:7–8, we are told that "men will look to their maker" and "they will not look to" their idols, their false gods. But we find that when Israel finally truly repents, they will not just ignore their idols, they will utterly destroy them, crushing them like chalk (Isaiah 27:9). Then we find in Revelation 6:9–10 some important information about the souls of believers in heaven who have been killed for the testimony of Christ. This is recorded in Revelation during the time of birth pains, as mentioned in Chapter 1 of this book. These died during the time between the battle of Damascus and the beginning of the tribulation, as the antichrist built his power base. "When they feel secure, he will destroy many." And then notice 2 Thessalonians 2:2–4:

> …Not to become easily unsettled or alarmed by some prophecy, report or letter supposed to have come from us, saying that *the day of the Lord* has already come. Don't let anyone deceive you in any way, for *(that day will not come) until the rebellion occurs and the man of lawlessness is revealed,* the man doomed to destruction. He will oppose and will exalt himself over everything that is called God or is worshiped, so that he sets himself up in God's temple, proclaiming himself to be God.

First in this passage, we need to establish what day it's talking about here. There has been much confusion and bickering about this. In the Old Testament, we have the Day of the Lord introduced to us, and it is *always* the tribulation period. I don't feel that we need to redefine it just for this passage. It is always the tribulation period! It is not the rapture (we'll discuss the rapture more thoroughly in Chapter 5 of this book). In this portion, the only time Paul addresses the rapture is in 2 Thessalonians 2:1, where he says, " …and our being gathered to him." The issue here is that the Thessalonian believers were told that they missed the rapture. This isn't an uncommon doubt, even for believers today. "What if I missed it?" Fortunately, it isn't in your hands or mine! But this is what spurred this discussion. Paul here is trying to put their minds at ease (2 Thessalonians 2:2). They were told that the tribulation (Day of the Lord) had started and they were still here. This had them all upset, so Paul realized that he needed to give them a little eschatology 101 (a basic lesson in end-time prophecies). In easing their worries about missing the rapture (our being gathered to Him), he addressed the events that must transpire before the tribulation (the Day of the Lord). He had already spoken to them about this very thing when he was with them face to face (2 Thessalonians 2:5)! He assures them, *in an effort to ease their minds*, that they haven't missed it because *certain things must happen before the Day of the Lord can occur.*

One of these things that must happen is "the rebellion" (2 Thessalonians 2:3). This isn't speaking of a general falling away. This is speaking of a sudden, malignant un-popularization (if I may make a word) of Christianity. Suddenly, it is no longer respectable to go to church. It is no longer respectable to read or carry a Bible. Leading someone to Christ is no longer tolerated. Prayer is not going to be seen in public. If someone is suspected of praying, they will be persecuted, likely put to death! This isn't suggesting that saved people will suddenly become unsaved. It is suggesting that all the hypocrites will stop play-acting and take an active stand against the truth. True believers will have to go underground in their belief. They will likely have to decide if their faith is worth dying for, because it will come to that. Many, out of fear or pressure, will not hear the gospel of truth. Christianity will become unpopular, even dangerous, worldwide! There have always been areas in the world where it is dangerous to be a Christian publicly. It will be unsafe to believe anywhere on earth! What will precipitate this attitude? We only have to look farther in the same verse. The other thing that must occur before the Day of the Lord is "the man of lawlessness is revealed." It is not coincidence that the "falling away" or "rebellion" is listed in the same verse as the mention of the antichrist's (man of lawlessness) revelation to the world. This *must* happen before the tribulation, and as we have seen, it will. This rebellion is what is mentioned in Isaiah 17:10. After the great revival of Isaiah 17:7–8, which occurs immediately *after* the Damascus battle (likely with nuclear weapons), the antichrist will squash it. Then the rebellion will occur.

Now I've mentioned that it is often said that the antichrist will come as a man of peace. And he may, but there is not one scripture that states that the antichrist will ever present himself as a man of peace! The types of the antichrist (types are like pictures, given to illustrate a future person or event) did present themselves initially as seeking peace, and on that basis, the antichrist himself may also, but he doesn't have to! I am aware of Daniel 8:25, which in the King James Version says, "…by peace he will destroy many," as I have already mentioned. This may be referring to the activities of the antichrist, but it may only be speaking about Antiochus Epiphanes. This is one of the times that it is difficult to determine the extent to which we apply this, and to whom. If it is indeed referring to the antichrist, it is the only one that speaks of his being a man of peace. There has been reference to the "white horse" of the Apocalypse in Revelation 6:2 with the rider holding "a bow, and he was given a crown, and he rode out as a conqueror bent on conquest." It has been said that this shows his initial peaceful facade because he had a bow but no arrows. The only thing here is that it doesn't say he was going out peacefully to conquer, just that he had a bow. It doesn't mention peace; it mentions conquering. We have mention of the antichrist's rise in Daniel 7:24, and it doesn't mention any peaceful rise. It says, "…he will subdue three kings." This is three of the ten kings of the ancient Roman Empire, from which the ten kings will arise. The ancient Roman Empire covers a lot of territory, and it never says that it has to encompass all of the ancient Roman Empire. It only has to come out of it. As has been mentioned, all the peoples of Psalm 83 are covered in the ancient

Roman Empire, and they are all represented in the people attacking Israel. They aren't necessarily countries, but they are people with specific leaders (kings, if you will). It also never says "countries" or "kingdoms," just "kings"! We are told that the antichrist will subdue three of them. We have found that Edom's children of Esau and the Philistines will have no survivors, and the children of Moab will have so few survivors that a slave (lower class, uneducated individual) could easily count them (Isaiah 16:14). This could be the three kings subdued by the antichrist. Will I guarantee it? No! It doesn't specifically say that these peoples, or kings, are subdued by the antichrist, but it is quite coincidental that three are mentioned as either utterly destroyed or so few remaining that an uneducated person could count them, and this is during the time that the antichrist will arise! (He will arise during a conflict that will happen before the Magog war, and the only one specifically mentioned as occurring before Magog is the Damascus battle.) This is not set in stone, but it seems likely by the clues given to us in Scripture. The coincidences are too strong to ignore. But please understand that all ten countries suffer differing degrees of damage, and most would be considered severe. Even Israel is considered to be killed (Isaiah 27:7, Isaiah 17:4–6). This doesn't sound too peaceful! The question here, though, is whether he comes to power before the Damascus battle or through it. By Daniel 7:24, it would seem that he gains power through the battle, not before. This is because he "subdues" three kings out of ten. He subdues three kings on his rise to power. He doesn't appear to exist on the world stage until he takes out these three kings. Ten kings are in power; ten peoples attack Israel. Of the ten kings that are in power, three are subdued by this little horn (king) that comes up among them. It makes me wonder if perhaps he is in an influential position behind the scenes. I say this because the rider on the white horse is going out to conquer. By the way, the rider on the white horse is not Christ! This is talking about the time before the tribulation—in fact, the beginning of the times of birth pains. Christ actually stands back at this time. We find the day of the Lord is at the beginning of the tribulation. Also we find that the day of the Lord follows these events (Revelation 6:16–17). If he were going forth at this time, it would be the end of the tribulation. Also, no crown has to be "given" to Christ! He is the rightful king! Some have said that this is speaking of the gospel being spread throughout the earth. This is grasping, quite frankly. You don't spread the gospel with a "bow." It is clear that the rest of the "riders" are speaking of the antichrist, and that is the subject of the first rider as well. It should be obvious that if the first rider is Christ, or His gospel, he is entirely unsuccessful in His conquest due to the record of the next three horsemen.

Another widespread problem we face today is that so many people are trying to identify the antichrist. God tells us that he won't be revealed until the restrainer is removed. This hasn't happened yet (we'll discuss this more thoroughly in Chapter 5 of this book). Until this happens, don't try! You'd be wasting your time! Just take God's word for it that he won't be revealed until the battle of Damascus.

I have already mentioned several "types" of the antichrist, fore-shadowings of the true man of sin. Christ told us in Matthew 24:11 and 23–26 that there would be many false prophets and false Christs in the last days. As I have already said, we have begun seeing them already. Many could be considered to be false Christs and types of the antichrist. Several were prominent during World War II. I have already mentioned Hitler. He was definitely a latter-day type of this evil man. Mussolini also was a modern-day type of the antichrist. Tojo of Japan would be a false prophet. He proclaimed that the Emperor of Japan was God. His goal was to bring the entire world under his sovereignty and worship. Then we have had more recent examples, which I have already discussed. Christ warns that we must not be deceived by these, even when they perform miracles, which the true antichrist will. In fact, it may be that there will be more than just he who will be able to perform miracles. By

Christ's word in Matthew 24:24, it seems that there may be several that will be able, by the power of Satan, to do this.

Perhaps the greatest example of a type of the antichrist is Antiochus Epiphanes, whom we have discussed at length. Another would be Alexander the Great, who would have been an antichrist type to a lesser extent. Even the Pharaohs of Egypt were, to a certain extent, types of the antichrist. Satan has been on the attack for centuries, and it will only grow stronger.

One of the greatest activities of the antichrist during the time of birth pains after his ascension to power is his accumulation of properties. He will amass much land (Daniel 11:39). We are told in Zechariah 11:15–17 that during that time, he will be set up as a "shepherd" to Israel:

> Then the Lord said to me, "Take again the equipment of a foolish shepherd. For I am going to raise up *a shepherd over the land who will not care for the lost, or seek the young, or heal the injured, or feed the healthy, but will eat the meat of the choice sheep, tearing off their hoofs."* Woe to the worthless shepherd, who *deserts the flock! May the sword strike his arm and his right eye! May his arm be completely withered, his right eye totally blinded!*

This is a very interesting passage! We are told that God raises up this "foolish shepherd." Indeed, God is sovereign. He certainly allows this to occur. This is a messenger of Satan. This concept of God raising up an evil leader is the same as God raising up Magog to punish Israel to bring them to repentance. We are told here that the antichrist will not care for Israel (the flock), but will only care for himself. This is in agreement with Daniel 11:39 and 43, where he is seeking worship, personal gain, and treasure. The Zechariah portion gives the impression that he opportunistically uses the people who settle the regions laid barren by the Damascus battle. Most of the settlers are Jewish, because there is such a vast storehouse of

Jews available worldwide to repopulate the area. So it would appear that he comes to power during the Damascus battle, perhaps instigating it as a ruthless grab for power. He overthrows three peoples or nations, takes their land, and subdivides it, if you will, for his own personal gain, making a fortune. By default, he becomes the "shepherd" to Israel. He also annexes Iraq, Syria, and other territories. The Israelites will take over the region and will be in subjection to him. During the Magog battle, he will lose control of Jordan when the Jews reject him. This may possibly occur while he is trying to save his possessions in Iraq (Daniel 11:41–44). At some time during his conquests, he receives a fatal wound to the head. I am not sure when he receives this wound, but I would lean to it being shortly after the Magog battle. This is because of the reference to this wound in Zechariah 11:17. It seems to be mentioned in connection with his abuse of Israel, "the flock." But it also seems to be after the end of hostilities of the Magog battle, because in Daniel 9:27, he is signing a "covenant" (probably a treaty) with the many. If he is being punished for his treatment of God's people, we have found that God doesn't treat them as His people until they repent (Jeremiah 30:14). They truly become God's people when they repent at the height of the Magog battle. Granted, God doesn't refer to Israel as "His people" in this verse, but He treats them as such. A parallel passage to Zechariah 11:17 is the much more well known portion, Revelation 13:3, 14. This refers to a wound to the head. It is referred to as a deadly wound. It has been suggested that he is killed and resurrected to life. That could be the circumstance here, but it really doesn't have to be the case. It could just be he receives a wound that would usually be fatal, but he survives. Anyway, people are amazed by it and by him, worldwide. I personally feel that he is indeed *killed*. This is because we are told that he "… once was, now is not, and will come up out of the *abyss* and go to destruction." This seems to indicate that he was indeed dead. We will cover this in more detail later in this chapter.

Please realize that we are told in Daniel 9:27 that the antichrist signs the covenant with the many, which will signify the beginning of the tribulation, the seventieth week of Daniel. We also have many verses that tell us that the tribulation begins when God intervenes at the height of the Battle of Magog. This is just another item that connects the timing of the Magog battle and the beginning of the tribulation.

This time begins with his signing that pact and is also intimately associated with the Battle of Magog and Israel's repentance at the height of it. There is much conjecture as to the contents of this covenant, from a peace pact to an agreement with nations to worship and pledge their allegiance to him. He is wounded with a "deadly wound," so his recovery will truly be miraculous, which goes along nicely with the lying signs and wonders that the Bible tells us of (Matthew 24:24). It is very possible that he isn't wounded in a battle but in an assassination attempt. It never says that he is wounded in battle, just that he is wounded fatally. It also doesn't say that he was wounded *before* the signing of the covenant. It may be right after.

Now, for just a minute, let's look at the wound as detailed in Scripture. Revelation mentions that he receives a wound to the head. It says it came from a "sword." This would be the result of a weapon of war. Zechariah mentions that his right eye is blinded and his arm is wasted away. It is an interesting fact that when a person receives damage to certain parts of the brain, it renders certain parts of the body crippled. It doesn't say which arm is crippled, but if it is a result of a wound to the head on the right side (right eye is blinded), it would be his left arm that is useless, and Revelation only mentions the head wound. This is because the right half of the brain controls the left half of the body, and vice versa. Whichever arm is crippled is only speculation though, because Scripture doesn't specify.

Okay, back to his activities during the time of birth pains. He is a shepherd to Israel, and Jews are trying to make their fortune in this newly vacated land. We are told in Isaiah 17:10–11 that when the Jews plant their crops, they will fail. Their farming will not be successful, because they have forgotten God (This is the falling away mentioned in 2 Thessalonians 2:3). God will not bless their endeavors at this point. When they reject the antichrist and turn to the true Christ, their crops will be blessed (Joel 2:23–27). In fact, this is the proof to the Jews that they are worshipping the true God. They will see their crops blessed as prophesied. It is interesting to note that it is when they see their crops being blessed, and for that matter, themselves being blessed as well, that they know that God (Christ) is in Israel. Not when they see *Him* face to face, but when they see His blessings! If they knew he was in Israel because they saw Him, this would only be a statement of the obvious. But they know He is there because they see His works!

Ezekiel 34 gives us a message for the antichrist (it is also a message to any "shepherd" of Israel, but will apply especially to the antichrist):

> The word of the Lord came to me: "Son of man, *prophesy against the shepherds of Israel*; prophesy and say to them: 'This is what the Sovereign Lord says: *Woe to the shepherds of Israel who only take care of themselves!* Should not shepherds take care of the flock? You eat the curds, clothe yourselves with the wool and slaughter the choice animals, but *you do not take care of the flock. You have not strengthened the weak or healed the sick or bound up the injured. You have not brought back the strays or searched for the lost. You have ruled them harshly and brutally.* So they were scattered because there was no shepherd, and when they were scattered they became food for all the wild animals. *My sheep wandered over all the mountains and on every high hill. They were scattered over the whole earth,* and no one searched or looked for them. Therefore, you shepherds, hear the word of the Lord: As surely as I live, declares the Sovereign Lord, because my flock lacks a shepherd and so has been plundered and has become food for all the wild animals,

and because my shepherds did not search for my flock but cared for themselves rather than for my flock, therefore, O shepherds, hear the word of the Lord: This is what the Sovereign Lord says: *I am against the shepherds and will hold them accountable for my flock. I will remove them from tending the flock so that the shepherds can no longer feed themselves. I will rescue my flock from their mouths, and it will no longer be food for them. For this is what the Sovereign Lord says: I myself will search for my sheep and look after them.* As a shepherd looks after his scattered flock when he is with them, so will I look after my sheep. *I will rescue them from all the places where they were scattered on a day of clouds and darkness. I will bring them out from the nations and gather them from the countries, and I will bring them into their own land. I will pasture them on the mountains of Israel, in the ravines and in all the settlements in the land.* I will tend them in a good pasture, and the mountain heights of Israel will be their grazing land. There they will lie down in good grazing land, and there they will feed in a rich pasture on the mountains of Israel. I myself will tend my sheep and have them lie down, declares the Sovereign Lord. *I will search for the lost and bring back the strays.* I will bind up the injured and strengthen the weak, but the sleek and the strong I will destroy. I will shepherd the flock with justice. As for you, my flock, this is what the Sovereign Lord says: I will judge between one sheep and another, and between rams and goats. Is it not enough for you to feed on the good pasture? Must you also trample the rest of your pasture with your feet? Is it not enough for you to drink clear water? Must you also muddy the rest with your feet? Must my flock feed on what you have trampled and drink what you have muddied with your feet? Therefore this is what the Sovereign Lord says to them: See, I myself will judge between the fat sheep and the lean sheep. Because you shove with flank and shoulder, butting all the weak sheep with your horns until you have driven them away, I will save my flock, and they will no longer be plundered. I will judge between one sheep and another. *I will place over them one shepherd, my servant David, and he will tend them;*

he will tend them and be their shepherd. I the Lord will be their God, and my servant David will be prince among them. I the Lord have spoken. *I will make a covenant of peace with them and rid the land of wild beasts so that they may live in the desert and sleep in the forests in safety. I will bless them and the places surrounding my hill. I will send down showers in season*; there will be showers of blessing. *The trees of the field will yield their fruit and the ground will yield its crops; the people will be secure in their land. They will know that I am the Lord, when I break the bars of their yoke and rescue them from the hands of those who enslaved them They will no longer be plundered by the nations,* nor will wild animals devour them. They will live in safety, and no one will make them afraid. I will provide for them a land renowned for its crops, and they will no longer be victims of famine in the land or bear the scorn of the nations. Then they will know that I, the Lord their God, am with them and that they, the house of Israel, are my people, declares the Sovereign Lord. You are my sheep, the sheep of my pasture, and I am your God, declares the Sovereign Lord.'"

Ezekiel 34:1–31

This most interesting portion is filled with end-times information. First, we find that this is prophetic in nature. Also, it is not directed only at the antichrist, although it does certainly include him. This theme of a shepherd only taking care of himself is mentioned in Zechariah 11:15–17 as relating directly to the antichrist. In the Zechariah portion, we find that he is feeding on the flock, not caring for them. Ezekiel tells us that these "shepherds" will treat Israel brutally. Again, this applies to many evil leaders of Israel. Then we find that it specifies shepherds at the time of Christ's first advent that led to the Jews scattering around the world. This specifically would include Caiaphas, Herod, and Pontius Pilate. These were the "shepherds" that were leading Israel in the time of Christ in different roles. Caiaphas was the high priest; Herod was the king of the region and appointed the high priest. It was a Herod that had

John the Baptist murdered. And Pontius Pilate was the governor of the area when Christ was crucified. All these were shepherds of Israel at the time of Christ. God tells us that He will hold the "shepherds" accountable. All the shepherds! This does apply to the antichrist. From this point on, it appears to apply mainly to the antichrist. God tells us He will rescue Israel from the mouths of the evil shepherds. He promises to regather them from throughout all the earth (Rosh Hashanah). Then in Ezekiel 34:17–22, God is giving a message to Israel specifically about how He will deal with them in the last days. Then He tells Israel that He will set Christ over them as a shepherd. We are told that Israel will know that He is God when He will "break the bars of the yoke and rescue them…" This is a reference to them turning from the antichrist to the true Christ. Then He will be their God, and they will be His people from then on.

In the next portion, we will look at the best portion dealing with the rise of the antichrist as described by Paul. This is found in 2 Thessalonians 2:1–12:

> *Concerning the coming of our Lord Jesus Christ and our being gathered to him,* we ask you, brothers, not to become easily unsettled or alarmed by some prophecy, report or letter supposed to have come from us, saying that *the day of the Lord has already come.* Don't let anyone deceive you in any way, *for (that day will not come) until the rebellion occurs and the man of lawlessness is revealed,* the man doomed to destruction. He will oppose and will exalt himself over everything that is called God or is worshiped, so that *he sets himself up in God's temple, proclaiming himself to be God.* Don't you remember that when I was with you I used to tell you these things? *And now you know what is holding him back, so that he may be revealed at the proper time. For the secret power of lawlessness is already at work; but the one who now holds it back will continue to do so till he is taken out of the way.* And *then the lawless one will be revealed,* whom the Lord Jesus will overthrow with the breath of his

mouth and destroy by the splendor of his coming. *The coming of the lawless one will be in accordance with the work of Satan displayed in all kinds of counterfeit miracles, signs and wonders, and in every sort of evil that deceives those who are perishing.* They perish because they refused to love the truth and so be saved. *For this reason God sends them a powerful delusion so that they will believe the lie* and so that all will be condemned who have not believed the truth but have delighted in wickedness.

In this portion, we have a lot of important information. First, we find that Paul is addressing the "coming of our Lord Jesus Christ." This can mean more than one thing. We find in the Old Testament prophecies that Israel will know that He is in Israel during the tribulation because of His miracles that he does on behalf of them. Is it speaking of this? No, I doubt it. Could it be His physical return to earth to reign as king? Possibly. But if Paul is keeping the subject in line with the rest of the sentence, that isn't it either, as we will see in Chapter 5 of this book. I believe that this is speaking of what he was talking to them about in 1 Thessalonians 4:16–17: the rapture. This is "our being gathered to him" when He comes for us. At least the "our being gathered to him" is certainly speaking of the rapture. Someone convinced the Thessalonian Christians that the tribulation had arrived and that they had missed the rapture. The "day of the Lord" is a synonym for the tribulation, as we have already found. This upset and confused these believers, because Paul had explained to them the proper order as rendered in 1 Thessalonians 4 and 5. Paul told them that they weren't appointed to wrath, and now they were afraid that they had misunderstood. It may be understandable that they would think they were in the tribulation, because there was great persecution at that time. Christians were being slaughtered for sport! Unfortunately, it will be worse during the tribulation period. It is suggested that the tribulation period is just the tribulation that we as believers endure throughout our life. This would be what the Thessalonian believers were suffering. Indeed, they suffered likely far worse than any of us have endured. But this horrible personal tribulation is not to be compared with the tribulation of the end times. Everyone on earth will endure extreme trouble. During the time leading into the tribulation and through it, over half of the earth's population will die from all nations around the world! It is packed into a time of seven years, when unprecedented disasters will become the norm. This is "the tribulation." Please don't confuse it with the events that we hear every evening on the news that cause us to exclaim, "Oh my, that poor family!"

Paul here is trying to ease their minds by explaining to them that they hadn't missed the rapture, because if they had entered the tribulation period, as they had feared, certain things would have had to have occurred. He bases this on several events that haven't occurred that must happen before the "day of the Lord" could come. First, there will be "the rebellion," and second, in fact hand in hand with the first event, "the man of lawlessness" is revealed. There has been much comment on the apostate condition of the world today, and I believe that this is mentioned in 2 Timothy 3:1–5. This is a general falling away. It was noticed and remarked about even back in the mid-nineteenth century as occurring, and it was thusly predicted that the second coming of Christ must be near on that basis. The falling away or rebellion of 2 Thessalonians 2 is a much more discrete event. It will not be "terrible times"; it will be "the Rebellion," a specific event. This comes from the Greek word *apostasia,* which means *a departure from the faith.* It is not an individual departure, but a departure as a whole. It has been suggested that this is speaking of the rapture, in that believers are raptured from the earth, leaving only the unsaved. This may be a neat way to support pre-tribulation teaching, but it doesn't have support from ancient usage. There are only two places where this is used in Scripture, 2 Thessalonians 2 and Acts 21:21, where Paul is being accused by some that he is causing Jews to forsake Moses's teaching of the Law. This would be to depart from the faith of Moses for the Jew. Since this is the only other usage in the Bible of this word (there are several usages of this word in the verb form in Scripture, which have varying meanings), we must look outside Scripture to find how it was used in that day, and it appears to mean *a forsaking of the faith*. So we must then consider that this isn't speaking of the rapture. Sorry! We do, on the other hand, have a record of an event that appears to align with this occurrence. This is found in Isaiah 17:7–10, as was mentioned earlier in this chapter.

After the Damascus battle, there is a great revival, but it is soon stopped. Let's read this portion.

> *In that day men will look to their Maker and turn their eyes to the Holy One of Israel.* They will not look to the altars, the work of their hands, and they will have no regard for the Asherah poles and the incense altars their fingers have made. *In that day their strong cities, which they left because of the Israelites,* will be like places abandoned to thickets and undergrowth. And all will be desolation. *You have forgotten God your savior; you have not remembered the Rock, your fortress.*
>
> Isaiah 17:7–10

I will end the quote here because the rest is irrelevant to this point. First, we find that it is speaking of the time immediately after the battle of Damascus (Isaiah 17:1–6). There will be a great revival! Then is mentioned the cities abandoned because of the Israelites (in the Damascus battle). Then, just as suddenly as the revival came, the falling away happens! You have forgotten your God, your Rock, *Christ!* How sad! How tragic!

I am convinced that this is what Paul is referring to in 2 Thessalonians 2:3. There is a falling away, and the "man of lawlessness" is revealed. The two seem to go hand in hand. They are mentioned in the same breath; I don't believe that is a coincidence. Then Paul reminds us that the antichrist is doomed to destruction, as is mentioned in several other scriptures (Daniel 7:26, 11:45, Revelation 19:19–20, etc.).

Paul then tells us that the antichrist will oppose God and everything that is worshipped. He doesn't just oppose the true God, but every god, so the true God just gets lost in the mix in the world's eyes. Being he doesn't accept any god, it is a small step to claim that he is god. After all, he has great power (given by Satan), and so he exalts himself above any god and demands worship. Paul then tells us in the clearest language that the antichrist will set himself up in the temple, demanding worship. Why does he set up in the Jews' temple instead of some other religious center? The reason is simple. All other religions accept him as their god; only the Jews, as a body, reject him. This is why the entire world is opposed to Israel (Zechariah 12:3). It is also why the antichrist forces himself on them; he doesn't need to force himself on any other nation. Luke 21:20 is a passage dealing with this in an example of multiple fulfillments. It was partially fulfilled at the destruction of Jerusalem and will be fulfilled again completely when the antichrist forcibly takes the temple. Christ tells us in Matthew 24 and Luke 21 about the type of the antichrist, Antiochus Epiphanes, and tells Israel to watch for it again. (Here Christ is explaining that this will be multiple fulfillment!) We are told by John in Revelation 13 that the false prophet (we will discuss him in greater detail later in this chapter), working with and for the antichrist, will set up an image of the antichrist in the temple, much as Antiochus Epiphanes did with a statue of Zeus before Christ. (Here again we see how the types of the antichrist parallel the actual man.)

The phrase found in 2 Thessalonians 2:6–7 has caused much controversy among students of the Bible. The "restrainer" of these verses is not made entirely clear in this portion. Most consider that it must be the Holy Spirit, and this is logical. God is the only power that is great enough to hold back the attack of Satan. But there is a problem with the ancient Greek dealing with this interpretation.

The possibilities have ranged from the Holy Spirit to the angel Michael to even the antichrist himself or Satan! The antichrist-as-the-restrainer theory is a result of circular reasoning and, upon close inspection, is completely illogical. It would result in the antichrist restraining himself until he takes himself out of the way so he can reveal himself! This isn't exactly a brilliant theory. It would have the result that the antichrist is in ultimate control. I mention it only because it is a theory that is being postulated as a viable interpretation. Please don't be fooled by this kind of study. The possibility of Satan as the restrainer is just as unlikely. It would not be realistic that Satan would restrain his minion, the antichrist, until God's timing was fulfilled. Remember, the tribulation is "the day of the Lord"! Also, the restrainer is limiting Satan, not supporting him. So these views are less than unlikely. So, eliminating these obviously faulty views, let's study some more likely ones.

First, let's consider the view of the Holy Spirit. As I have already said, this isn't unlikely, except that some of the language would seem not to support this, according to some students of the Greek who understand it better than I do. Even they tell me that it isn't impossible, but they feel uncomfortable with it because it isn't proper grammar. Some feel that it is not likely that there would be a change in gender from verse 6 to verse 7 if it were the Holy Spirit. They feel that He would always be referred to in the masculine gender. Others feel that this is entirely proper, being that the word *spirit* (*pneuma*) is referred to as both neuter in its generic form and masculine when referring to the person of the third person of the Godhead. By far, the most popular view is that it is the Holy Spirit. This may not be a good reason though. I never accept a viewpoint just because it is popular. It needs the verification of God's Word.

Second, we'll look at the idea of it being Michael the angel. I personally don't feel that this is likely, because he simply isn't powerful enough. Satan was the leading angel when he was created as Lucifer (Isaiah 14:12–17), and as such, he was a most powerful angel

(Ezekiel 28:14–19), if not *the* most powerful angel. I don't feel comfortable with the notion of God assigning an angel to restrain Satan over a long period of time. I believe God would have to do this with some other agency. Also, as it is recorded in Daniel 10:10–14, the conflict here seems to be quite a contest. Angels aren't omnipotent, and it took three weeks for the message to get through. The record of Michael's battle in Revelation 12:7–17 doesn't refer in any way to restraining the antichrist. It is a battle in heaven between Satan and his angels and Michael and the angels of God. This is where Satan is thrown to the earth for the last three and a half years of the tribulation (when things get really bad!). This is not when the restrainer steps aside; this is when the powers of heaven force Satan out of heaven. The antichrist is already very active and present by this time. Michael is in heaven, not on earth restraining, for the last two thousand years. And there is no scripture that would infer that Michael is the restrainer.

A third view is that the restrainer is the Church, the body of Christ. Perhaps, but not by the power of the people in it, but by the power Jesus Christ indwelling the believers in this church. This is possible. When the church is removed at the rapture, then Jesus Christ is removed from that role as restrainer, and until the second coming, He is not present on earth *physically.*

Another view is that the active agent of restraint is a program set in motion by God himself. This would be the stewardship, or administration (*oikonomia*, from which we get our word *economy*), of grace that Paul mentions in Ephesians 3:2. Or perhaps the whole Mystery that Paul speaks so much about also in Ephesians 3:3, 9, Colossians 1:26–27.

Whatever the agent of restraint actually is might just be irrelevant. The restrainer is ultimately God! Whether it is through His church, the Holy Spirit, Jesus Christ and His church, or a God-instituted program that must run its course before these things can happen, God is still ultimately responsible for the restraint of the antichrist. I realize that the ramifications of this seem to hold special significance to some people, but there is no doctrine that hinges entirely on this issue, regardless of claims.

We will address this again in Chapter 5 of this book.

Second Thessalonians 2:7 also makes an interesting statement, that the "secret power of lawlessness is already at work" but is being restrained. The King James version says that the "mystery of iniquity doth already work." Paul explains his use of the word "mystery" in Ephesians 3:5, 9. It is something that is hidden in God, never before revealed! So following this reasoning, this "secret power of lawlessness" was something new. It was "secret"! The concept of the antichrist (as beast, foolish shepherd, or whatever) was not new to Paul's day. This was mentioned long before Christ. So Paul here was speaking of something else. Perhaps it was Satan's attack on believers saved by grace that Paul was addressing here. This would be the lie that the tribulation had begun, even though certain events that must occur first, hadn't. This could be the beginning of this "mystery" of lawlessness. It could be the program that will ultimately result in people being fooled by the great deceiver, Satan, through the antichrist that the Devil began all the way back in Paul's day. It is interesting to note history. There have been several that would have been good candidates for the antichrist, beginning with Antiochus Epiphanes, long before Christ (types of the antichrist would not be the secret power of lawlessness; it was not a mystery), but after Paul's day, we see that there were several of them. While types of the antichrist are not the "secret" or "mystery," they would feed on this lawlessness. In fact, they will numb the world to the activities of the real antichrist, thus becoming part of the "mystery of iniquity." There came the Gnostic cults of the early church, which tried to pervert the gospel of Christ and even today are causing confusion. (The so called "lost books of the Bible.") There is a long list of books that are claimed to belong to scripture. I will mention only a few of them, such as "the Gospel of Thomas," "the Gospel of Mary," "the Gospel of the Egyptians," "the Gospel of the Truth," and "the Letter of Peter to Phillip." These claim to be gospels, but are in contradiction to God's canon of scripture, and most if not all were written well past the time that these people lived by a group called the "Gnostics." They were a popular cult that flourished mainly between 200 to 400 AD, but there are still some who subscribe to their false teachings. The Dead Sea Scrolls are very popular today, but they were written in part by a group of skeptics that existed around the time of Christ that took the truth and twisted it to their own ends, which is Satan's method of operation. Also there is the "Book of Enoch" and the "Book of Jashur," which has parts actually quoted in scripture, but these books are not scripture because they were corrupted before Christ was born. The parts quoted in scripture are reliable, but the rest should be treated as unreliable. The "Book of Enoch" today is actually used in Satan and or angel worship! If it isn't in the canon of scripture it isn't God's Holy word! This would be part of the "mystery of iniquity." Substituting another gospel other than that which Paul preached in Galatians 1:8, John, in Revelation, speaks of the wrong doctrines creeping into the early churches even while he was alive. This is the secret power of lawlessness, the Mystery of iniquity. This is softening up the world to hear another gospel, which is that the man of sin is god. Especially today (and from the past 200 years), we find cults springing up. These will embrace the antichrist as god when he appears. He will fit their doctrine. The only ones who won't embrace him are true believers. He will be very persuasive.

We find in 2 Thessalonians 2:8 that after the restrainer is removed, the antichrist is revealed. We will not know who he is before the restrainer is removed. When he is revealed, the only ones who will know that he is the antichrist will be true believers. All true believers will know him for what he is (Matthew 24:24). Every unsaved will be taken in by him (Revelation 13:8). When He arises, he will come up through a conflict, most likely the battle of

Damascus (Daniel 7:24). I will not waste my time trying to guess who he is. If you have a likely candidate, he is probably just another mini-antichrist, a false Christ that the true Christ warned us of. We won't know the real one until he comes to power.

In 2 Thessalonians 2:9, we find that he will be working through the power of Satan and will deceive many through great signs and wonders. He will perform miracles!

In 2 Thessalonians 2:10 and 11, we find an interesting statement. God tells us that the unsaved are unsaved because they have rejected the truth. They haven't loved the truth. Christ is the way, *the truth,* and the life. They haven't worshiped Christ. They instead are deceived into believing the antichrist can replace God, but it will only deceive the unsaved. God will not send the lie; that will be the antichrist's activity. God will just allow the lie to be believable. God will not lie. Those who will not trust in Christ will be doomed forever.

So in this portion, we find that the Thessalonian believers were being lied to, that the tribulation had started—not that the rapture had come specifically, but that the tribulation had started and they were still here. By implication, they realized that if the tribulation were here, they had missed the rapture. This upset them! Paul started out his discourse on this subject by first addressing the issue of Christ coming for them in the rapture, "the coming of our Lord Jesus Christ and our being gathered to him." This is the only reference to the rapture that Paul will make in this passage. This shows us that this is what they were primarily concerned with; they didn't want to be left behind. I suppose I can't blame them, since they were told that it came from Paul himself. Paul chides them for being so gullible after he told them how it would be. He tells them to not be so easily alarmed (gullible). Part way through this discourse, he asks, "Don't you remember when I told you this?" He tells them that they shouldn't believe anything that disagrees with what he told them already, even if it comes in a letter from Paul himself! What they are not to believe is that " ... the day of the Lord has already come." Young's Literal translation reads, " ... that the day of Christ hath arrived." This would be the tribulation period (Revelation 6:16–17). They were afraid that the tribulation period was upon them; it was here! Paul cautions them again to not be fooled by false statements (2 Thessalonians 2:3), because "that day" will not come unless certain things happen first. "That day" *does not refer to the rapture!* It refers to the day that they were told was upon them, the day of the Lord, known as the seven years of tribulation. The conditions that have to happen first are that the world will reject Christ and that the antichrist would be revealed, together, so it seems, in the context of this portion.

Then Paul goes even farther in telling them of events that must be met before even the antichrist can be revealed. The one who is restraining the work of Satan in his ultimate plan to bring the antichrist on the scene must be taken out of the way of keeping him down, of holding him back from his evil plans (2 Thessalonians 2:6–7). Only then can the antichrist be revealed. What is this restrainer? We can eliminate some things from the list. First, it isn't the antichrist himself, which would be nonsense. Likewise, it isn't Satan. It certainly isn't any human government (I didn't cover this earlier, but it is a position that some take). Human government will embrace the antichrist with open arms and wet kisses! It has to be some aspect of God; either it is the Holy Spirit himself, the indwelling Holy Spirit in the Church, the body of Christ, the body of Christ church and Christ Himself, or a program that is instituted by God that must be completed before these things can occur. This doesn't leave the Holy Spirit gone from the earth; it just leaves Him not in the role of indwelling believers on this earth. Why would it be important to God to remove His church before these things happen? It is His nature to protect his own! Look at Noah and the flood. He wouldn't send the flood until Noah and his family was safe on the ark. Look at righteous Lot. He wouldn't destroy Sodom and Gomorrah until they were out of town! Look at the children of Israel in Egypt. He protected them from the death angel. He will spare His church from wrath, because it is His nature! Certainly there will be people saved during the birth pains and the Tribulation period, and they will have to face great persecution. God tells us this over and over. But He will rescue all he can before that awful day arrives. Many believers will have to die for their faith, but remember, *all unsaved will die for their lack of faith*!

An interesting portion comes to mind that may shed some light on this issue as to what will keep the antichrist back and what will be taken out of the way. This portion tells us that there is only one thing that *must* occur before there is a substantial change in the way God deals with people. Romans 11:1–32 gives us some great insight into the events of the end time.

> I ask then: *Did God reject his people? By no means! I am an Israelite myself,* a descendant of Abraham, from the tribe of Benjamin. God did not reject his people, whom he foreknew. Don't you know what the Scripture says in the passage about Elijah—how he appealed to God against Israel: "Lord, they have killed your prophets and torn down your altars; I am the only one left, and they are trying to kill me"? And what was God's answer to him? "I have reserved for myself seven thousand who have not bowed the knee to Baal." So too, at the present time there is a remnant chosen by grace. And if by grace, then it is no longer by works; if it were, grace would no longer be grace. What then? What Israel sought so earnestly it did not obtain, but the elect did obtain. The others were hardened, as it is written: "God gave them a spirit of stupor, eyes so that they could not see and ears so that they could not hear, to this very day." And David says: "May their table become a snare and a trap, a stumbling block and a retribution for them. May their eyes be darkened so they cannot see, and their backs be bent forever." Again I ask: *Did they stumble so as to fall beyond recovery? Not at all! Rather, because of their*

transgression, salvation has come to the Gentiles to make Israel envious. But if their transgression means riches for the world, and their loss means riches for the Gentiles, how much greater riches will their fullness bring! *I am talking to you Gentiles. Inasmuch as I am the apostle to the Gentiles,* I make much of my ministry in the hope that I may somehow arouse my own people to envy and save some of them. For if their rejection is the reconciliation of the world, what will their acceptance be but life from the dead? If the part of the dough offered as firstfruits is holy, then the whole batch is holy; if the root is holy, so are the branches. If some of the branches have been broken off, and you, though a wild olive shoot, have been grafted in among the others and now share in the nourishing sap from the olive root, do not boast over those branches. If you do, consider this: You do not support the root, but the root supports you. You will say then, "Branches were broken off so that I could be grafted in." Granted. But they were broken off because of unbelief, and you stand by faith. Do not be arrogant, but be afraid. For if God did not spare the natural branches, he will not spare you either. Consider therefore the kindness and sternness of God: sternness to those who fell, but kindness to you, provided that you continue in his kindness. Otherwise, you also will be cut off. *And if they do not persist in unbelief, they will be grafted in, for God is able to graft them in again.* After all, if you were cut out of an olive tree that is wild by nature, and contrary to nature were grafted into a cultivated olive tree, how much more readily will these, the natural branches, be grafted into their own olive tree! *I do not want you to be ignorant of this mystery, brothers, so that you may not be conceited: Israel has experienced a hardening in part until the full number of the Gentiles has come in. And so all Israel will be saved, as it is written: "The deliverer will come from Zion; he will turn godlessness away from Jacob. And this is my covenant with them when I take away their sins."* As far as the gospel is concerned, they are enemies on your account; but as far as election is concerned, they are loved on account of the patriarchs, for God's gifts and his call are irrevocable.

> Just as you who were at one time disobedient to God have now received mercy as a result of their disobedience, so they too have now become disobedient in order that they too may now receive mercy as a result of God's mercy to you. For God has bound all men over to disobedience so that he may have mercy on them all.

This portion starts out with an interesting question: "Did God reject His people?" to which Paul responds, "By no means!" Now, if this ended there, it could be argued that God is reassuring us that He doesn't reject believers (which, of course, He doesn't). But Paul makes the intention of his question clear: "I am an Israelite myself." So this portion is dealing with a change in God's program that believers were observing at that time. God was dealing primarily with Gentiles. Paul refers to Jews as God's people, and Paul claims that essentially, it hasn't changed; it is just interrupted. But definitely interrupted! Paul also makes an interesting point about God rejecting people. He asks if God rejected His people "whom He foreknew." Paul's point here is, why would God reject someone He calls "His people," in light of His foreknowledge? If God knew someone would inevitably reject Him, why would He call them, "His people" to start with? God does foreknow everything; that is one of God's attributes! But we do find that God has punished them by *most* Jews having their eyes darkened to the truth (Romans 11:7–9). God assured Elijah that He had kept a remnant of Israel believing when Elijah thought he was alone. Indeed, today there are many Jews saved by grace as, in fact, was true in Paul's time. God has kept a group of His people, Israel, saved during this time, despite not dealing with Israel directly, as He had in the past.

Paul goes on to ask in Romans 11:11–12, "Did they stumble as to fall beyond recovery?" Again, the assertion is made, "Not at all!" So to all the substitution theorists, Israel is not beyond hope! In fact, Paul goes on to say that the reason God is dealing with Gentiles primarily is to make Jews jealous. Then Paul goes on to say, essentially, "Fortunate Gentiles!" Because of the sin of Israel rejecting their King, Christ, salvation has come to the Gentiles. But Paul then goes on to ask, "If their sin brought salvation to the (gentile) world, how much more will their "fullness" bring?" (Both NIV and KJV use the word *fullness*. NASB says their *fulfillment*). Young's Literal Translation words it as, "and if the fall of them [is] the riches of the world, and the diminution of them the riches of the nations, how much more the fullness of them?" Actually, I believe this most clearly presents God's meaning here. We find in Exodus 19:5–6: "Now if you obey me and keep my covenant, then out of all nations you will be my treasured possession. Although the whole earth is mine, you will be for me a kingdom of priests and a holy nation."

We find that Israel was supposed to be a kingdom of priests. As a kingdom of priests, they were to dispense faith in the true God to the world. They failed. God said to them, " … If you obey me and keep my covenant." They didn't! The perfect response hasn't happened to this point. Paul is saying here, if Israel's failure has brought salvation to the whole world, think how great it would have been if they had just obeyed in the first place! Think how great it will be when they fulfill their true calling! When they fully obey God and do things His way, imagine how great that will be! Matthew 24 tells us that the gospel of the kingdom will be preached throughout all the earth during the tribulation. At that time, Israel will indeed begin behaving like a "kingdom of priests."

Then in Romans 11:13, we find that Paul is making a claim to a special office. He is the apostle to the Gentiles. This is an interesting claim, and we will study this in greater detail later in this book series. Paul is speaking to Gentiles here. He tells us that he hopes, through his ministry, to arouse envy in some of his fellow Jews to bring them to salvation. Then Paul assures us that their salvation would bring even greater salvation to the world, life from the dead!

Then in Romans 11:16, Paul starts to explain to the Gentiles about being grafted into the main root. He goes on to explain in the verses following that the Gentiles are a "wild olive shoot" and have been grafted in to share the sap from the root (which is God); we, as Gentiles, shouldn't become arrogant and boast over the natural branches. Paul reminds us here that we don't support the root, but the root supports us. We aren't indispensable. Paul tells us that just because the natural branches (Israel) were broken off so we (Gentiles) could be grafted in, not to get cocky about it. They were broken off because of unbelief, and we Gentiles can be broken off too. He tells us to "be afraid." Sobering words! He tells us that if God didn't spare the natural branches, He sure won't spare us either! Paul tells us in Romans 11:22 that we should consider the kindness and sternness of God—kind in that He extended salvation to us but stern to those who fell. Then he tells us that the Gentiles had better continue in faith, or they will be cut off as well. Paul tells us that if Gentiles turn from God, He will graft the Israelites back in, and it will be easier for God to do that than to graft in the wild shoots, the Gentiles.

Then in Romans 11:25–26, we find that Paul refers to "this mystery." We find the word *mystery* appears twenty-two times in the Bible (at least in the King James Version. Sometimes it is translated "secret" in other versions), all in the New Testament. Mark mentions it once, when he tells us that the kingdom of God is a mystery to those who don't believe. Four references are in Revelation, written by John. John refers to *mystery* as things hidden in visions, which need interpretation by God in each case. Paul refers to *mystery* seventeen times. He explains that "this mystery" was something hidden in God, which God revealed to him by special revelation. Paul's "mystery" is unique, in that it seems to announce a special program instituted by God. Throughout his writings, Paul mentions this mystery and gives certain details about it. We will study this "mystery" issue later in this book series also, but there seems to be some relevance to the mystery of Paul and the change of how God deals with man. It seems to involve going from dealing with

Gentiles in general to dealing with Jews again as His chosen people. We find this in these two verses, that when "the full number of Gentiles has come in," the "hardening" of the Jews will end! This will result in *all Israel* being saved! Here we do have a great change in God's program, indeed. Now please understand that God doesn't change. But we do find that God's methods of dealing with man have changed from time to time and will continue to do so. If you claim that God's methods have not changed, then you need to obey the whole Law of Moses! As of about nineteen hundred years ago, that ended, and not just as a result of Christ's death on the cross, as we also will see later. We have already found that at the time of the Magog battle, all the surviving Jews will be saved, without exception. Paul states that fact here again in Romans 11:26–27.

We find in Romans 11:29 that God's gifts are irrevocable. His promises to Abraham are going to be fulfilled just as God promised. Then, in the rest of this portion, Paul mentions again that God is only dealing directly with us because Israel has disobeyed. God will have mercy on all. This is because he offers forgiveness to all.

Now there is an aspect of the "mystery" which is exclusively a "Paulism." This is the Church, the body of Christ. We find six references to this Church, and it is only mentioned in Paul's epistles. This Church, the "body of Christ" is entirely peculiar to Paul's writing, and we have some insight to this right in Romans. Romans 11 speaks of the "mystery" (verse 25), and then he goes on with his explanation of how the Jews will be grafted in again. The last four verses of Romans 11 are Paul reveling in God's wisdom and knowledge. He is worshiping God there. I didn't quote these verses because they are not on the topic we are studying, but Romans 12 picks up the thought again. He begins Romans 12 with "Therefore." When I attended Bible College, I was always instructed to find out what "therefore" was there for. When he begins chapter 12, he is saying, *because of what was in Romans 11, you should do something.* That something that we should do is to live in a way that seeks to be as close to God as possible. Not to be proud of ourselves, but to have faith in Him. This is because everyone who is a believer in this age is a member of Christ's body, (Romans 12:4–5). Let's look at Romans 12:1–8:

> *Therefore*, I urge you, brothers, in view of God's mercy, to offer your bodies as living sacrifices, holy and pleasing to God—this is your spiritual act of worship. Do not conform any longer to the pattern of this world, but be transformed by the renewing of your mind. Then you will be able to test and approve what God's will is—his good, pleasing and perfect will. For by the grace given me I say to every one of you: *Do not think of yourself more highly than you ought, but rather think of yourself with sober judgment,* in accordance with the measure of faith God has given you. Just as each of us has one body with many members, and these members do not all have the same function, *so in Christ we who are many form one body,* and each member belongs to all the others. We have different gifts, according to the grace given us. If a man's gift is prophesying, let him use it in proportion to his faith. If it is serving, let him serve; if it is teaching, let him teach; if it is encouraging, let him encourage; if it is contributing to the needs of others, let him give generously; if it is leadership, let him govern diligently; if it is showing mercy, let him do it cheerfully.

In this portion, we have Paul telling us that because we are grafted into the root by the mercy of God, we need to humble ourselves and not be proud of ourselves. This mystery of God letting us, as Gentiles, directly partake of the sap of the root is revolutionary in Paul's day. But he got it by revelation directly from God (Ephesians 3:2). Paul refers to this Mystery as the administration, or stewardship, of the grace of God. This grafting into the root (which is Christ) makes us members of the body in Christ. This body of Christ Church is only found in the mystery of Paul, given to him in revelation by God. We, the many grafted-in branches, are the many members of the body, grafted into Christ.

From this, we have a logical explanation as to the "what" of the restrainer (neuter gender), which is the Church, the body of Christ. In the Bible, we have the Church referred to in the neuter gender. We also have the "he" restrainer (masculine gender), which would refer to Christ himself. Christ comes to retrieve us when He raptures His church away. This would in no way remove the Holy Spirit from His work on this earth, continuing to convict mankind of sin and saving those who will be saved during this terrible time. Christ comes in the clouds to take His Church (the body of Christ) out of this world. Then this program of the "mystery," which includes the body of Christ Church, will end, the Church, which restrains the antichrist, will be removed (just as God couldn't destroy Sodom and Gomorrah until Lot and his family left), and Christ goes with it (we are His body on this earth).

I realize that isn't simple. Peter even said that it was hard to understand, but it is important not to twist Paul's message (2 Peter 3:15–16).

In the next portion, we will explore a well-known passage that deals with the rise and early years of the antichrist's reign. This is Revelation 6:1–17, and this includes the "four horsemen of the apocalypse":

> I watched as the Lamb opened the first of the seven seals. Then I heard one of the four living creatures say in a voice like thunder, "Come!" I looked, and there before me was a white horse! *Its rider held a bow, and he was given a crown, and he rode out as a conqueror bent on conquest.* When the Lamb opened the second seal, I heard the second living creature say, "Come!" Then another horse came out, a fiery red one. *Its rider was given power to take peace from the earth and to make men slay each other. To him was given a large sword.* When the Lamb opened the third seal, I heard the third living creature

say, "Come!" I looked, and there before me was a black horse! Its rider was holding a pair of scales in his hand. Then I heard what sounded like a voice among the four living creatures, saying, "*A quart of wheat for a day's wages, and three quarts of barley for a day's wages, and do not damage the oil and the wine!*" When the Lamb opened the fourth seal, I heard the voice of the fourth living creature say, "Come!" I looked, and there before me was a pale horse! *Its rider was named Death, and Hades was following close behind him. They were given power over a fourth of the earth to kill by sword, famine and plague, and by the wild beasts of the earth. When he opened the fifth seal, I saw under the altar the souls of those who had been slain because of the word of God and the testimony they had maintained. They called out in a loud voice, "How long, Sovereign Lord, holy and true, until you judge the inhabitants of the earth and avenge our blood?"* Then each of them was given a white robe, and they were told to *wait a little longer,* until the number of their fellow servants and brothers who were to be killed as they had been was completed. I watched as he opened *the sixth seal. There was a great earthquake. The sun turned black* like sackcloth made of goat hair, *the whole moon turned blood red, and the stars in the sky fell to earth,* as late figs drop from a fig tree when shaken by a strong wind. *The sky receded like a scroll, rolling up, and every mountain and island was removed from its place.* Then the kings of the earth, the princes, the generals, the rich, the mighty, and every slave and every free man hid in caves and among the rocks of the mountains. *They called to the mountains and the rocks, "Fall on us and hide us from the face of him who sits on the throne and from the wrath of the Lamb! For the great day of their wrath has come, and who can stand?"*

First in this portion, we find the rider on the white horse. The rider held a bow. I have heard from the time I was a child that this means that he comes peacefully because he doesn't have arrows. This is to make it go with the portion in Daniel that speaks of Antiochus Epiphanes starting out peacefully but then becoming brutal later. This was because they didn't know that it was not speaking of the antichrist. Now I don't believe that it is impossible for him to come on peacefully; types of the antichrist have certainly done so and, as a model of the antichrist, it could be likely. It is just that no scripture that speaks directly of the antichrist says specifically that he comes on peacefully. What gives me reason to pause on this issue is the wording of this verse. He goes out with a bow. It was told to me that he doesn't have arrows. It doesn't say that! It just says that he goes out with a bow. I prefer not to build a case on what *isn't* said, especially when it goes on to say, " … he rode out as a conqueror *bent on conquest.*" If he's bent on conquest, it doesn't sound peaceful. Also, in Daniel 7:24, we are told that when he arises, he will *subdue* three kings. This doesn't sound peaceful. Now I realize that there are modern-day examples of conquering by intimidation, and I guess that is a possibility. Hitler did it before he invaded Poland with Austria and the Sudetenland. But he only did it with the threat of annihilation hanging over their heads. But as I said, there is no scripture speaking expressly of the antichrist that says he comes on peacefully. I believe that the white horse is the antichrist's rise to power and prominence, his subduing of three kings.

Next we find the fiery-red horse and its rider. He is given power to take peace from the earth and make men kill each other. This may lend some strength to the idea that he comes on peacefully, because it is here that he is given power to *take* peace from the earth. But let's look at this portion carefully. He is bent on conquering in the previous portion. He subdues three kings. There are ten kingdoms involved in the attack on Israel. While there is war and three kings are subdued, I don't believe it takes in the whole earth. Revelation 6:4 says he is given power to take peace from the earth. I don't see this leaving out any area. Also, we will find that it isn't the antichrist doing the killing here. He gets men to kill each other. The first one was given a crown. This indicates that he was given a leadership role. In this one, he is given a *large* sword. This is indicative of great war capability. It seems to me that he uses international rivalries to cause strife, which he uses for his own personal gain. Perhaps he sells arms to both sides of a dispute, or maybe he urges both sides to war and takes the land of the losers. Who knows? But we do know that he is ruthless and greedy. This would be likely, but we can't know the specific scenario until it happens. God's Word doesn't tell us.

In the next one, we find a black horse with a rider. The rider carries a set of balances in his hand. Balances were used in ancient times to do day-to-day commerce, the buying and selling of goods, such as food, and we find that this is what this pertains to. We find that food is being sold at a premium—a quart (approximately, it stands for a meal's worth) of wheat for a day's wages or three meal's worth of barely (a lower grade of grain) for a day's wages. Forget rent and a new car. Especially forget gasoline! There is a portion that I believe speaks of this event. It is found in Isaiah 17:11. This portion tells us that because people have forgotten God, God will not bless them, and their crops will fail. When Israel repents and rejects the antichrist, the Jews *know that God is in Israel because their crops are blessed* (Joel 2:23–27). There is no more famine in Israel! I cannot say that the red and black horses come at different times. They may come together but show two entirely different phases of events related to the antichrist, or they may be sequential, following in order. We are told in Isaiah 17 that first, there is the battle of Damascus, followed by a great, worldwide but short-lived revival. Apparently, something squashes it (the antichrist, most likely). Then there is a worldwide famine (this is also found in Matthew 24:7). These events mesh with the Revelation portion well. Even the revival meshes with it, as we will see shortly, although not chronologically. (Certain parts do not come in a particular order but occur throughout the time of the seals.)

But before we look at that, let's look at Revelation 6:7–8. This is the rider of the pale horse. We find that the rider of this horse is named. The other riders aren't named, but this one is. It is Death. Hades (another name for hell) follows close behind. This covers the whole period of birth pains, from beginning to end. It is a general covering of the results of the antichrist's activities. It is not the antichrist specifically, as we are told; it is Death and Hades. Death is a direct result of the activities of the antichrist, and Hades is a result of death without Christ, so this "horse and rider" is a result of the antichrist's evil schemes. Here we find that *one quarter* of the earth's population dies! This seems to be during the whole time of the birth pains, not just limited to a certain part of it, although it will intensify as things progress. Things will steadily get worse. We find that during this time, there are two major battles, Damascus and Magog (Russia and her allies versus Israel), famine, pestilence, perhaps other wars, animal attacks, and if anything was missed, death. As was already mentioned, this goes hand in hand with Matthew 24:4–8.

Now we'll discuss the next seal. (The four horsemen were the first four seals.) This one and those following are not represented by horses. This fifth seal is very interesting. I have found while writing this book series that many of the obscure portions come to life and bring the deepest messages, and this one is no exception. I always have found this seal more or less parenthetical in my understanding of it, but as I studied for this book series, it showed me some things I never considered. First, we find that John sees the souls of those killed for the testimony of Christ. Now we have to ask, "Is this just the ones killed during the birth pains, or is it martyrs killed because of Christ throughout all time from Jesus onward?" This portion gives the answer!

The people who were killed for the testimony of God cried out to God, asking Him, "How long is it going to be before you avenge our blood *on those who live on the earth*?" If they were looking for vengeance for their death (which they were), and they were looking for vengeance on those who were *alive*, it could only be those killed during the birth pains, or at least very near it! I would have to believe that it is speaking of those killed during the birth pains. Now it can and should be asked, "How do you know it isn't those killed during the tribulation?" That is found in the same verse. They are asking how long before God avenges their blood. This very question locates the timing of this event. When the tribulation is poured out upon the earth, *that is God's vengeance poured out on unbelieving* mankind (Ezekiel 38:19, Jeremiah 30:11, 20, 23–24, just to mention a few)! That will be God's vengeance on their murderers. Obviously, when they ask the question, the tribulation hasn't happened yet. The tribulation hasn't truly begun yet. Will it be a terrible time? Certainly! But *it isn't God's wrath being poured out.* It is man's and Satan's wrath. We find that God tells them to wait a little longer, that there are more of their brothers and fellow servants that need to be killed. This has to be fulfilled. We will find God's wrath begins shortly in this chapter of the Bible!

The sixth seal is definitely key in understanding the timing of the seals as birth pains and not tribulation. It is also the beginning of God's vengeance being poured out. Now we find that a great earthquake occurs. The sun is darkened, and the moon looks like blood! The "stars in the sky fell to the earth." The heavens depart like a scroll that is rolled up. *Every mountain and island is moved out of its place*! Oh my! No, I don't want to be there when that happens! Everybody on earth is terrified! They hide and beg the mountains to fall on them. Why? Because they want to be hidden from "him who sits on the throne and the wrath of the Lamb." Then we find this key statement: "For the great day of their wrath has come, and who can stand?" This is the "day of the Lord"! We have already shown where this is recorded elsewhere in this book series, but I will briefly repeat it here. Ezekiel 38:18–22 mentions an "earthquake" that is felt around the world! Every wall will fall to the ground! Wow! Joel 2:30–31 tells us that there will be fire and pillars of smoke, the sun will be darkened, and the moon will look like blood! Sound familiar? Here we find the earthquake that is felt around the earth. As I have already noted, volcanoes are not specifically mentioned in the Bible and are lumped together under the inclusive term "earthquake." Revelation tells us that every mountain and island is moved out of its place. Now please don't confuse this with a later event in the tribulation, when every island is not to be found; that will come later! This one is peculiar because this is the only one where the moon has the appearance of blood. The later one just darkens the moon. This event comes at the end of the Magog battle with God's intervention on Israel's behalf. We find this to be true in the Ezekiel portion with the Joel portion. Joel says that it will come just before the "day of the Lord." Revelation 6:17 has the people crying out, "the great day of their wrath has come." This marks the beginning of the day of the Lord, after the first five seals and in the middle of the sixth seal. Joel tells us that the "earthquake" is just before the day of the Lord. I believe that this is because God intervenes on Israel's behalf. There is great destruction and then, shortly after the battle is over, the antichrist signs the covenant with "the many." This will officially start the tribulation.

There are several explanations as to what exactly occurs with this "earthquake." The sun being darkened is rather self-explanatory, if we assume that it is, or accompanies, a volcano. By the description in Joel, I feel that this is very likely with the "pillars of smoke." The smoke, gasses, and ash that accompany a massive volcano would darken the sun and make the moon change color. This has been observed on a local scale many times.

The "stars" falling to the earth is a little more difficult to explain, but not impossible. There is more than one possibility for this event. One could be that the volcano-earthquake is powerful enough to send rocks into space, where they re-enter the atmosphere like meteorites. This isn't at all unlikely, especially in light of the description of this seismic disturbance. It is believed that such large volcanoes elsewhere in the solar system have sent rocks into space. Another possibility is that this whole event is triggered by a meteor fall, causing the earthquake. In this scenario, a volcano isn't even necessary, because a large enough meteor strike would produce the same effect, spewing smoke and dust into the atmosphere. It too could cause a shock felt around the world, causing mountains to fall. By the way, the word translated *stars* in the Greek means *strewn over the sky*. This description, then, could match either of these scenarios.

The sky receding like a scroll is a description of what it looked like to John. This is likely a description of the clouds of dust and gasses rolling around the world and blocking out the view of the sky. I can't say for certain what the explanation is, but it will look like the sky is being rolled up like a scroll.

Then, as already mentioned, *every mountain and island* is moved out of its place. Wow, that's some earthquake! This agrees closely with Ezekiel 38:19–22.

It is interesting to note that Ezekiel's passage gives us even more insight into these events. Ezekiel mentions torrential rains, hail, and brimstone accompanying this earthquake. It is known that volcanoes produce their own storm systems, involving rain, lightening, and in some cases, hail. These are mentioned here. What else is mentioned is *brimstone*! This is sulfur. Sulfur is very often found in great quantities in volcanic activity. Of course, if a meteor were to strike with enough penetration, it too could liberate sulfur from the molten rock underlying the earth's crust. We need to remember that this event is caused by God's fury. He will bring these events to pass as He sees fit. What I have suggested here is just speculation, but it is speculation that fits the biblical description. Please note that the Bible says that God sends an earthquake. This is a seismic disturbance. This can involve either volcanism or meteor strikes. Either fits the biblical description, and since God does tell us that it is a worldwide seismic event, there are certain natural things that accompany such an occurrence. These things are aptly described in the scriptures, so my speculation is not out of line.

Then we find that the people of the earth beg the mountains to fall on them because they know that this is the wrath of Christ and that the day of the Lord is come. This is an interesting comment. It shows that they *know* who God is. They aren't unbelievers, as such, but remember what James said: "You believe there is one God. Good! Even the demons believe that—and shudder" (James 2:19). They believe in God but don't have faith in God. In fact, they are in open rebellion against Him! This sounds familiar. Remember 2 Thessalonians 2:3? It tells us that there will be a falling away. This is also translated as *the rebellion*. These people are in rebellion against God! They have swallowed the lie (2 Thessalonians 2:10–12), whatever it is. This isn't denying God's existence though; it's rebellion!

The next portion is one of the classic passages dealing with the antichrist. It is Revelation 13. This deals with his rise, his reign, and certain details of his activities.

> *And the dragon stood on the shore of the sea. And I saw a beast coming out of the sea. He had ten horns and seven heads, with ten crowns on his horns, and on each head a blasphemous name.* The beast I saw resembled a leopard, but had feet like those of a bear and a mouth like that of a lion. The dragon gave the beast his power and his throne and great authority. *One of the heads of the beast seemed to have had a fatal wound, but the fatal wound had been healed. The whole world was astonished and followed the beast. Men worshiped the dragon because he had given authority to the beast, and they also worshiped the beast and asked, "Who is like the beast? Who can make war against him?"* The beast was given a mouth to utter proud words and blasphemies and to exercise his *authority for forty-two months.* He opened his mouth to blaspheme God, and to slander his name and his dwelling place and those who live in heaven. *He was given power to make war against the saints and to conquer*

them. And he was given authority over every tribe, people, language and nation. All inhabitants of the earth will worship the beast—all whose names have not been written in the book of life belonging to the Lamb that was slain from the creation of the world. He who has an ear, let him hear. If anyone is to go into captivity, into captivity he will go. If anyone is to be killed with the sword, with the sword he will be killed. *This calls for patient endurance and faithfulness on the part of the saints. Then I saw another beast, coming out of the earth. He had two horns like a lamb, but he spoke like a dragon. He exercised all the authority of the first beast on his behalf, and made the earth and its inhabitants worship the first beast, whose fatal wound had been healed. And he performed great and miraculous signs, even causing fire to come down from heaven to earth in full view of men. Because of the signs he was given power to do on behalf of the first beast, he deceived the inhabitants of the earth. He ordered them to set up an image in honor of the beast who was wounded by the sword and yet lived. He was given power to give breath to the image of the first beast, so that it could speak and cause all who refused to worship the image to be killed. He also forced everyone, small and great, rich and poor, free and slave, to receive a mark on his right hand or on his forehead, so that no one could buy or sell unless he had the mark, which is the name of the beast or the number of his name.* This calls for wisdom. If anyone has insight, let him calculate the number of the beast, for it is man's number. *His number is 666.*

Revelation 13:1–18

In this portion, we find the "beast" rising out of the sea. The "dragon" was on shore waiting for him. The King James Version doesn't mention the dragon on shore, but NIV and NASB do. It appears that the "beast" is more than just the antichrist—but includes him. It seems that this beast is the devil's attempt to destroy the plans of God, past, present, and future. The antichrist is specifically the head with the fatal wound. It would seem that the antichrist is the culmination of Satan's plans for world ownership. He appears to embody all the power that Satan has used to overthrow God throughout the ages. We will also find that the antichrist embodies all the aspects of Satan's attacks on God. The antichrist is the wounded head, and he is also the beast himself. Fortunately, we are assured frequently in Scripture that this is doomed to failure. Now, as we study this, brace yourself; this is going to be very deep. (Frankly, I wanted to chicken out at this point!)

In Revelation 17:7–11, we find the interpretation of this beast and its various components. Now realize that the Revelation 13 discourse is from the aspect of the antichrist already in power during the tribulation; the tribulation is in progress, by interpretation. The explanation as found in Revelation 17 is based in John's day. I will try to show this as we go along.

> Then the angel said to me: "Why are you astonished? I will explain to you the mystery of the woman and of the beast she rides, which has seven heads and ten horns. The beast, which you saw, once was, now is not, and will come up out of the abyss and go to destruction. The inhabitants of the earth whose names have not been written in the book of life from the creation of the world will be astonished when they see the beast, because he once was now is not, and yet will come. This calls for a mind with wisdom. The seven heads are seven hills on which the woman sits. They are also seven kings. Five have fallen, one is, the other has not yet come; but when he does come, he must remain a little while. The beast who once was, and now is not, is an eighth king. He belongs to the seven and is going to his destruction."
>
> Revelation 17:7–11

First we will discuss the seven heads. The seven heads represent two things. First, they are seven hills, upon which a great city sits. We will study this aspect in greater detail later, because it doesn't directly deal with the antichrist as it applies to this part of the study. The other aspect deals with the antichrist specifically. The seven heads are also seven kings. In John's day, we find that five of the kings (heads) have fallen, one is, and the other (the antichrist) is not yet come. Now, as the text says, the beast (antichrist) is an eighth king and belongs to the seven.

This is very difficult to understand. It appears that the seven kings are seven kingdoms that have tried, or will try, for world domination. The heads (kings) representing kingdoms that have attempted world domination seem to be consistent with Daniel's visions, but Daniel didn't include this many. Daniel mentioned only four kings up to John's time: Babylon, Medo-Persian, Greece, and Rome. This may be because Daniel was beginning with the kingdom of the time and was not concerned with the one that was already past, which may be Egypt. There are those who also offer Assyria as a candidate. Assyria was overthrown by Babylon. Egypt was not interested in world domination, but they were interested in keeping Israel from becoming a nation, and that is sufficient in God's eyes to put them on the list of seven. Assyria, on the other hand, was violent. It was interested in world domination. I believe Assyria to be a great candidate for one of the kings John saw as heads on the beast. Assyria was the nation (capital, Nineveh) that was in power in Jonah's day. They were so violent that Jonah wanted them all dead. In fact, Jonah wanted them to not go to heaven! That's why he went the other way on the ship. He knew God would forgive them, and he wanted no part of it! That would give us Egypt, Assyria, Babylonia, Medo-Persia, Greece, and Rome. These all cover the same basic area, and they all were bent on domination of Israel. There have been several others since that time, but they haven't been as successful as the last one will be. Germany in World War II was bent on destroying Jews. There were others who also were intent on destroying Jews. God never let any of them be successful, but He still allowed them to persecute the Jews because of their rejection of the true Messiah. The kingdom of the antichrist will again try to destroy the Jews, but at that time, God will be directly protecting them. He will only be bent on their destruction because Israel will be the only country that will not worship him. The world may think that Israel rejected their Messiah again and will turn against them. Or the world may just think that Israel was right in the first place, seeing that they are in rebellion against God. The antichrist will be the seventh king, and he will embody all of them. He will be the fulfillment of all of the devil's schemes from time past.

Some people relate the ten kings of Daniel 7 to this portion in Revelation 17. They say that since he overthrows three of the ten, this makes him the eighth. This would make sense until you examine it. The ten kings were all contemporaries of each other. The seven kings of Revelation 17 (which are the seven heads of Revelation 13, lest we forget) were one after the other, not contemporaries. The ten kings of Daniel were at the rise of the antichrist. Five of the seven kings of Revelation were before the time of John.

The thing that is most confusing about this is the statement, "He once was, now is not, and yet will come." With the statement, "The beast who once was, and now is not, is an eighth king. He belongs to the seven and is going to destruction." How could he be one of seven and be the eighth? I believe that the answer is in Scripture. It isn't plainly visible, but it does seem to be there. When you look at the passage in Revelation 13:3, you find that the world was astonished and followed the beast when he received the fatal wound and was healed. In Revelation 17:8, the world was astonished when they see the beast, *because he once was, now is not, and yet will come*! This is speaking of his receiving the fatal wound!

If you look at Jeremiah 30:8, it is speaking of the time of the Battle of Magog, when Israel turns to Christ. In that day, the Lord says He will "Break the yoke off their necks and will tear off their bonds; no longer will foreigners enslave them." The seventh head, the king that is not yet, will come, and will enslave Israel. This is what Egypt did to Israel; they were enslaved by Egypt. The antichrist will enslave Israel. At the Battle of Magog, they will reject the antichrist—perhaps they will be the ones delivering the fatal wound! That would be conjecture, but he will receive a fatal wound. I am beginning to believe that the fatal wound will come immediately *after* he signs the covenant with "the many." This will set in motion the seven years of tribulation, but the antichrist will be in power for forty-two months—three and a half years. This is the *last three and a half years of the tribulation.* During the time that he is first king, during the birth pains, he enslaves them. When he comes back as the eighth king, he desires to destroy them because they have rejected him (and perhaps assassinated him). This way, he is definitely of the seven, he was, is not, and will be again. He would be off the scene for the first half of the tribulation, but he will come back. There really is no mention of him during the first half of the tribulation except of his signing of the covenant. If indeed the wound is fatal, as I said, it is a miracle for him to be resurrected. Indeed, the world would wonder after him. The resurrection is flawed though. He is blind in one eye (the right one) and loses the use of an arm (Zechariah 11:15–17).

For some time while preparing this book series, I concluded that Satan actually raised the antichrist from the dead, from the abyss (Revelation 17:8, and 11). This bothered me, but it seemed that there was no alternative. Then, finally, God gave me the correct understanding! There are some very important reasons why this couldn't be.

As you recall from Revelation 13:3–4, the antichrist receives a fatal wound to the head but is healed. Then the world wonders after him and worships him. We find also in Revelation 17:8 that after he comes up out of the abyss, the world will be astounded. The unsaved world will believe that Satan has the power to *raise the dead!* The problem with this view is that if Satan can indeed raise the dead, then Satan also can have victory over death and the abyss. If that were possible, there would be no eternal punishment for sin.

Satan could actually get people out of it. Satan is betting on people believing this, and indeed, most people will believe it (Revelation 13:3–4, and Revelation 17:8)!

Now you may rightfully ask, "If Satan doesn't do it, then who does it?" The answer is found in 2 Thessalonians 2:9–12:

> The coming of the lawless one will be in accordance with the work of Satan displayed in all kinds of counterfeit miracles, signs and wonders, and in every sort of evil that deceives those who are perishing. They perish because they refuse to love the truth and so be saved. For this reason God sends them a powerful delusion so that they will believe the lie and so that all will be condemned who have not believed the truth but have delighted in wickedness.

God sends them a "powerful delusion." Does this mean that God lies? No, of course not! God cannot lie! Titus 1:2: "A faith and knowledge resting on the hope of eternal life, *which God, who does not lie*, promised before the beginning of time."

So we find that God raises the antichrist from the abyss. It never says that Satan raises him. It does say that God sends a powerful delusion. Satan claims the power to raise the dead when God is the one who, in fact, raised him. If God didn't raise him, the events of Revelation wouldn't come to pass. It isn't a lie, but Satan makes a lie and uses this event to delude the whole world into believing the lie. That lie is that Satan is worthy to be worshipped and is as powerful as God, that Satan can protect humanity from the eternal wrath of God!

We are told that this is a "powerful delusion." Indeed it will be! Satan's man, who was killed, is again walking the Earth! Christ himself tells us in Matthew 24:24–25: "For false Christs and false prophets will appear and perform great signs and miracles to deceive even the elect—if that were possible. See, I have told you ahead of time."

This delusion is powerful enough that the *very elect would be deceived if that were possible.* Thankfully, this isn't possible! Also thankfully, He told us ahead of time!

There are some very popular views that the antichrist is not a person, but a system, either a religious system or a political system (or both). To claim this, you have to ignore many scriptures. Daniel 11:36–45, Zechariah 11:15–17, 2 Thessalonians 2:3–11, especially verse 4, and much of Revelation, just to name a very few.

Okay, back to Revelation 13: We have discussed the seven heads, now we will go back to the ten horns. Right off the bat, I'm going to say these ten horns aren't the same ten horns that Daniel saw! This set of ten horns is working in cooperation with the antichrist, and he doesn't subdue any of them. They receive power from the antichrist (Revelation 17:12–18). We will discuss this more later.

Now we find that the beast is likened to a leopard, a bear, and a lion. We find this also in Daniel 7:4–6. These are a reference to the Babylonian empire, the Medo-Persian Empire, and the Greek empire. This is represented by three of the five heads that have fallen of Revelation 17:10. This is to relate the beast to the Daniel portion.

Then we find that this beast is empowered by "the dragon." This is none other than Satan himself.

Now in Revelation 13:3, we get to the fatal wound, which we already discussed. This is where he comes back as the eighth king and the entire world is amazed by him—so amazed that the whole world worships him (with the exception of Israel and any believers in the true God, Jesus Christ).

We find in Revelation 13:4 that men also worship Satan, who gives power to the antichrist, and they ask, "Who can make war with him?" My guess is that he takes credit for stopping Russia in the Battle of Magog, but this is conjecture. The reason that I say this is because he is fighting against Russia and Ethiopia and the others in the Battle of Magog as told in Daniel 11:36–45. Seeing he is set against them at that point, when God intervenes on behalf of Israel, I don't think it is too much of a stretch to believe that he would take credit for it. Also, three and a half years after he is killed, he is again walking the earth, and Satan will likely take credit for that as well.

We find in Revelation 13:5 and 6 that he blasphemes God and is given power for forty-two months, as I have already mentioned. This is after he has had power before the tribulation for an unspecified length of time (Zechariah 11:15–17, Revelation 6, Daniel 7, etc.). The forty-two months is his stint as the *eighth* king. The unspecified rule is his stint as the seventh king.

In Revelation 13:7, we find a disturbing portion. We find that he is given power to make war with the saints (living believers) and to conquer them! This was mentioned first in Daniel 7:21, where it says about the same thing! We do find in Revelation 15:2 that the ultimate victory goes to the believers and Christ. But it will seem that he has destroyed all believers. We find that Israel is protected in the wilderness from him (we will discuss this in greater detail in chapter 3 of volume 2). We are told in Daniel 7:21–22 that he will wage "war against the saints, defeating them until the ancient of days came and pronounced judgment in favor of the saints of the most high ... " So he will be winning the war against true believers on earth during the tribulation until God intervenes! Praise the Lord for his divine intervention! The kingdom on earth is set up after that. It seems that it is just a matter of time before all believers are killed, but God interrupts the antichrist's evil plans. This seals his doom.

We are told in Revelation 13:8 that everyone on earth who is not saved will worship the antichrist. Then we are told in Revelation 13:9 and 10 to listen closely! If anyone is to go into captivity, he will go into captivity, and if anyone is to die, he will die. This is not going to be good, but stick it out!

Then we find another beast coming on the scene. There has been much confusion about these two "beasts." I probably should have mentioned it sooner, but some believe that the first "beast" is the false prophet. This cannot be so, as I will explain. It is the second beast that is the false prophet; the first beast is the antichrist. This is because the second beast directs worship to the first beast. This would be the role of a false prophet; to cause someone to worship a false god, just as the role of a true prophet would be to direct worship to God.

We are told that he had two horns like a lamb, but spoke like a dragon. This indicates that he is essentially a wolf in sheep's clothing! He looks Godly, but speaks the things of the Devil. I believe that it is much easier to identify the false prophet than it is the antichrist. We are told that the antichrist's identity will be hidden in 2 Thessalonians 2, but the Bible never claims that the identity of the false prophet is hidden. He looks like the lamb, but speaks the words of Satan. We are also told in Revelation 13:12 that he has all the authority of the first beast and he causes the world to worship the first beast (whose wound was healed).

I know that there are many people who at first will be offended by this, but please bear with me. To identify him, let's go to Revelation 17.

Let's start with Revelation 17:1, which introduces the theme of the chapter and the one following. This is "the punishment of the great prostitute, who sits on many waters." We are told in Revelation 17:2 that the "kings of the earth committed adultery and the inhabitants of the earth were intoxicated with the wine of her adulteries." This shows that this "prostitute" has worldwide influence. We find in Revelation 17:3 that this woman sits on the beast. There is a description of this prostitute. She is dressed to the nines—fine clothes, jewelry, and a golden cup full of her adulteries. She was drunk with the blood of the saints. The false prophet is likely the representative of this prostitute. He is probably her leader. I say this because it appears that the antichrist seeks legitimacy from the prostitute, and the false prophet is in the business of giving the antichrist legitimacy. We already discussed the beast in this portion. The beast has seven heads. We find that the seven heads represent two things; first they represent seven hills that the woman sits on. Secondly, as we have already found, they represent seven kings. Now we will discuss the hills. Then the story of the prostitute carries on again in Revelation 17:15, following. The waters are the people of the earth. Then the woman is the great city that rules over the kings of the earth. I have heard for some time that this is speaking of Rome. This is inescapable. Rome was then and still is known as the "city of seven hills." Now please bear with me. I am not condemning anyone today. During the tribulation period, though, it is another story. How does Rome influence the kings of the earth today? In fact, how does it influence everyone on earth? This is only through the Roman Catholic Church. I do not claim that the Roman Catholic Church is the great prostitute—yet. Not today. But something will happen. I believe that there are many truly saved people in this organization—today—people who claim that only through Christ's death on the cross and His resurrection can we be saved, and they trust in that. I have already alluded to the rapture. In this event, *all* true believers will be snatched away from this earth. What will be left in our churches? Just the Pharisees, the hypocrites, the ones who pretend to be saved. There will be pretend Christians left from every denomination, Catholic and protestant. It is just that the Roman Catholic Church is the largest organization and, as such, will seem to speak for all Christendom. I recently heard a cardinal speak about a prophesied "antipope." *He* called him an "antipope." This can happen, because believers are gone. When people begin turning to Christ again, it will not be through organized religion. It will mostly be underground, especially after the "falling away." This "antipope" will likely be the false prophet. The reason I feel that the Pope of the tribulation is the false prophet is because the great city that sits on seven hills rides on the beast's back. The reason that it is called a "prostitute" is because it has left it's intended (Christ) for personal gain (the favor of the antichrist). It no longer serves God in any way. It says that this great prostitute is "drunk with the blood of saints." This is because it will be instrumental in the betrayal and death of true believers (Revelation 6:9–11, 13:7).

We find in Revelation 13:13–14 that this false prophet will do miracles on behalf of the antichrist to deceive the inhabitants of the earth. He will erect an image of the antichrist (in the temple, Daniel 9:27, 2 Thessalonians 2:4). He will be able to cause the image to come to life (Revelation 13:15), and everyone will worship this image. He (the false prophet) will cause everyone to receive a mark on their forehead or the back of their hand, and without this, they will not be able to buy or sell. It will be a "security device" of some sort. It will be either the name of the antichrist (this is who the false prophet directs worship to) or the number of his name, which is 666. The King James Version also says "his mark." This doesn't seem to be in the oldest manuscripts, so I personally doubt this will be included, but it may be. There is much conjecture as to the identity of this "mark." Some believe that it will be a tattoo; some that it will be a "bar code"; and some that it will be a microchip. The Bible doesn't say! It could be anything! The only thing to be sure of though, is that true believers of the time will know it when they see it. No one will take it accidentally!

While we are on the subject of the antichrist and Rome, there are even more scriptures that go with this. In Daniel 2, King Nebuchadnezzar dreamed of a tremendous statue with a head of gold, chest and arms of silver, belly and thighs of bronze, legs of iron, and feet partly of iron and partly of baked clay. Daniel explains the vision as being of four world empires. The first was Babylon, Nebuchadnezzar's kingdom, next was the Medo-Persian Empire, third was Greece, and fourth was Rome. The last three of these were future to Daniel at the time of the dream. The Medo-Persian Empire came on while Daniel was still alive to witness it. The last empire mentioned was the Roman Empire. It extended to the feet, which were iron mixed with clay. This showed a mixed empire, loosely held together, extending into the end times. Much has been said about the "ten toes." Daniel doesn't mention "ten" toes, so the number of toes is not significant. (The number ten is significant with Daniel's later vision of the beast with ten horns.) This iron and clay is most likely the Roman catholic church of Revelation 17! It is this church (and all organized Christendom) with all believers removed. This also may explain Daniel 9:26, which says, "…The people of the ruler to come will destroy the city and the sanctuary…" Many have identified the antichrist as "Roman" because of this passage, when it may be that he is merely the leader of the apostate Roman Catholic Church. This may be how he is of the people who destroyed the temple and Jerusalem. Romans destroyed these, the city, and the temple. He will be leading the latter-day Romans. As was mentioned, the Roman Catholic Church will ride the antichrist until he kills it.

Another note on Revelation 17: the antichrist will hate the "prostitute," even though he is partnered with it. This is probably because he doesn't want to share the glory with anyone, especially a church. In a twist of the plot, he will have the prostitute church destroyed when he is through with it. We will study this in greater detail in chapter 3 of volume 2.

In the next portion, we will briefly cover the "abomination that causes desolation" mentioned by Christ. The primary portion dealing with this is Matthew 24:15–20. Other scriptures covering this are Mark 13:14–17 and Luke 21:20–24.

> So when you see standing in the holy place "the abomination that causes desolation," spoken of through the prophet Daniel—let the reader understand—then let those who are in Judea flee to the

mountains. Let no one on the roof of his house go down to take anything out of the house. Let no one in the field go back to get his cloak. How dreadful it will be in those days for pregnant women and nursing mothers! Pray that your flight will not take place in winter or on the Sabbath.

Matthew 24:15–20

Here we find Jesus Christ telling His disciples about the time in the tribulation when the antichrist will have his image put up in the Temple. We mentioned this while going over Revelation 13, as well as other places, so I will not belabor the point here. The antichrist will commit this desecration of the Temple when he comes to power as the eighth king, the beast of Revelation 13 and 17. Daniel speaks of this in Daniel 9:27.

> He will confirm a covenant with many for one "seven." *In the middle of the"seven" he will put an end to sacrifice and offering. And on a wing of the temple he will set up an abomination that causes desolation,* until the end that is decreed is poured out on him.

Daniel 9:27

Here we have the "abomination that causes desolation" that Christ mentioned. The antichrist signs the covenant and then, three and a half years later, the image is set up in the temple. This ushers in the last half of the tribulation, known as "the Great Tribulation." Much is said in Scripture about the last three and a half years of the tribulation. Much less is said of the first half.

The Mark 13:14–17 passage is basically a restatement of Matthew 24:15–20, but Luke 21:20–24 will give us some more interesting details on this subject.

> *When you see Jerusalem being surrounded by armies, you will know that its desolation is near.* Then let those who are in Judea flee to the mountains, let those in the city get out,

and let those in the country not enter the city. *For this is the time of punishment in fulfillment of all that has been written.* How dreadful it will be in those days for pregnant women and nursing mothers! *There will be great distress in the land and wrath against this people.* They will fall by the sword and will be taken as prisoners to all the nations. Jerusalem will be trampled on by the Gentiles until the times of the Gentiles are fulfilled.

It is said that this was fulfilled in 70 AD with the destruction of Jerusalem. It was only *partially* fulfilled. Definitely, armies surrounded Jerusalem when it was destroyed. This is so Jews will recognize it when it happens again. It is obvious that this rendition is speaking of the same message as Matthew 24 and Mark 13. These are both clearly speaking of end-times matters. Also, this portion tells us, "For this is the time of punishment in fulfillment of all that has been written." All end time wraths that have been prophesied throughout the Old Testament are the "Day of the Lord." This is the time of tribulation. This theme is reinforced in Luke 21:23, where it says, "There will be great distress in the land and wrath against this people." The great wrath is the tribulation (Joel 2:11, 31, Zephaniah 1:14, Malachi 4:5). Also, the time of the Gentiles is mentioned in Revelation 11:2. When the tribulation is over, the time of the Gentiles is over. What this portion is telling us specifically is that the antichrist will take the temple by force, just as the Romans took it by force when they destroyed Jerusalem.

It is in 1 John and only in 1 John that we find the term *antichrist.* As such, I need to go over the scripture here: "Dear children, this is the last hour; and as *you have heard that the antichrist is coming, even now many antichrists have come.* This is how we know it is the last hour" (1 John 2:18).

This short portion gives the title of "antichrist." It also gives us some other important information. First, we see that there is a specific "antichrist." John refers to *the* antichrist. Then he goes on to say that there are many antichrists. So there are two types of antichrists, the one and only antichrist and the *types* of antichrist. We have discussed these throughout this book series. John goes on in 1 John 2:22 to tell us a trait of the antichrist, and that is that he denies Jesus is the Christ. The antichrist definitely will claim that he is the Christ, the Messiah, or perhaps more likely, he will unseat the true Christ. In doing so, he must deny the true Christ.

Now we come to the demise of the antichrist. We are assured throughout Scripture that he will not ultimately succeed. This is found in Revelation 19:20 and 20:10, as well as many others. We are also told in 2 Thessalonians 2:8 that he will be destroyed by the spirit of His (Christ's) mouth and the brightness of His coming. In Daniel 11:45, we are told that he will come to his end without help.

We find in Revelation 19:20 that the beast and the false prophet will both be thrown alive into the lake of fire. Here they will exist for all eternity. This is the reward for their selfish ambition and deception, not only of the world, but also of themselves. Then in Revelation 20:10, we find that the devil joins them in the lake of fire after a thousand years. Then all unbelievers will join them. How sad! How hopeless! There is no escape and no hope. Dear reader, please don't be numbered among this group.

Now we will recap this chapter. We started with an examination of the names of Christ as found in the Old Testament. These tell us much of about His character and His deity. We find that he is clearly called God in the Old Testament prophecies of him. We also discussed the names of the antichrist all through the Bible. It is obvious that he overestimates his own importance and power. He is the "little horn," the "beast," "abomination," "foolish shepherd," and "the man doomed to destruction," among others.

Then we looked into Christ's prophecy of him. First we find that there will be many who will come in Christ's name, masquerading as Christ, and we are told that we must not be deceived by them. Christ mentions Daniel's prophecy of the abomination that causes desolation. We found that this was originally fulfilled by Antiochus Epiphanes, but that this is just a snapshot of things to come in the end time. This, we found, will be fulfilled finally by the antichrist as told to us by Paul in 2 Thessalonians 2:4. We are told that in the last times, there will be a time of military upheavals, as well as geological disturbances. We are seeing these things begin now, but it will get much worse. There will also be famines and disease. We found that during this time, there will be a great revival, but it will be short lived. The antichrist will snuff it out (along with most believers). People will be in open rebellion against God. When they see the things of the "apocalypse" begin, they will know what it is, but they still will not turn to Christ. We find that there will be many that will turn from the faith and will betray each other. This is speaking of the time during the tribulation, because the Jews are said to be hated because of Christ's name. They will not be hated because of Christ before the tribulation, because it is at the beginning of the tribulation that they, as a nation, turn to Christ. We find that before that, God treats them as an enemy. People will betray each other for their faith in Christ, not only during the tribulation, but also during the time of "birth pains." We also found that the Jews will not be fooled by the antichrist; they will reject him (perhaps they will assassinate him). We found that the rest of the world will accept the antichrist and will have no sympathy for Israel, because they have forsaken the god of the world. The world will think that they are rejecting the god that is true. We found that when Israel turns to Christ, they will all believe. All the Jews who survive the Battle of Magog will be saved!

We found that the "gospel of the kingdom" will be preached throughout the entire earth despite the antichrist's attempts to stifle it. This gospel of the kingdom is not the same as the gospel we preach now. It is similar, in that to be saved from our sins we still need to trust in what Christ did on the cross, but the difference is to stand firm for Christ because His return is near, in our lifetime if we survive the tribulation and the murderous plans of the antichrist, and we will see Him soon as king. He will set up His prophesied kingdom on this earth within just a very few years. We learned that the antichrist will be empowered by Satan to perform great miracles that will deceive many. We learned that it is impossible for true believers to be fooled by the antichrist.

We learned how the antichrist will come to power. There will be ten kings (leaders of peoples) who will attack Israel. Most of these are listed in Psalm 83. This is likely at the battle of Damascus. He will subdue three kings, and this will be his rise to power. The three kings that he will subdue are probably southern Jordan, central Jordan, and the Palestinians. I don't know that we can be perfectly sure of this until it happens. Much land will be desolated, and he will move in and take it over. He will be very greedy and will dole out land for a price or as a reward for people's worship. Jews from all over the world will be able to move in to the area and set up house-keeping, and he will be the "shepherd" over the land. Essentially, Israel will be subservient to him. They will have to answer to his wishes. At that time, Israel will accept him. He will use them for his own gain and will "eat them up." Many lands will be annexed, making Israel very large. Israel will control Iraq (and their oil fields). It is right after the battle of Damascus that there is a revival, which he destroys.

We found that he will elevate himself above God and anything that is worshipped. He will blaspheme the true God and will have the (misplaced) trust of the entire world. We have a detailed rendition of his activities during his rise through the Magog battle in Daniel 11:36–45. Daniel tells us that he will come to his end without help. But we found that his end will happen after the tribulation. We found that the antichrist will not be able to get control of the area of central and southern Jordan. Israel will deny it to him, because they will at this time reject him as their shepherd. We will find in volume 2 that this is important, although during this battle, he will plunder Egypt, Sudan, and Ethiopia. I believe that it is likely that the antichrist takes credit for the true God's intervention in the Battle of Magog. Thus, he will build an aura of invincibility. This will come in handy for him when he receives a fatal wound. I do believe that it will truly be fatal because of the passage in Revelation 17, which says, "he was, he is not, but he will be," and that he comes up out of the abyss and will go to destruction. When he is resurrected, he will have remnants of a wound that will leave him blind in one eye and with a lame arm.

We found that much can be learned from the types of the antichrist that God chose to show us in His word, Antiochus Epiphanes in particular. It seems in Daniel 8 that there is some smearing of the application from him to the antichrist in the end time. Daniel tells us that the explanation concerns the distant future. I believe that he means it applies to the time of the tribulation. It is interesting that the antichrist is never said to be a peacemaker, even though some of his types are. Who knows? He may appear to be peaceful at first, but the Bible never says so.

We found that the "day of the Lord" cannot come until the rapture occurs and that the "day of the Lord" is the tribulation, although I wouldn't stand on this just to prove it. We will study this in much greater detail in future chapters of this book series, especially chapter 5 of this book. We found this because the Thessalonian believers were told that they had missed it. Paul reassures them, giving them several things that must come to pass before the day of the Lord can come. He told them that there would be a great rebellion, or falling away, and the "man of sin" (antichrist) would be revealed. This is likely the falling away found in the Isaiah 17 portion detailing the battle of Damascus and its aftermath. He also told them that the antichrist couldn't be revealed until the "restrainer" is removed. He referred to the restrainer in both the neuter and masculine gender. This is most likely speaking of the "body of Christ" church and Christ himself. The genders fit the grammar and the usage in the

Bible. This would also support a pre-tribulation rapture. Again, if that were all the support I had, I wouldn't claim that it was probable. We learned that Paul speaks of the "mystery" and that it was a special message from God, given to him through revelation. It is found that the rapture is part of this "mystery," according to 1 Corinthians 15:51–53. We also found that the Church, the body of Christ, is another part of this "mystery" peculiar to Paul's teaching (Romans 11–12).

We found that we should stop trying to identify the antichrist! (I hope!)

We also found that Israel will know that they are worshipping the true Messiah when he blesses their crops and they have plenty. They will then know that Christ is in Israel, not when they see him! The just will still live by faith, not by sight!

It becomes obvious that the earthquake of Joel 2, Ezekiel 38, and Revelation 6:12–17 are speaking of the same thing, the midpoint of the Battle of Magog, when God intervenes on Israel's behalf and Israel repents, and the start of the tribulation period. We also found that it is more than likely that this earthquake will include some great volcanic activity.

We learned that three of the four horsemen of the apocalypse are all the antichrist in his early reign (as the seventh head of the beast in Revelation 13, 17). The forth horseman is Death with Hades. We found that the entire first six seals are before the tribulation proper and are during the time that Christ calls "birth pains." The sixth seal introduces the tribulation period. We found that the signing of the covenant with the antichrist will start the seven years of tribulation. We also found that there is no mention of the antichrist during the first half of the tribulation. I believe that it is likely that he receives the fatal wound right after he signs the covenant. He dies, is resurrected (comes up out of the abyss), and is king again, being both the seventh head (king) and the eighth king, the beast himself, of Revelation 17.

We learned that one fourth of the world's population will die during the time of birth pains, but that the tribulation will be worse! (Those crazy people who say, "Wouldn't it be exciting to live through that?")

We learned about the image of the beast in the temple and the mark of the beast, which is either his name or the number of his name, 666.

We studied the false prophet and found that he is likely an evil, unbelieving pope. The antichrist probably gets his legitimacy by a cover of the apostate Roman Catholic Church (all true believers are gone by that time) directed by this pope.

I don't believe that the ten horns of Daniel 7 are the same ten horns of Revelation 13 and 17. It is impossible, because the ten horns of Revelation work in cooperation with the antichrist, and the antichrist subdues three of the horns in Daniel. Also, it cannot be the seven heads of the beast, because the ten horns of Daniel are all contemporaries, and the horns of Revelation are one after the other.

We found that the true believers will not be fooled by the antichrist, and no one will accidentally take the mark of the beast.

Last of all, we learned that the antichrist and the false prophet will be thrown alive into the lake of fire, forever!

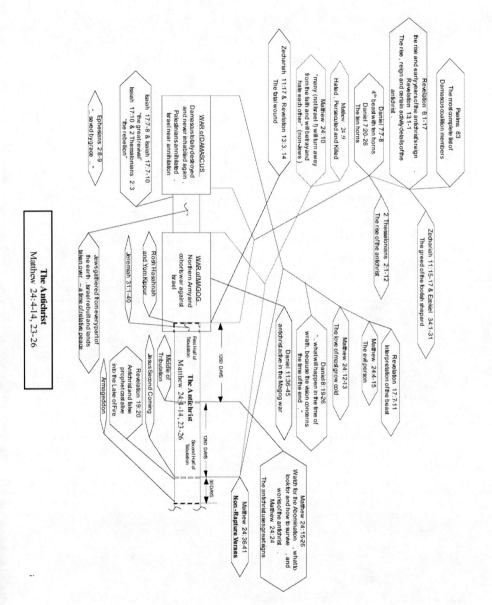

The Antichrist Event Line

CHAPTER 5

*Prophecies Concerning "The Body of Christ" Church
1 Corinthians 12:12–31*

Now we'll study the information that we are all waiting for. We'll be studying what is in the Bible that applies specifically to us (at the time of the writing of this book series). We will have to identify "us." It may seem strange, but much of Christianity is misidentifying who we are. We will find that we have a unique place in God's plan, and it's an honored place!

I want you to do yourself a favor and come to a conclusion that I had to arrive at before I began to study to write this book series. I realized that there are many sincere believers who disagreed with the ideas that I had been brought up with. I was raised a pre-tribulation, pre-millennial, we-are-raptured-and-then-the-seven years-of-tribulation-will-begin Christian believer. I realized that I was being rather arrogant. I decided to empty myself of all my preconceived ideas and just study God's Word and let Him tell me what the truth was. I decided to claim John 14:26, which reads: "But the counselor, *the Holy Spirit*, whom the Father will send in my name, *will teach you all things* and will remind you of everything I have said to you."

You'll notice that I don't quote "Bible scholars" and commentaries in this book series. It was Bible scholars and commentaries that gave me my position, at least the ones that I accepted and read. There is a vast supply of scholars and commentaries that gave a very different view of eschatology (the study of end times). On every aspect of the end times, there are a great number of scholars writing commentaries that disagree with one another, all of them well studied and sincere, all of them experts. First of all, I decided to not trust any of them. This is not to disrespect any of them. They all love God with their whole heart; if they didn't, they wouldn't have taken the time and great bother to write a book (trust me on that!). But every scholar has one flaw: *they're human! I'm human too!* That's the reason I beg you to read this book series with a Bible in your lap. *Don't take my word for anything.* Read what I've presented to you and *study it out for your self from God's Word.* We find in Acts 17:11 that the Berean believers were noble because they *didn't* take Paul's word for things but studied the scriptures for themselves, as it pertained to Paul's messages. Don't study it from so and so's commentary or the notes in your study Bible's margin. These things are not God's inspired word! Only the Bible is God's Word, and I'm not going to include paraphrases as God's Word. They are someone's idea of what God is trying to tell you. They are only an idea commentary on God's Word, and if the writer has the wrong idea, the wrong doctrine will result. In this book series, I have used, for the most part, five Bibles that are good to different degrees. First, I've used the New International Version (NIV). This has never been my favorite Bible for most applications, but I've found it to be probably the most true to the original as it applies to end-time prophecy study! I intended to use it as the text for this book series because it reads easier than the other translations and then correct the problems as I went along, but to my pleasant surprise, it needed very little correction! I was very surprised about that. Secondly, I used the King James Bible (KJV). This is, of course, the old standard. It's good but can be difficult to understand. Also, in some places, it truly isn't as close to the original language as is necessary. But don't get me wrong! It is very good! Third, I used the New American Standard Bible (NASB). This is usually my favorite translation. It is over all the most faithful to the original of any of the translations. I referred to it frequently as I studied. Fourth, I used the Amplified Bible (AMP). This is not too bad, but it does stray from being the translation it should be. The idea of the Amplified Bible is to give all the nuances of the original language, and the translators definitely tried, but in doing so, they occasionally strayed into the pitfall of paraphrasing God's Word. So while being helpful, I also needed to be very careful in my handling of this version. Last of all, I decided to try Young's Literal Translation (YLT). This is very cumbersome to read, much more so than the King James Version. It has the same difficulties as any translation but can give another view of the nuances of the verses being studied. With all of these translations, I also used Strong's Exhaustive Concordance and Lexicon. This is a very good helper and will not give you any preconceived notions. It is not doctrinal. In the lexicon, it gives you the meaning of the words used throughout the entire Bible, along with their root meanings and derivations. This is invaluable in a word study, especially if you are not fluent in the original language of God's Word (I am not). Those who are well versed in the Bible's original languages have told me that Strong's is an excellent and helpful resource. It will give you all the nuances of a word that is used in God's Word without being in a particular context. You then can arrive at what the original author was trying to tell you.

As you study, pray often for God's guidance. He will be faithful to you and give you great understanding as you go if you are sincerely interested in learning God's truth, not in trying to prove your preconceived idea. This is paramount! Let God guide you. He wants to; you (and I) just have to be willing. It's scary but rewarding! But if you go at God's Word to prove your point, you'll learn nothing.

Okay, the introduction for this chapter is out of the way; let's get on with what God has for us in His Word.

There is much discussion on the subject of the "rapture." First of all, "rapture" is not a word that you'll find in Scripture. That doesn't mean that it's unscriptural though! The way this concept was arrived at is through the translation into the Latin of the word for *snatching away*. It is, as I understand it, *rapare*, which means *snatching away*. The "snatching away" is found in 1 Thessalonians 4:13–5:11 as follows:

> Brothers, we don't want you to be ignorant about those who fall asleep, or grieve like the rest of men, who have no hope. We believe that Jesus died and rose again and so we believe that *God will bring with Jesus those who have fallen asleep in him.* According to the Lord's own word, *we tell you that we who are still alive, who are left till the coming of the Lord, will certainly not precede those who have fallen asleep. For the Lord himself will come down from heaven, with a loud command, with the voice of the archangel and with the trumpet call of God, and the dead in Christ will rise first. After that, we who are still alive and are left will be caught up together with them in the clouds to meet the Lord in the air. And so we will be with the Lord forever.* Therefore encourage each other with these words. Now, brothers, about the times and dates we do not need to write to you, for you know very well that *the day of the Lord will come like a thief in the night. While people are saying, "Peace and safety," destruction will come on them suddenly, as labor pains on a pregnant woman, and they will not escape. But you,* brothers, are not in darkness so that this day should surprise you like a thief. You are all sons of the light and sons of the day. We do not belong to the night or to the darkness. So then, let us not be like others, who are asleep, but let us be alert and self-controlled. For those who sleep, sleep at night, and those

who get drunk, get drunk at night. But since we belong to the day, let us be self-controlled, putting on faith and love as a breastplate, and the hope of salvation as a helmet. *For God did not appoint us to suffer wrath but to receive salvation through our Lord Jesus Christ.* He died for us so that, whether we are awake or asleep, we may live together with him. Therefore encourage one another and build each other up, just as in fact you are doing.

This is the prime passage dealing with the event commonly referred to as the "rapture." Paul starts out giving the Thessalonian believers words of comfort about their believing relatives and friends who have died. Paul uses the euphemism "fallen asleep," but it is clear that he is referring to physical death. He tells us that we who are still alive at the coming of the Lord will not go before the ones who are "asleep": dead. Notice that he will come back with the ones who have died, (2 Corinthians 5:8, "… *to be away from the body and at home with the Lord*" shows that when we die we immediately go to be with him and we will be waiting for the time when we will be given our new bodies), then he will raise the ones who have died. Their souls, their awareness, and consciousness will be with Christ in heaven until he returns with them to raise them from the dead. Interesting! They are with Him, but they still need to be raised. We will discuss this shortly, as Paul talks about it to the Corinthian believers. This event will happen with a loud command, with the voice of the archangel, and with the trumpet call of God. This is the signal used throughout the Old Testament to signal a gathering, an assembly. We discussed the significance of trumpet calls in chapter 2 of this book in dealing with the fulfillment of the Feast of Trumpets, Rosh Hashanah. There will be these events, and the dead "in Christ," those who have believed and subsequently passed away, will be raised from the dead as the very first part of this "rapture." Then believers who are left that are still alive will be snatched away into the clouds, and we will meet the Lord in the air. We are told that from that point on, we will always be with the Lord. This is for our comfort. So here we have the order of the rapture. But the timing still hasn't been discussed. We will get some insight into this in the verses of 1 Thessalonians chapter 5. The first thing Paul tells us in this chapter is that we don't need to know the times or the dates of the rapture. He then tells them that the day of the Lord will come as a thief in the night. He tells them that it will come when people are saying "peace and safety." This goes along with Ezekiel 38:8, 11, where Ezekiel tells the reader that Magog and her cohorts will attack Israel, who has recovered from war and where they were all living in *safety*. This is indeed the beginning of the "day of the Lord." Paul is telling them about the coming tribulation. But we find that he is assuring them that believers will not have to go through it. He tells them that they aren't in darkness, that the day should overtake them. The unsaved world *is* in darkness; the day will overtake them. Paul is not even suggesting that the day could overtake them if they dozed. Because in verse 9, he assures us that God did not appoint *us* to suffer wrath. He is including himself with the rest of *us*. He assures us that we are to receive salvation. It cannot be speaking of spiritual salvation here, because he is speaking of himself and "brothers," Christian brothers, people who have already been spiritually saved. He is speaking of physical salvation in that day! Also notice that he didn't say, "We are not appointed to *God's* wrath," just "wrath." That is important, as we will see. So in this portion, we find Paul assuring the Thessalonian believer that believers will not face the tribulation! Now I realize that there seem to be scriptures that appear to contradict this view. We will study these shortly; bear with me. There is another passage that gives us some more insight into the "rapture."

Let's look at 1 Corinthians 15:51–54:

> Listen, *I tell you a mystery: We will not all sleep, but we will all be changed– in a flash, in the twinkling of an eye, at the last trumpet.*

For the trumpet will sound, the dead will be raised imperishable, and we will be changed. For *the perishable must clothe itself with the imperishable, and the mortal with immortality.* When the perishable has been clothed with the imperishable, and the mortal with immortality, then the saying that is written will come true: "Death has been swallowed up in victory."

Well, there's Paul's "mystery" again! This part of the mystery is that we will not all sleep, but we will be changed, in a flash, in a split second, and the timing of this event is at the "last trumpet." If you'll recall, in the 1 Thessalonians 4 portion, we found that the dead will be raised at the "first trumpet." We will be raised at the "last trumpet." There are two trumpet calls, one for the dead and one for the living. When we are changed, he tells us, this "perishable" must put on the "imperishable"; this "able to die" must put on the "inability to die"! This mortal must put on immortality. How cool is that? We will be suddenly changed, in a split second! Paul tells the Thessalonian Christian that we will be "snatched away." This infers a sudden, apparently violent (although it won't hurt us) act. We'll be gone faster than the eye can perceive! In that sudden moment, we will be given the perfect immortal bodies that are discussed earlier in 1 Corinthians 15. There is another passage that is popularly referred to as the rapture.

Let's study Matthew 24:29–41:

Immediately *after the distress of those days* "the *sun will be darkened*, and the *moon will not give its light*; the *stars will fall* from the sky, and the heavenly bodies will be shaken." At that time the sign of *the Son of Man will appear in the sky*, and all the nations of the earth will mourn. *They will see the Son of Man coming in the clouds of the sky, with power and great glory.* And *he will send his angels with a loud trumpet call, and they will gather his elect from the four winds, from one end of the heavens to the other.* Now learn this lesson from the fig tree: As soon as its twigs get tender and its leaves come out, you know that summer is near. Even so, when you see all these things, you know that it is near, right at the door. I tell you the truth, this generation will certainly not pass away until all these things have happened. Heaven and earth will pass away, but my words will never pass away. No one knows about that day or hour, not even the angels in heaven, nor the Son, but only the Father. *As it was in the days of Noah, so will it be at the coming of the Son of Man.* For in the days before the flood, people were *eating and drinking, marrying and giving in marriage,* up to the day Noah entered the ark; and *they knew nothing about what would happen until the flood came and took them all away.* That is how it will be at the coming of the Son of Man. Two men will be in the field; *one will be taken* and the other left. Two women will be grinding with a hand mill; *one will be taken* and the other left.

Let's study this passage carefully. First, we find the events following are immediately *after* the distress of those days, after the tribulation. Remember, Paul said that believers aren't appointed to suffer wrath, but this event is immediately *after* the wrath. But despite this problem, the people who embrace the post-tribulation view arrive at their conclusion simply because they assume that Paul and Christ are speaking of the same thing. First, there will be the effects of a great earthquake with volcanism again. I believe that this is recorded in Revelation 16:17–21, as I mention in chapter 4 of volume 2. Then we find Christ telling us that at that time, He will appear in the clouds of the sky with power and great glory. Those who call this the rapture say that this is the same as 1 Thessalonians 4:17, because we meet Him in the clouds. And then we find that He will send His angels with a loud trumpet call, and they will gather the elect. Again, they say this is the rapture. At first glance, I would think so as well, if I read no further. But let's read on. Where do they gather His elect from? "The four winds," specifically, "from one end of *the heavens* to the other!" It doesn't mention anything about gathering them from the earth! Even if you suppose that "the four winds" is speaking of the earth, it doesn't say it. Furthermore, the wording appears to specify heaven. Well, there is a small problem, and I would have no problem with it if that were all, but there's more! He goes into the story of the fig tree, which I mention in chapter 4 of volume 2. The fig tree is a fig tree, not the nation of Israel! Anyway, going on, Christ tells us that His coming will be as it was in the days of Noah. Well, how was that? They were eating and drinking and marrying and giving in marriage, that's how it was. They were simply living their lives! That is the whole point. They were doing what people do every day throughout all of history. Christ tells us that this is what He means here. He explains it well. Then he tells us that they didn't know anything was going to happen until the flood came and *took them all away.* The flood took them! The flood didn't rescue them, it killed them, and it killed them all except for eight people! Then Christ tells us that this is how it will be when he comes back. Two men will be in the field; one is *taken*, not rescued—killed! Doomed! There is no way anyone listening to Christ would have gotten anything different from this. First Thessalonians hadn't been written yet. Two women will be grinding with a hand mill; one is taken—dead—just as the flood *took* the people who were unsuspecting in the days of Noah! This isn't the rapture! The ones taken aren't saved; they are doomed! The ones left behind are saved to go into the kingdom! So despite some similarities, Christ doesn't mention the rapture, only the second coming. Obviously, the saved ones Paul was speaking of were saved, because they *were* taken. The ones Christ was speaking of were saved because they were *left behind!* People need to read this carefully! Paul and Christ were speaking of two different things.

So Matthew does not mention the rapture. The same holds true for all the Gospels. None of them mention the rapture! I wonder why? We'll keep studying.

There is, in fact, only one verse that may be speaking of the rapture outside of Paul's Epistles, and I will only say *may be*; if it is referring to the rapture, it is very obscure. This is found in Revelation 3:10; it is speaking to the church of Philadelphia: "Since you have kept my command to endure patiently, *I will also keep you from the hour of trial that is going to come upon the whole world to test those who live on the earth.*"

This keeping from the hour of trial may be speaking of the rapture. I certainly couldn't prove it from this passage. The hour of trial that is going to come upon the whole earth certainly seems to be speaking of the tribulation period. If God keeps them from it, it would likely be through the rapture. If it is speaking of the rapture, it is the only non-Pauline passage that does, but I wouldn't have a problem with that anyway. Revelation was written after Paul's epistles. There is another portion in Revelation that many people claim is a reference to the rapture, Revelation 4:1: "After this I looked, and there before me was a door standing open in heaven. And the voice I had first heard speaking to me like a trumpet said, '*Come up here*, and I will show you what must take place after this.'"

It is claimed that since John was ordered to "Come up here," it must be speaking of the rapture. Why was John ordered "up here?" It was to receive the Revelation. It wasn't to be rescued! There was a clear purpose to this summons. This is not speaking of the rapture. There are no Old Testament portions that speak of the rapture. There are several that speak of the resurrection, but that is an event that accompanies Christ's second coming (Isaiah 49:6, Isaiah 25). They are mentioned in reference to earthly events. Their earthly reign will begin on this earth but will move to the New Earth upon this earth's destruction. Are there any other prophecies concerning our time? Well, yes. Let's look at 2 Timothy 3:1–9:

> But mark this: There will be *terrible times in the last days.* People will *be lovers of themselves, lovers of money, boastful,*

proud, abusive, disobedient to their parents, ungrateful, unholy, without love, unforgiving, slanderous, without self control, brutal, not lovers of the good, treacherous, rash, conceited, lovers of pleasure rather than lovers of God- having a form of godliness but denying its power. Have nothing to do with them. They are the kind who worm their way into homes and gain control over weak-willed women, who are loaded down with sins and are swayed by all kinds of evil desires, always learning but never able to acknowledge the truth. Just as Jannes and Jambres opposed Moses, so also these men oppose the truth- men of depraved minds, who, as far as the faith is concerned, are rejected. But they will not get very far because, as in the case of those men, their folly will be clear to everyone.

First, Paul tells us that there will be terrible times, and then he goes on to elaborate. It sounds like a newscast. I know that people have said this for over a hundred years. In fact, there was a group in the 1800s that claimed that Christ's return was imminent because this prophecy was then fulfilled. If only they knew! It is so much worse today, and yes, it could get worse. This description is not terribly specific. It could be said to be fulfilled at almost any time, but look at the list. For years, the "me generation" has been proclaimed. "You've got to look out for number one!" "Money makes the world go around." "Anything you can do, I can do better!" "Come on, have a little pride!" etc. I can't help but feel this is rather indicative of our times! It is still not specific, but it is a prophecy and it is being fulfilled. We just don't know to what extent it will have to be fulfilled. This ungodliness is not the same one mentioned in 2 Thessalonians 2:3. In fact, let's look at 2 Thessalonians 2:1–12:

Concerning the coming of our Lord Jesus Christ and *our being gathered to him,* we ask you, brothers, not to become easily unsettled or alarmed by some prophecy, report or letter supposed to have come from us, saying that *the day of he Lord has already come.* Don't let anyone deceive you in any way, for *that day will not come until the rebellion occurs and the man of lawlessness is revealed,* the man doomed to destruction. He will oppose and will exalt himself over everything that is called God or is worshiped, so that he sets himself up in God's temple, proclaiming himself to be God. Don't you remember when I was with you I used to tell you these things? And now *you know what is holding him back, so that he may be revealed at the proper time.* For the secret power of lawlessness is already at work; *but the one who now holds it back will continue to do so till he is taken out of the way.* And *then the lawless one will be revealed, whom the Lord Jesus will overthrow* with the breath of his mouth and destroy by the splendor of his coming. The coming of the lawless one will be in accordance with the work of Satan displayed in all kinds of counterfeit miracles, signs and wonders, and in every sort of evil that deceives those who are perishing. They perish because they refused to love the truth and so be saved. For this reason God sends them a powerful delusion so that they will believe the lie and so that all will be condemned who have not believed the truth but have delighted in wickedness.

What Paul is discussing here is the coming of our Lord Jesus and *our being gathered to him.* This is speaking specifically of the rapture. The rapture is the one thing that is concerning the Thessalonian believers here. They are afraid that they have missed it! The reason they think that they have missed it is because someone gave them false information; they were told that the day of the Lord had already happened. The day of the Lord is the tribulation period. They knew from talking with Paul that they would be raptured before the tribulation, so they were frightened. That's why this is concerning "our being gathered unto Him," when the information they had received said that the tribulation had already come. So, in an effort to calm them, Paul gives them a set of events that must happen before the day of the Lord can happen. The first things that must happen (Paul lists them together) is the rebellion must occur and the man of sin must be revealed. This is mentioned in Daniel 8:23. In this Daniel portion, it mentions the rebels becoming completely wicked and a stern-faced king arising. This is the antichrist. The pattern fits perfectly, as I mentioned in chapter 4 of this book. The circumstances are a match between Daniel and 2 Thessalonians. This man of sin, man of lawlessness, will be revealed, and there will be a great rebellion. If you will recall from chapter 1 of this book, after the battle of Damascus, there is a revival (Isaiah 17:7), but it is quickly squashed, and most everyone turns their back on God (Isaiah 17:10). I believe that this is also speaking of the same thing, the great rebellion. It coincides with the rise of the antichrist. We find that he will come up in a conflict and will "subdue" three kings (Daniel 7:24). We find that the antichrist is fully in power at the Battle of Magog (Daniel 11:36–45, Revelation 6.) The sixth seal is the place where God intervenes on Israel's behalf at the height of the Battle of Magog; the antichrist is already in power in the first seal. So there is actually quite a bit of corroborating evidence in Scripture backing up the rise of the antichrist and the rebellion.

Then we find that something is holding back the revealing of this "man of lawlessness"; it is the "what" of 2 Thessalonians 2:6. This is an interesting reference, when you consider the Greek that it was written in. The word *what* is in the neuter gender, so this eliminates some things that could be referred to by this word. But anyway, this "what" is holding back the man of lawlessness. But then we find in the very next verse that the restrainer will continue to hold back the antichrist until "he" is taken out of the way! The gender changed! For the Greek, this is a very interesting bit of information. Many have supposed that it is speaking of the Holy Spirit. He would certainly have the power to hold the antichrist back, and it was supposed that he would be taken out of the way when believers were raptured. This seems entirely logical, except He doesn't fit the "what." Furthermore, it has been pointed out to me that the Holy Spirit is very active here on earth after we are gone, so

He isn't really taken out of the way! I then spoke with someone who is literate in the ancient Greek, and he explained to me that there is only one answer to this problem. Paul refers to us as the "body of Christ" church. As a church, it would be referred to as a "what," neuter gender. Being we are baptized into Christ when we are born again, Christ dwells in us (Colossians 1:27). Thus, when the rapture occurs, the "body of Christ" church is removed—this is the neuter gender "what" (the church would properly be neuter gender), and as Christ is in us (and there is no reference to Christ being physically on the earth until the second coming), Christ Himself is removed as well—this would be the "he." In fact, this is the *only* possible solution! No other explanation can explain the change in gender without offending proper Greek grammar, regardless of whom it would be speaking of. Only after the body of Christ church and Christ Himself are removed can the antichrist be revealed!

So, according to this portion, the rapture will have to be before the tribulation. The tribulation cannot occur until the rebellion occurs and the antichrist is revealed, and that cannot happen until the restrainer is removed, which is us (the body of Christ church) and Christ Himself. That will only happen after the rapture occurs! From this, the snatching away has to be before the tribulation; in fact, it has to be some time around the battle of Damascus, because he is revealed when he subdues three of the ten kings. Because we have to be gone before the antichrist will be revealed, and he is in power for an indefinite length of time before the tribulation happens. It is probably the battle of Damascus that has to happen at the time he is revealed (so we have to be gone by then), and Israel has to recover, and then Russia has to attack, and Israel has to repent and turn to Christ. There are a lot of events that will happen after we are gone, after the body of Christ church is gone and the tribulation starts. I was astounded when I learned this! I say "probably" in reference to the battle of Damascus because there is no scripture that specifically states that he will be revealed then, but the evidence is very compelling.

Well, I guess this eliminates the midtribulation view of the rapture as well! But this raises even more questions. Why is Paul the only one to give any meaningful teaching on the rapture and, for that matter, the body of Christ church and his "mystery"?

We already studied Romans 11, as it deals with the grafting in of wild branches on the olive tree after breaking off the natural branches. This is metaphorically referring to Gentiles and Israel, as Paul explains in the text. This goes on from Romans 11 verse 1 through verse 24. Now we'll pick up the narrative with Romans 11:25–12:8:

> I do not want you to be ignorant of this *mystery*, brothers, so that you may not be conceited: *Israel has experienced a hardening in part until the full number of the Gentiles has come in. And so all Israel will be saved, as it is written:* "The deliverer will come from Zion; he will turn godlessness away from Jacob. And this is my covenant with them when I take away their sins." As far as the gospel is concerned, they are enemies on your account; but as far as election is concerned, they are loved on account of the patriarchs, for God's gifts and his call are irrevocable. Just as you who were at one time disobedient to God have now received mercy as a result of their disobedience, so they too have become disobedient in order that they too may now receive mercy as a result of God's mercy to you. For God has bound all men over to disobedience so that he may have mercy on them all. Oh, the depth of the riches of the wisdom and knowledge of God! How unsearchable his judgments, and his paths beyond tracing out! "Who has known the mind of the Lord? Or who has been his counselor?" "Who has ever given to God, that God should repay him?" For from him and through him and to him are all things. To him be the glory forever! Amen. Therefore, I urge you, brothers, in view of God's mercy, to offer your bodies as living sacrifices, holy

and pleasing to God-this is your spiritual act of worship. Do not conform any longer to the pattern of this world, but be transformed by the renewing of your mind. Then you will be able to test and approve what God's will is-his good, pleasing, and perfect will. For by the grace given me I say to every one of you: Do not think of yourself more highly than you ought, but rather think of yourself with sober judgment, in accordance with the measure of faith God has given you. *Just as each of us has one body with many members, and these members do not all have the same function, so in Christ we who are many form one body*, and each member belongs to all the others. We have different gifts, according to the grace given to us. If a man's gift is prophesying, let him use it in proportion to his faith. If it is serving, let him serve; if it is teaching, let him teach; if it is encouraging, let him encourage; if it is contributing to the needs of others, let him give generously; if it is leadership, let him govern diligently; if it is showing mercy let him do it cheerfully.

As we study this, I want us to take notice of Paul's use of the word *mystery*. Paul uses it more than any other Bible author. Paul also has a theme associated with his use of this word. It seems to accompany a special message that he received from God. Just here, he gives the reason for the hardening of the hearts of the Jews. It is so the full number of Gentiles can come in, that is, to be saved. We find again that Paul reasserts the fact that at some time, all of Israel will be saved. It hasn't happened yet, but it certainly will. But the point here is that the Jews being put to the side for a time for the salvation of the Gentiles is a mystery, something that was an unheard-of circumstance prior to Paul's mention of it. That is a characteristic of Paul's "mystery," something unheard of until then. The mystery isn't that Israel will turn against God. The prophets have spoken of that for many years. It isn't that they will turn again to God, every one of them; this also has been spoken of from old. The mystery was that God would turn to the Gentiles and deal with them as the primary recipient of His mercy and grace, that God would make Gentiles as important as the Jews, indeed, equals. In fact, *during this time of God bringing in the full number of Gentiles*, this "mystery," there are no longer any "Jews" or "Greeks" (Gentiles); we are all one in Christ (Galatians 3:28, Ephesians 3:6). When Paul said these things, it was new, revolutionary. Many Jews balked at the idea of not being the sole possessor of God's favor. It was even difficult for Peter (2 Peter 3:15–16).

It is interesting to note what the word *mystery* in the original language means. It is translated from the Greek word *musterion*. It comes from a derivative of *muo*, which means *to shut the mouth*. It means a *secret* or *mystery* (through the idea of silence imposed by initiation into religious rites). This is found in Strong's Exhaustive Concordance and Lexicon, #3466 Greek. It appears that a more correct translation would be *secret*.

Paul goes on to remind us that we need to have the correct perspective. No one is more important than another; we are all members of one team—the *body*. He tells us we are *one body in Christ*. Let's read what Paul told the Ephesian believers in Ephesians 4:1–16:

> As a prisoner for the Lord, then, I urge you to live a life worthy of the calling you have received. Be completely humble and gentle; be patient, bearing with one another in love. Make every effort to keep the unity of the Spirit through the bond of peace. *There is one body* and one Spirit—just as you were called to one hope when you were called—one Lord, one faith, one baptism; One God and Father of all, who is over all and through all and in all. But to each one of us grace has been given as Christ apportioned it. This is why it says: "When he ascended on high, he led captives in his train and gave gifts to men." (What does "he ascended" mean, except that he also descended to the lower, earthly regions? He who descended is the very one who ascended higher than all the

heavens, in order to fill the whole universe.) It was he who gave some to be apostles, some to be prophets, some to be evangelists, and some to be pastors and teachers, *to prepare God's people for works of service, so that the body of Christ may be built up* until we all reach unity in the faith and knowledge of the Son of God and become mature, attaining to the whole measure of the fullness of Christ. Then we will no longer be infants, tossed back and forth by the waves, and blown here and there by every wind of teaching and by the cunning and craftiness of men in their deceitful scheming. Instead, speaking the truth in love, *we will in all things grow up into him who is the Head, that is, Christ. From him the whole body, joined and held together by every supporting ligament, grows and builds itself up in love, as each part does its work.*

The first thing significant to this study is that there is one body. This seems important, as Paul includes this with one Spirit, one hope, one Lord, one faith, one baptism, one God, and one Father. Wow! Heavy company! This tells me at least that this is an important item! Then we are told that God gave different abilities to believers to do various works. He mentions different things that believers do that support and encourage and instruct fellow believers. He then tells us that this is to build up the body of Christ. Then, as he dwells on the subject of the body of Christ being built up, he tells us, "We will in all things grow up into him who is the Head, that is, Christ." So here we find that the "body of Christ" is a separate entity from Christ, who is the Head. The body grows up into Him, the Head, Christ. (For some reason, Peter states that this is difficult to understand! Go fig!) In the last verse of this portion, as well as the context of this whole portion, we find that Paul seems to identify the "body" as the group of believers of which we are a part. Well, I guess I cheated a little. Paul already identified the body earlier in this book of Ephesians. In Chapter 1:22–23, he gives us the answer: "And God placed all things under his feet and appointed *him to be head over everything for the Church, which is his body*, the fullness of him who fills everything in every way."

If you read earlier in this chapter, you will find that this is speaking of Christ (Ephesians 1:20). The Church is the *body of Christ*! Hmm, isn't that interesting? We have a special title! How do I know that it is the title of the present church? Romans 11:11–12 tells us that Israel's fall has brought salvation to the world, and the salvation of the Gentiles may make the Jews envious. Israel still rejects Christ. As a nation, Israel still doesn't accept Christ. The program that Paul speaks of is to win gentile souls until the time when God will deal with Israel again as a nation (Romans 11:11, 24–27). We are in a program where the vast majority of believers are gentile. Are Jews not allowed to be saved now? Yes, they are certainly allowed to be saved, but they need to be saved the same way as any Gentile, just as Gentiles had to be saved by being proselytized into Judaism under the Law (Numbers 15:14–16, among others). There is no longer Jew or Greek; all are one in this program (Galatians 3:28). Let's look at a couple of other scriptures that deal with the church being called "the body" of Christ. Colossians 1:18, 24.

> Colossians 1:18: And *he is the head of the body, the church*; he is the beginning and the firstborn from among the dead, so that in everything he might have the supremacy.
> And Colossians 1: 24: Now I rejoice in what was suffered for you, and I fill up in my flesh what is still lacking *in regard to Christ's afflictions, for the sake of his body, which is the church.*

Okay, the church is clearly called Christ's body. But we will only find this distinction in Paul's epistles. Nowhere in any other scripture will you find any Bible author refer to the church as "the body" or "Christ's body." No other scripture even *hints* at it, just Paul!

There are some scriptures written by Paul that seem to support the idea that the church is the *bride* of Christ. Let's look at them. We'll start with Ephesians 5:22–33:

Wives, submit to your husbands as to the Lord. For the husband is the head of the wife as *Christ is the head of the Church, his body,* of which he is savior. Now as the church submits to Christ, so also wives should submit to their husbands in everything. *Husbands, love your wives, just as Christ loved the church and gave himself up for her* to make her holy, cleansing her by the washing with water through the word, and to present her to himself as a radiant church, without stain or wrinkle or any other blemish, but holy and blameless. *In this same way, husbands ought to love their wives as their own bodies. He who loves his wife loves himself.* After all, *no one ever hated his own body,* but he feeds and cares for it, *just as Christ does the church- for we are members of his body.* "For this reason a man will leave his father and mother and be united to his wife, and the two will become one flesh." This is a profound mystery—but I am talking about Christ and the church. However, *each one of you also must love his wife as he loves himself,* and the wife must respect her husband.

This is an interesting passage, which many use as support for the church being the bride of Christ. However, Paul never claims that the church is Christ's bride, just that husbands should love their wives as Christ loved the church. Does Christ love the church? Yes, of course! How much? So much that he gave his life for it! And that's how much a husband should love his wife! In fact, twice Paul identifies the church as Christ's body, never as his bride! Another interesting fact: Paul tells husbands to love their wives as *their own bodies*! And Ephesians 5:29 says, "No one ever hated his own body, but feeds and cares for it, *just as Christ does the church ...*" Here Paul is relating Christ's love for the church as how someone loves *his own body*! There's another thing, and it has to do with the NIV translation of this portion. In referring to the church, it repeatedly calls it "her." The term in the original language is gender non-specific. It is translated every time in the King James as "it." Okay, well, I guess this isn't a good bride-of-Christ passage. But now, let's look at the very best passage supporting this church being Christ's bride. Let's turn to 2 Corinthians 11:2.

> I am jealous for you with a godly jealousy. I promised you to one husband, to Christ, so that I might present you as a pure virgin to him.
>
> 2 Corinthians 11:2 (NIV)

Well, this sounds pretty convincing at first. In fact the King James Version reads:

> For I am jealous over you with godly jealousy; for I have espoused you to one husband that I may present you as a chaste virgin to Christ.
>
> 2 Corinthians 11:2 (KJV)

Well it doesn't specifically come out and say you're Christ's bride, but at first glance, it sure appears that way. It is interesting, when you begin to do a word study, that the word translated *espoused* in KJV or *promised* in NIV is only used once in the entire Bible. The word *espoused* is used many times, but is always a different word! This word can mean *espoused*, but it can mean *joined* or *fit together*, just as well! It would seem that if Paul were stressing the marital aspect of this relationship, he would have used a more common word for the engagement instead of this obscure one. Also, the word *husband* can mean *husband*, as well, but it simply means *man*, over three times to every one where it means *husband*. In the context, it seems more likely that Paul was admonishing the Corinthian believers to live godly lives, because he led them to Christ. It's a sort of "don't embarrass me," and, even more so, a "don't harm yourselves spiritually" situation. If you are familiar with the Corinthian believers, you will know that that could be a real concern. Paul loved them and wanted them to grow in Christ and be examples to the world. So, even this portion isn't necessarily speaking of the church as the bride. In fact, Paul *never* calls the church "the bride," just as the other Bible authors *never* call the church "the body"! Why would that be? Let's look at Paul's message and see if we can find out. First, let's see if Paul has any special mission. Let's turn to Romans 11:13 and see what it says.

Romans 11:13: "*I am talking to you Gentiles. Inasmuch as I am the apostle to the Gentiles, I make much of my ministry…*"

Here we find that Paul does indeed have a special mission. He is the apostle to the Gentiles! He goes on to say that through this ministry, he hopes to move some of his own people (Jews) to envy that some may be saved. His heart is still with his fellow Jews, but He has come to bring salvation to the Gentiles. He is specifically *the* apostle to the Gentiles! What does it say about the mission of Peter and the twelve? Let's read Galatians 2:6–9:

> As for those who seemed to be important—whatever they were makes no difference to me; God does not judge by external appearance—*those men added nothing to my message. On the contrary, they saw that I had been entrusted with the task of preaching the gospel to the Gentiles, just as Peter had been to the Jews. For God, who was at work in the ministry of Peter as an apostle to the Jews, was also at work in my ministry as an apostle to the Gentiles. James, Peter and John,* those reputed to be pillars, gave me and Barnabas the right hand of fellowship when they recognized the grace given to me. They *agreed that we should go to the Gentiles, and they to the Jews.*

First we find that the "pillars" of the faith added nothing to Paul's message. By the context, it appears that what is meant here is the other apostles didn't minister with Paul and Barnabas. They agreed to fellowship with them but not to preach or minister with them. They, in fact, recognized that Paul was given a special mission from God to the Gentiles, as special a mission as Peter had been given to the Jews. Paul agreed with Peter, James, and John that they should go to the Jews, while Paul and Barnabas would go to the Gentiles. So it's obvious that Paul had a special mission. Let's examine it further. Let's look at Ephesians 3:1–11:

> For this reason I, Paul, the prisoner of Christ Jesus for the sake of you Gentiles- Surely you have heard about the *administration of God's grace that was given to me for you, That is, the mystery made known to me by revelation,* as I have already written briefly. *In reading this, then, you will be able to understand my insight into the mystery of Christ, which was not made known to men in other generations as it has now been revealed by the Spirit to God's holy apostles and prophets. This mystery is that through the gospel the Gentiles are heirs together with Israel, members together of one body, and sharers together in the promise in Christ Jesus.* I became a servant of *this gospel* by the gift of God's grace given me through the working of his power. Although I am less than the least of all God's people, this grace was given me: *to preach to the Gentiles the unsearchable riches of Christ,* and to make plain to everyone *the administration of this mystery, which for ages past was kept hidden in God,* who created all things. His intent was that now, through the church, the manifold wisdom of God should be made known to the rulers and authorities in the heavenly realms, *according to his eternal purpose* which he accomplished in Christ Jesus our Lord.

First, let's examine the word *administration.* This is the Greek word *oikonomia.* According to Strong's, it means: *administration (of a household or estate); specifically a (religious) "economy": dispensation, stewardship.* (#3622, from 3623)

If you look at the word *oikonomos,* we find that it comes from the Greek root words *oikos* (#3624), and *nomos* (#3551). *Oikos* means *a dwelling; by implication, a family; home, house (hold), temple.* And we find that *nomos* means *law.* So the word essentially means house-law, or how God rules his household. We get our English word *economy* from this word. One of the ways it is translated is *admin-*

istration, as it is used here in the NIV. This isn't a bad translation. When you go from one president to another, you have a change in the administration. While you operate in the same basic framework of rules, the way things operate can be somewhat different. This is essentially what is happening here. While God's grace is extended to all, and has been throughout all of history, the way God administers His government changes periodically. For instance, before Abraham, God did not order circumcision for worship; with the Abrahamic covenant, it was commanded by God. Did God change? No! But the way humanity worshiped Him did. It was a sign of obedience to God. It was required (Genesis 17:9–14). It was required through the time of the Law of Moses (Leviticus 12:3). Now, under this "administration," it is no longer a requirement. In fact, in the early church, there was a big argument among the Jewish believers and the gentile believers about this issue (Acts 15:1–11, Galatians 5:1–6). Paul states that we will not be more righteous if we practice circumcision as Gentiles, and we shouldn't pursue it for religious reasons. This is just one ramification of the change in administration. The difference in this change of administration is that it isn't the leadership that is changed, but the people that are being dealt with and the amount of God's Word that is revealed to them.

Paul, here and only here, calls it the "administration of grace." It is grace as opposed to law, specifically the Law of Moses. Is this inferring that grace is a new concept? Certainly not! Grace was operative from the time of Adam and Eve, when they fell into sin. It is that now the centerpiece of this administration is "grace." It is its main feature, whereas under the Law of Moses, the centerpiece was the "Law." Everything revolved around the framework of the Law and its commandments. The element of grace entered when someone sinned; there was a means of restoring their relationship with God. This was accomplished with animal sacrifice. Animal sacrifice wasn't even the means of salvation; it was intended for restoration of the relationship (Psalms 51 the whole chapter, but especially verses 12, 16–17). Today, we cannot restore our relationship with God by sacrificing an animal; we are under a new administration. God hasn't changed, but the people he is dealing with have. The church is presently a Gentile-based organization, or, at least, it doesn't respect one race over another. All are equal in God's sight. Where the "law" enters today is just as a guide for us to know what God considers to be sin and something to be avoided (Romans 3:20, Galatians 3:24–29).

Next, we find that this administration was given to Paul to dispense to this church, the body. Paul calls this administration the "mystery." This explains his use of the term more than anyone else in the entire Bible. He was given this administration as the "mystery." The word *mystery* means *to shut the mouth*, as I have already mentioned. It was a secret hidden in God until the time of Paul. God then revealed it to Paul through revelation. It wasn't something that was told to him by any other human agent. It came straight from God himself! It wasn't revealed to the other apostles before it was revealed to Paul; it is his! Paul claims special insight into this mystery. He has an understanding of it, as it is only then being revealed to God's apostles and prophets. He tells us that it was not made known in other generations, ever! You won't find it in the Old Testament; you won't even find it in the Gospels! Christ Himself didn't mention it! It wasn't Christ's ministry; Christ was a minister to the Jews. Romans 15:8 tells us this, as does Matthew 15:24. Let's read these verses.

Romans 15:8 says; "For I tell you that *Christ has become a servant of the Jews* on behalf of God's truth, *to confirm the promises made to the patriarchs.*"

Christ was a servant to the Jews. The King James Version says: "Jesus Christ was a minister of the circumcision…" and "to confirm the promises made unto the fathers." When I first read this, I was shocked! It amazed me to learn that He didn't minister on this earth to the Gentiles as well as the Jews! But let's read Christ's word on this:

"He answered, '*I was sent only to the lost sheep of Israel*'" (Matthew 15:24).

Christ is saying these words. He said, "I was sent *only* to the lost sheep of Israel." Wow! He was sent to minister only to the lost sheep of Israel. This is the story of the woman (this was not a parable) who came to Him for the healing of her demon-possessed daughter. At first, Christ refused, saying, "It is not right to take the children's bread and toss it to their dogs." Ouch! Christ called her a dog, and by implication, He called all Gentiles dogs. Why? This is because He was sent only to the Jews. Her response was, "Yes, Lord, but even the dogs eat the crumbs that fall from their masters' table." This is a very interesting response. She exhibited humility and faith. Christ honored this faith and healed her daughter. Was Christ trying to be mean? No. Number one, He knew what her response would be; after all, He is God. Secondly, He had to make the point that He was sent (by the Father) only to the lost of Israel. Christ tells us what His ministry on this earth was to be. This is found in Matthew 5:17: "Do not think that I have come to abolish the Law or the prophets; *I have not come to abolish them but to fulfill them.*"

Christ's ministry was not to bring an end to the Law of Moses, but to fulfill it, to bring it to all that it was supposed to become. Did this happen while He was on earth? No, not yet, but it will happen when He comes back at His second coming. Every bit of the Law of Moses will be fulfilled when He comes back as King and rules this world, eventually destroying sin entirely.

Christ was not a minister to the mystery. Does His life and sacrifice on the cross apply to us in this time? Absolutely! Without what He did for us, we would all be destined for a lost eternity, an eternity in the lake of fire! His life, death and resurrection are what all of history past, present, and future hinge on. Salvation for all mankind and throughout all ages is available because He lived on this earth (Hebrews 4:14–16), died for the sins of the entire world (1 Corinthians 15:3), and rose from the dead (1 Corinthians 15:4). But his *ministry on this earth* revolved around and applied specifically to Israel; this is His word, not mine! We need to differentiate between His *life* and His *ministry*. His life applies to all, but His ministry, those he came specifically to serve, was the Jews. It is easy to confuse the two, but remember that His life is an example to all. For instance, He was tempted in all ways but was yet without sin. He walked in our shoes. Because of this, we can approach Him boldly (Hebrews 4:14–16). Wow! This applies to all. He urged people to obey the Law of Moses (Matthew 5:17–19). This applies to Israel. This was a part of His *ministry*.

Now going on with our study of Ephesians 3:1–11, we'll pick it up at verse 6. We find that a large part of this mystery is that Jews and Gentiles are heirs together and members of one body, equals! In this church of Christ's body, Gentiles are no longer dogs just because they're Gentiles; we are equal in God's sight. That is quite a revolutionary concept for the Jews of the Bible, especially in view of Christ's response to the Canaanite woman. But this was because Christ was a minister to the Jews, and at the time of Christ's confrontation with this woman, the Jews properly considered Gentiles "dogs." At that time, to be saved, a Gentile had to become proselytized as a Jew, and at that point, she wasn't.

Next, we find Paul making an interesting comment. He claims to have become a servant of this *gospel*. Is this a different gospel than Peter and the twelve were preaching? Well, a little. Both preached that salvation came through Christ's sacrifice on the cross, but let's look at Peter's message found in Acts 21:20: "When they heard this, they praised God. Then they said to Paul: 'You see, brother, how many thousands of *Jews have believed, and all of them are zealous of the Law.'*"

We have already found that, under Paul's teaching, we are not under the Law, but the Jews were saved and were praised by the early disciples (James, one of the twelve, and the other elders) for being *zealous* of the Law of Moses. Were they wrong? No! This was the Gospel of the circumcision of Peter and the rest of the twelve (Galatians 2:7–9, as already quoted). Let's look at Galatians 2:7 in the King James Version: "But, contrariwise, when they saw that the *gospel of the uncircumcision* was committed unto me, as the *gospel of the circumcision* was unto Peter."

The wording in the King James Version implies that Paul preached a gospel tailored to the Gentiles as Peter preached one tailored to the Jews. In the NIV, it more seems to imply that Paul was just exclusively to preach to the Gentiles and Peter to the Jews, but with no difference in content. Which is correct? Let's study this a little more. We've already noted that James praised the Jewish believers for being zealous of the Law of Moses (Acts 21:20). Paul doesn't urge the Gentiles to follow the Law of Moses. On the contrary, he discourages it! Let's read Galatians 2:16:

> Know that *a man is not justified by observing the law,* but by faith in Jesus Christ. *So we, too, have put our faith in Christ Jesus that we may be justified by faith in Christ and not by observing the law, because by observing the law no one will be justified.*

Here we find that Paul strongly discourages following Moses's Law. There seems to be a difference. Is there more? Let's look at James 2:20–24:

> You foolish man, do you want evidence that faith without deeds is useless? Was not *our ancestor Abraham* considered *righteous for what he did* when he offered his son Isaac on the altar? You see that his faith and his actions were working together, and his faith was made complete by what he did. And the scripture was fulfilled that says, "Abraham believed

God, and it was credited to him as righteousness," and he was called God's friend. You see that *a person is justified by what he does and not by faith alone.*

This is the famous "faith without works is dead" portion. ("Faith without works is dead" is the wording in the KJV.) Please note that James is speaking to the "twelve tribes scattered among the nations" (James 1:1). We, as Gentiles, are not members of the "twelve tribes"! Do we therefore reject anything written in his book series? No! We can learn from the principles presented here. But we need to understand who this book is addressed to specifically—the twelve tribes! In this portion, James is arguing that faith alone is not enough to save (justify) a person and that he must produce works to prove his faith. To James, the believer needs faith that produces works; the faith alone will not be sufficient, just as works alone are not sufficient and never were (Isaiah 64:6). There are many sermons preached on this topic every year. What does Paul say on this issue? Let's look at Romans 4:1–5:

> What then shall we say that Abraham, our forefather, discovered in this matter? *If*, in fact, *Abraham was justified by works, he had something to boast about*—but not before God. What does the scripture say? *"Abraham believed God, and it was credited to him as righteousness."* Now *when a man works, his wages are not credited to him as a gift, but as an obligation. However, to a man who does not work but trusts God who justifies the wicked, his faith is credited as righteousness.*

Paul starts out with, "If… Abraham was justified by works, he had something to boast about." What does Paul's message state about works in the Christian life? Let's look at Ephesians 2:8–9: "For it is by grace you have been saved, through faith—and this not from yourselves, it is the gift of God—*not by works, so that no one can boast.*"

In this portion, we find that salvation is not by works, because God doesn't want people to be able to brag that they were good enough to make it to heaven on their own merit. Salvation is a gift! In Ephesians 2:10, it goes on to say that "…we are created in Christ Jesus to do good works, which God prepared in advance for us to do." We are to do good works, not for salvation, not even to prove our faith, but because when we are saved, God makes us a "new creation" (2 Corinthians 5:17), capable of good works. We are to do this out of love for God. But we aren't justified by works! Abraham believed God, and it was credited to him as righteousness. Paul goes on to say in Romans 4:5, "However, to a man *who does not work* but trusts God who justifies the wicked, *his faith is credited to him as righteousness.*" We are not justified by what we do. God gives tasks to do, and we will be rewarded for the things we do for Him, but our salvation doesn't hinge on it. Works do not justify us! This is a very different message than what James preached! Is James wrong? Is Paul wrong? No on both counts! Their messages are to two different audiences, one Jewish and one gentile. Abraham was indeed justified by faith, purely by faith! But as the father of the Jews, he was justified by proving his faith with a sign, which was his action of sacrificing his son (or starting to). Both messages are correct, even though both appear opposed to each other. Paul tells us that Jews require a sign (1 Corinthians 1:22). Abraham's sign of his faith was this sacrifice. Works were a large part of Jewish worship, and this is borne out in their zealousness of the Law of Moses, and properly so. This circumstance of two proper messages being preached, one to the Jews and one to the Gentiles, went on until the Jews were put aside for good and were scattered throughout the world. This final rejection by the Jews culminated with Acts 28:26–28. Let's read this portion:

> Go to this people and say, "You will be ever hearing but never understanding; you will be ever seeing but never perceiving.

For this people's heart has become calloused; they hardly hear with their ears, and they have closed their eyes. Otherwise they might see with their eyes, hear with their ears, understand with their hearts and turn, and I would heal them." *Therefore I want you to know that God's salvation has been sent to the Gentiles, and they will listen!*

From this point on, Jews and Gentiles received the same message. No longer was anyone to follow the Law of Moses—until the sacrifice will begin again during the tribulation. At that point, the Jewish form of worship will resume. But for a while, there were two messages being taught, one to the Jews and one to the Gentiles, all based on Christ's sacrifice on the cross but with slight differences depending on the intended audience. This has caused confusion for generations, but Paul stressed the distinctions of his gospel and the "mystery" frequently. Why did God not just end the program to the Jews when they rejected Him at the stoning of Stephen (Acts 7:54–60)? Certainly God knew the outcome before they rejected Him the third time in Acts 28. Of course He knew the outcome, but He needed to give them every opportunity to repent so no one could accuse Him of not giving them every chance, and also because of what it says in Romans 10:21: "But *concerning Israel* he says, '*All day long I have held out my hands* to a disobedient and obstinate people.'"

Here we find that God is prolonging His offer to the Jews, even though they are disobedient and obstinate. God loves them. He was unwilling to just give up on them, and He will renew His offer to them again in the future, and they will accept it! There is much comfort in this characteristic of God. He will not just give up on you when you are disobedient and obstinate. He hasn't given up on me when I'm that way, either.

An interesting passage to note is Galatians 1:8–9:

But even if we or an angel from heaven should preach a gospel other than the one we preached to you, let him be eternally condemned! As we have already said, so now I say again: If anybody is preaching to you a gospel other than what you accepted, let him be eternally condemned!

We find here a passage where Paul is condemning any other gospel being taught to these people. Who are these people being written to here? Galatians; Gentiles! Some Jewish believers had come to them demanding that they follow Moses's Law (Galatians 3:1–2, 5:1–6). This caused a difficult contention between Jewish and gentile believers. Paul here is warning, first, Jewish believers not to apply their gospel to gentile believers and secondly, for the Galatian believers (and by implication all gentile believers) not to be reliant on the law for salvation. This is the purpose of the book of Galatians.

Okay, going on with the Ephesians 3 portion, we find in verse 9 that Paul reiterates the point that his message is a "mystery, which for ages past was kept hidden in God." He wishes to make it perfectly clear that this is something new, something you won't find mentioned in Isaiah, for instance! But even though this is something hidden of God from ages past, it is still according to His eternal purpose. It was just then being revealed to Paul and the believers in his time.

So there is a distinction between the body of Christ church and the bride of Christ. This is good, because for the bride of Christ to be the body of Christ is illogical. Christ will not marry himself!

Let's review some of the Old Testament passages that deal with the church as the bride. Perhaps the best portion in the Old Testament is Hosea 2:14–20. I cover this in chapter 5 of volume 2, so I will not spend a lot of time with it here except to point out that God is speaking to Israel in this chapter (verses 1–2, 11, 13, 15, 23) and to mention that God is going to marry her (verses 14–20). This is obviously not a "mystery"; it has not been hidden in God. Let's look at another portion. Let's read Isaiah 54:5–8:

For *your maker is your husband*—the Lord Almighty is his name—the Holy one of Israel is your redeemer; he is called the God of all the earth. *The Lord will call you back as if you were a wife deserted and distressed in spirit*—a wife who married young, only to be rejected, says your God. *"For a brief moment I abandoned you, but with deep compassion I will bring you back. In a surge of anger I hid my face from you for a moment, but with everlasting kindness I will have compassion on you," says the Lord your redeemer.*

This is of course a prophecy of God's turning His back on Israel for rejecting Him when they rejected Christ throughout the book of Acts. He scattered them throughout the nations of the world, but He will bring them back. He refers to it here as "For a brief moment I abandoned you, but with deep compassion I will bring you back." And "I hid my face from you for a moment, but with everlasting kindness I will have compassion on you." It is clear that He is referring to Israel and that He will marry her (verse 5).

Now these are good portions, but there is one even more convincing. It is found in Isaiah 62:1–5. Let's read it:

For Zion's sake I will not keep silent, *for Jerusalem's sake* I will not remain quiet, till her righteousness shines out like the dawn, her salvation like a blazing torch. The nations will see your righteousness, and all kings your glory; you will be called by a new name that the mouth of the Lord will bestow. You will be a crown of splendor in the Lord's hand, a royal diadem in the hand of your God. No longer will they call you Deserted, or name your land Desolate. But *you will be called Hephzibah, and your land Beulah; for the Lord will take delight in you, and your land will be married. As a young man marries a maiden, so will your sons marry you; as a bridegroom rejoices over his bride, so will your God rejoice over you.*

When you understand this portion, it speaks so clearly of God's eventual marriage to Israel (remember, Christ is God!). God, here, is speaking this "for Zion's sake" and "for Jerusalem's sake." This couldn't be clearer that it is speaking of Israel! Then in verse 4, we find that Israel will be called Hephzibah. I wondered what that meant, so I searched it out. It means *my delight is in her*. Then we find that the land is called Beulah. Again, at first, it meant nothing to me until I searched out the meaning of this word. *Beulah* means *married*! The verse goes on to explain this, but at first I didn't realize it. The Lord will take delight in Zion, Jerusalem, and "*your land will be married*"! This is so clearly speaking of the nation of Israel and the land of Israel being *married to God*! I was confused momentarily by the phrase, "so will your *sons* marry you." The word *sons* can also mean *builder*. I believe that this is the correct interpretation of this verse. Indeed, Israel's builder will marry her. Marrying one's "sons" is not logical. I know it could be argued that Christ was the "Son" mentioned in Isaiah 9:6, and I suppose that could explain it, but *builder* is a much stronger and clearer argument, and it's logical. By the words of the Old Testament, it is absolutely certain that Israel is the bride of Christ! This is no "mystery." The "mystery" is clearly defined in Ephesians 3:6. Let's read it again: "This mystery is that through the gospel *the Gentiles are heirs together with Israel, members together of one body*, and sharers together in the promise *in Christ Jesus*."

Another passage which speaks it just as clearly or maybe more so is Colossians 1:24–27:

> Now I rejoice in what was suffered for you, and I fill up in my flesh what is still lacking in regard to Christ's afflictions, for the sake of *his body, which is the church*. I have become its servant by the commission God gave me to present to you the word of God in its fullness—*the mystery that has been kept hidden for ages and generations, but is now disclosed to the saints.* To them God has chosen to make known among the Gentiles

the glorious riches of *this mystery, which is Christ in you*, the hope of glory.

The mystery is that Jews and Gentiles will be fellow heirs, of one *body*. Does this mean Gentiles become Jewish? No! That isn't a mystery. That is how Gentiles were saved from the time of Moses. It is that Gentiles are saved without becoming Jewish and Jews are saved in the same manner as Gentiles—if they decide to trust Christ. This is brought out clearly in Colossians 3:11: *"Here there is no Greek or Jew, circumcised or uncircumcised, barbarian, Scythian, slave or free, but Christ is all, and is in all."*

The point of Jews and Gentiles being one is that there is no longer the distinction of races that there was just a short time before this was written. Christ is in all! We are all members of *one body*, the body of Christ, the church. The Jews saved under the Law of Moses were clearly the bride. There is much scriptural evidence for this, as I have quoted. But "here," as Paul said, under this "mystery," the Jews and Gentiles, all believers, are in the body of Christ church. This is a new administration! We have a new set of rules to play by, never before revealed to man. The Colossians portion tells us that the church is His body, Christ's body, and it is made up of believers that are saved under the administration of this mystery. Paul re-emphasizes the fact that it was hidden in God for ages but is now being shown to believers (remember, saints are living believers). He even tells us that the mystery is Christ dwelling in you, in me. We are in His body.

There is even more proof that something happened *after* the salvation of Paul. We have found that there are many places where Paul tells us that his message is something hidden in God, never before revealed. But we find another place in Scripture that gives us a definitive distinction between Paul's message and the ministry of the others. This is found in Acts 3:24: "Indeed, *all the prophets from Samuel on, as many as have spoken, have foretold these days.*"

This is speaking for the time of Pentecost. Everyone in the past was speaking of it! All the prophets spoke of it. It was no mystery! Paul's message, on the other hand, was hidden, never before known by man. Something changed! It changed with Paul. It changed by God's revelation to Paul.

Okay, that long explanation out of the way, what does it mean for prophecy about us? Truly, there are a few things that will become evident. As the body of Christ, we will be present at the wedding; we will be a part of the groom. We will be married to Israel, united forever. As such, we will have the right to dwell in the New Jerusalem. "So will we be with the Lord, forever" (1 Thessalonians 4:17).

Will we have any special role to fill in regard to being Christ's body? Yes! We find in John 5:22 a responsibility given to the Son, Christ, by the Father: "Moreover, the Father judges no one, but *has entrusted all judgment to the Son.*"

Who has *all judgment* been given to? The Son, Jesus Christ! What does that have to do with us? Let's read 1 Corinthians 6:2–3: "Do you not know that *the saints will judge the world*? And if you are to judge the world, are you not competent to judge trivial cases? Do you not know that *we will judge angels*? How much more the things of this life!"

Whoa! Didn't we just read that *all* judgment was given to the Son? Yes we did! We are members of the Son! We are members of His body! This has tremendous implications! We will have an awesome responsibility. We will judge the world and angels! We can only do this as members of His glorious body! There can be no other explanation!

In Revelation, we find an interesting verse. It is Revelation 20:4. It reads: "I saw thrones on which were seated *those who had been given authority to judge.*"

I will end the quote here because it goes on to other groups of people. John saw thrones, on which were seated those *who had been given authority to judge*! According to 1 Corinthians 6:2–3, they would be us! The body of Christ church will judge the world. That has been *given* to us! What an awesome responsibility (even a little scary, when I think about it now)! This shows a part of our distinction, a part of our special calling.

We find that Christ is head over the bride (this is what all the marriage analogy is referring to; Ephesians 5:23), but He is also head over His body the church (Colossians 1:18).

Also, as described earlier in this chapter, we will be rescued before wrath is poured out on the world! Why? Because Christ loves us *as His own body*! We will have to be out of here before any of the prophesied events of the Old Testament can come to pass that is dealing with end-time events. We will be snatched away in a split second! And we will be given new bodies that won't suffer. We have to be gone *before* the antichrist can come on the scene! The antichrist has to be on the scene and established before the tribulation can begin; in fact, he has to be here for an undetermined length of time before the tribulation can happen! Wherefore, comfort one another with these words indeed!

Okay, now we will recap what we covered in this chapter.

First, I begged you to study from a disciple's viewpoint. Just learn from God's Word. Claim Christ's promise in John 14:26 that the Holy Spirit will teach us all things. Pray for His guidance, and He will teach you. Remember that all commentaries, study Bible margin notes, and sermons are man's ideas of what God is trying to tell us. They are not inspired by God! Only God's Word is inspired by God. Even translations have problems—*every* translation. You need to study carefully, seeking the meaning of words in the original language to the best of your ability to understand what *exactly* God is trying to tell us. For most things, the meaning is obvious, but in a deep study such as this, it sometimes becomes important to be picky. Like when we studied the meaning of *horse* (in chapter two of this book). It means *leaper* and can be referring to horses, swallows, cranes, or anything that appears to leap or fly. That gives us a much clearer understanding of what prophecy speaks of in reference to modern times. I beg you to study this book series with a good translation present and open, not a paraphrase. Paraphrases are just a shallow commentary on the Bible. Again, it is not God's inspired Word. Don't even trust me. Don't trust anyone who will tell you they cannot be wrong. Only God can be one hundred percent correct. Be in communication with God; ask for His guidance. He wishes to give it to you!

First, we studied a subject that is much discussed today: the *rapture*. We found that *rapture* is not a word found in the Bible; it comes from the Latin translation of the word for *snatching away*, as found in 1 Thessalonians 4:17, where we are said to be "caught up." This is the "snatching away" that the original language says. The Latin translation is the word *rapare*, which means *snatching away*. So *rapture* is an okay word; it isn't truly unscriptural. We found another rendition of this in 1 Corinthians 15:51–54. We found in these portions that the rapture is going to be sudden, it will be signaled by trumpet blasts (as any assembly in the Bible times was), and it will be for the protection of God's children. He frankly wants us "out of Dodge" before things get messy. It is God's nature to protect His children. He wouldn't destroy the world at the flood until Noah and his family were safe; He wouldn't destroy Sodom and Gomorrah before Lot and his family were out. We are snatched away because He loves us and will not let us suffer the horrors of the tribulation. Anyone who wants to go through it simply doesn't understand how horrific it will be. But we found that we are not appointed to wrath. Even more, we found in 2 Thessalonians 2 that the antichrist cannot even be revealed until we are out of the way. What a relief that is! Paul definitely speaks words of comfort! We aren't even appointed to the antichrist's wrath!

Then we studied a portion that is often assumed to be speaking of the rapture. But we found that Matthew 24 does not speak of the rapture but of the second coming of Christ to this earth as king. We found that there are discrepancies between the Thessalonian portion and the Matthew portion. Perhaps *discrepancies* may be a bad word;

maybe *distinctions* would be better. We found that in the Thessalonian portion, the ones "taken" were saved, rescued. In Matthew, the ones taken are destroyed! Truly a big difference! The Matthew portion comes *after* the distress of those days; the Thessalonian portion comes before the wrath and, in fact, before the antichrist is revealed! This also is a big difference. We found that there is no reference to the "rapture" in any of the Gospels and no clear reference to the rapture anywhere except in Paul's writings. There may be an obscure mention of it in Revelation, but if so, it would have been written long *after* Paul had revealed this "mystery" to the world.

We found that the only prophecy of conditions before the rapture is very obscure and mentions that people will become selfish, mean, unloving, etc. This could be speaking of any time, but it is certainly truer today than it was just a few years ago. How far will it go? We cannot know. This goes with the rapture coming as a thief in the night. It is a secret, and God isn't telling us, no matter what any preacher or evangelist or any other false prophet that sets dates will tell you. You'll know the date when you find yourself in the clouds (but you probably won't care at that point). I must say that any person who claims that Christ has to rapture us by such and such a year is lying! God tells us over and over that it is not for us to know.

Next, we studied our identity. We found that we are clearly called the body of Christ church by Paul. We found that Paul is the apostle to the Gentiles, and with his ministry, there is no longer any difference between Jew and Gentile. We found that Paul never refers to us as the "bride." Even though Christ's love for the church is compared to that of a husband and wife, it is also compared to one's love for one's self, and then Paul reaffirms that we are His body. The other portion often cited as Paul's proof that we are the "bride" in 2 Corinthians 11:2 is, in fact, not saying this in the original language. It is telling the Corinthian believer that Paul led them to the Lord, so they should live like godly people.

There are, on the other hand, many scriptures that refer to Israel as the bride, even in the Old Testament. So it appears that we are not the bride of Christ, although it will have only a small difference. We will still live in the New Jerusalem, we will always be with Christ, we will be united with Israel (through marriage). One difference is we will judge the world and angels. We find that God the Father gave *all* judgment to the Son (Christ), but we will judge at the start of the earthly kingdom. We can only do this as the body of Christ. We are indeed part of Him!

We studied many distinctions between what Paul taught and what Peter, James, and the rest of the twelve taught. The twelve were called the apostles to the circumcision, where Paul was called the apostle to the uncircumcision: Gentiles. The twelve, as apostles to the Jews (circumcision), praised the Jewish believers for their zealousness for the Law of Moses. Paul, on the other hand, admonished his gentile believers to not follow the Law! So there were distinctions between their messages, though both taught that faith in Christ was the central theme. Paul called his message the "mystery." It is a word that means *secret*, or *to shut the mouth*. No one else called their message the mystery, just Paul. Paul seems to emphasize the mystery aspect of his message. He pointed out that it was hidden in God for all time past and was just then being revealed to people as it was given to Paul. We find that Paul claimed that we were under a new administration from God. Not that God had changed, but the primary people that God was dealing with changed. He was primarily dealing with Gentiles now. We found that there were distinctions between what James taught about Abraham's faith (equal with works, works support the faith) and what Paul taught about Abraham's faith (justified by faith, apart from works).

We also found that Christ was a minister to the Jews only while he was on earth. We also found that his life applies to all times and generations; but His time on earth was as a minister to the Jews. He came to fulfill the Law, to complete it! We found that during the earthly kingdom, when He is king over the whole earth, there will be temple worship. This will be the fulfillment of the Law.

We found that the Jewish message was finally put on hold entirely at Acts 28:26–28, when the Jews rejected Christ as their Messiah for the third time.

All of this was to show that Paul had a special mission and that it was to a special people, the believers of the body of Christ. We will have a special position in prophecy. We will have a place as Gentiles in the New Jerusalem. Other gentile believers that are saved outside the frame of the Law (during the time of the Law they would have to become proselyte Jews) or the body of Christ will have a place in the New Earth outside the New Jerusalem, but they will have free access to the New Jerusalem. We will learn more about them in volume 2. As members of Christ's body, we are also heirs of the promises made to Abraham.

Because we are a special people, we will be raptured before the tribulation or any aspect of it. We will even be raptured before the "birth pains" Christ spoke of! We will be given the right to judge angels and the world! We will have a special place at the wedding of the Lamb. We will only be able to claim these things if we have placed our trust in Christ to save us from our sins. Without that, we are facing eternity in the lake of fire! Be sure of your eternal status. You can know that you are saved (1 John 5:13)! Be sure! It's more important than life itself! If you have never trusted in Christ, you will face the horrific judgments of the tribulation if you are still alive when it comes. It isn't worth it! Then you will only face eternal punishment. Christ has given us all every opportunity. He loves us so much that He gave His life so we wouldn't have to face eternal judgment and tribulation. Don't spurn that love!

Next we will have the conclusion. Don't skip it! In the conclusion, we will cover all that we have studied in this book and tie it together in a logical, scriptural sequence of events. We will see how it all fits together!

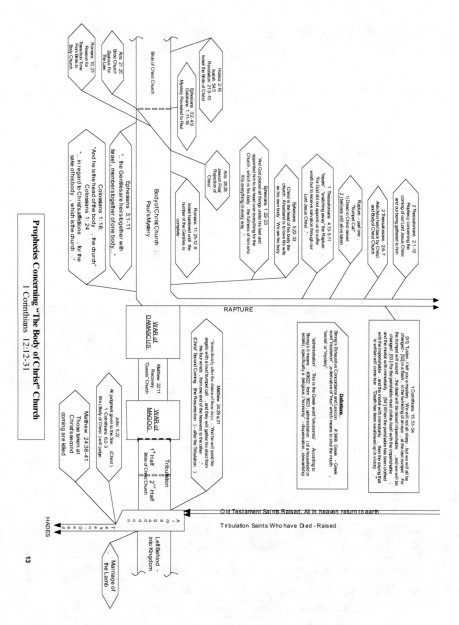

Prophecies Concerning "The body of Christ" Church Event Line

CONCLUSION
TO VOLUME 1

In this conclusion, I will strive to tie the contents of volume 1 into a logical, chronological order. In deference to those who place greater importance on one piece of scripture over another, I started with the words of our Lord, Jesus Christ. In doing so, we discovered that Christ never mentioned the rapture! There is a part of His message that is often considered to be the rapture, and there are some strong similarities, but on closer examination, we found that it couldn't be the rapture at all. Christ's Olivet discourse states that those who were "taken" were destroyed, the same as those unsuspecting ones who were "taken" by Noah's flood! Those taken by Paul's rapture were to be "ever with the Lord," saved! This is proof that the two portions are speaking of completely different events.

This explanation out of the way, we will start with the first prophetic event that we will be able to see. This is the rapture. The word *rapture* is never found in Scripture. This is because our word *rapture* is from a translation of the Greek word for *to snatch away* into the Latin word *rapare*. So while the word *rapture* is not found in Scripture, the concept of the rapture certainly is. We are told in 1 Thessalonians 5:1 that we have no need to know the times or the dates that the "day of the Lord" will be. God doesn't tell us the date of the rapture either, and Paul is likely lumping the rapture with the day of the Lord, since the day of the Lord cannot come without the rapture anyway. There is a very popular movement of people who want to put dates to these things. People try to calculate it like God can be outsmarted. There is a big problem with doing that. When the date comes and goes and we are still here, it makes Christianity look stupid, and worse, the one making the prediction is a false prophet. According to Scripture, anyone who makes a prophecy that doesn't come true is a false prophet. Christ tells us that in the last days, there will be many false prophets. The penalty for this under the Law was death by stoning. It is a serious infraction. Do not set dates that God doesn't give us. Even the time of the tribulation may be short of seven full years, because Christ said it may be shortened to save his people. So even people who are here to see the beginning of the tribulation can only say, "It will be seven years or less from now." Do not set dates!

We found that the rapture has to come before the antichrist can be revealed, because the thing that is holding him back (neuter gender; the church; the body of Christ) and He who is holding him back (masculine gender, Christ himself, who lives in us) has to be taken out of the way. The rapture will do just that.

We found that the reason Paul is the only one who speaks of the rapture is because of Paul's special mission. He was the apostle to the Gentiles. The body of Christ church is a gentile organization. Peter and the other eleven were the apostles to the circumcision, the Jews. The Jews as a nation have been set aside for the time being. They will be dealt with as a nation at the end of the period Christ calls the "birth pains" or the "time of sorrows" (KJV). Paul speaks frequently of the mystery given to him. This mystery includes the rapture. The word for *mystery* in the original language means *to shut the mouth*. Paul says it was "hidden in God." It was never revealed before Paul. Even Christ was called a minister to the Jews. His life is to all mankind of all periods of history, past, present, and future.

But His ministry was specifically to the Jews. Christ himself claims that is the case!

This is the reason Paul is the only one who makes specific mention of the rapture.

After believers are raptured, the battle of Damascus can begin. In this battle, it is likely that the antichrist will come to power. There will be ten nations that will attack Israel and nearly completely destroy her. Israel will counter attack before being completely destroyed and will nearly destroy her attackers. The attacking countries will not be able to recover, but Israel will recover because she has Jews living all around the world. They will be able to repopulate Israel and the lands of her attackers. Israel will be bigger than ever. She will be about the size that was promised to Abraham! Hmmm ... fulfilled prophecy! How exciting!

Immediately after this battle (which will probably be nuclear), there will be a great revival. Many will turn to Christ, but with the rise of the antichrist, this revival will be quickly snuffed out. If you are a believer, you will have to worship underground. To worship openly would be suicide. It will be open season on believers. The unbelievers will be officially encouraged to kill those who are saved. Genocide will be a way of life. This was why the early Christians could be concerned that they had missed the rapture. Things were happening that will happen again but on a much greater scale. It will be global! The world will believe that God has abandoned them and wants to destroy them. Any who repent and are saved will be in mortal danger. The unsaved will believe that Satan can beat God!

During this time there will be widespread famine. Crop failure will become the norm. This is because God isn't blessing mankind. Still people will be in open rebellion against God.

During this time, the antichrist will be in a leadership position over Israel. He will give out land either for money or as a reward for worshipping him. Israel will recover and will assume that they are at peace. Israel will become very wealthy. They will control Iraq's oil fields. Finally, Russia and her allies will attack Israel to gain much plunder. This will likely be her oil fields and the goods that they have earned her. They will mount the greatest military force ever to exist on the face of the earth and will move to wipe Israel off the face of the earth. At this time, Israel will recognize her helpless situation and will all regather to the nation of Israel in fulfillment of Rosh Hashanah, their Feast of Trumpets. Trumpets were used by Israel in ancient times to call an earnest assembly and to examine themselves before God. They will earnestly seek God, and in doing so, they will repent and accept Christ as their Messiah and Savior. They will do this as a nation. This is in fulfillment of their Yom Kippur, their Day of Atonement. At that point, God will intervene and kill the army attacking His people. The antichrist will likely take credit for this and will claim he was the power behind the miraculous change of fortune. Israel will not be fooled. The antichrist will broker a peace treaty with many nations (not with Israel), and he will then be killed.

We found that the first six seals were before the tribulation. This is proven by the wording of the fifth seal. The martyred souls under the throne in heaven ask how long it will be before God will pour out His wrath on those living on the earth who killed them. This statement is loaded with information. The people who killed them are still living on the earth, and God has not yet begun to pour out His wrath. These martyrs are a specific group of believers who will accept Christ after the rapture and give their lives for it. Not everyone who gives himself to Christ will die for it, but many will. We find that the tribulation will begin with the next seal. The rebellious unbelievers will note that the "great day of their (Him who sits on the throne and the Lamb) wrath has come, and who can stand?" They know but will not repent. They beg the rocks and mountains to fall on them and hide them from God! The sixth seal introduces the tribulation.

The events of the tribulation and the times to follow will be covered in the second volume of this book series. The second volume will take us through the tribulation and the many events that will follow. It will relate these events to many Jewish holidays and ceremonies. These ceremonies are well explained by end-time prophecy. They are given to Israel to give her a view of these events and so she will recognize them as they come. We will see the body of Christ church's role throughout the end-time events of future history. We will examine in detail the marriage of the Lamb and the thousand-year reign and its significance in Jewish rituals. We will examine the final destruction of this heaven and earth and what God tells us of the world to come! Don't miss it! (The second volume completes this book series, and more importantly, it completes our study of future events into eternity!)

BIBLIOGRAPHY

1. New International Version (NIV):
    Scripture quotations taken from the *Holy Bible, New International Version* ®, Copyright© 1973, 1978, 1984 by International Bible Society. Used by permission of International Bible Society. "NIV" and "New International Version" are trademarks registered in the United States Patent and Trademark office by International Bible Society. http://www.ibs.org

2. King James Version (KJV):
    Scripture quotations taken from the *Holy Bible, King James Version* The KJV is public domain in the United States.

3. New American Standard Bible (NASB)
    Scripture quotations taken from the *New American Standard Bible*®, Copyright © 1960, 1962, 1963, 1968, 1971, 1972, 1973, 1975, 1977, 1995 by The Lockman Foundation Used by permission." (www.Lockman.org).

4. Wycliffe New Testament:
    The *American Standard Version* (ASV) was originally published in 1901 by Thomas Nelson & Sons. The copyright for the ASV is now expired and it is now public domain.

5. Amplified Bible (AMP):
   Scripture quotations taken from the Amplified® Bible, Copyright ©
   1954, 1958, 1962, 1964, 1965, 1987 by The Lockman Foundation
   Used by permission." (www.Lockman.org)

6. Young's Literal Translation Bible (YLT):
   Scripture taken from the *Young's Literal Translation Bible*
   The YLT is public domain in the United States.
   No copyright information available.

7. Strong's Exhaustive Concordance and Lexicon: Copyright © 1995,
   1998 by Thomas Nelson Inc.

8. Original Manuscripts:
   Dictated by the Great I AM, the Triune God; penned by the
   servants of the same Triune God being the Prophets, Scribes,
   Disciples and Apostles.

Other Items:

9. Event Lines:
   War of Damascus, War of Magog, Yom Kippur, The Antichrist,
   Prophecies Concerning the Body of Christ Event Line,
   Tribulation, First Half, Tribulation, Temple Rebuilt, Second Half,
   Armageddon and the Second Coming, Marriage of the Lamb and
   the Judgment of the Righteous, Millennial Reign of Christ, Final
   Rebellion and Judgment and the New Heaven and Earth, Fullness
   of Times, Conclusion *were produced specifically for this book series by
   the author and/or those mentioned in the Dedication.*